D1602524

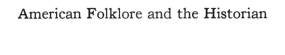

American Folklore and the Historian

# American Folklore
# & *the Historian*

Richard M. Dorson

The University of Chicago Press · Chicago and London

2257

International Standard Book Number 0-226-15868-3
Library of Congress Catalog Card Number: 75-149093

The University of Chicago Press, Chicago 60637
The University of Chicago Press, Ltd., London

To my colleagues in the History department
of Indiana University

# Contents

Preface                                                    ix

Acknowledgments                                            xi

1. Fakelore                                                 3

2. A Theory for American Folklore                          15

3. A Theory for American Folklore Reviewed                 49

4. Folklore in Relation to American Studies               78

5. The Question of Folklore in a New Nation               94

6. Folklore Research Opportunities in
   American Cultural History                              108

7. Oral Tradition and Written History:
   The Case for the United States                         129

8. Local History and Folklore                             145

9. Defining the American Folk Legend                      157

10. Print and American Folktales                          173

11. The Identification of Folklore in
    American Literature                                   186

12. Folklore in American Literature:
    A Postscript                                          204

    Index                                                 211

# Preface

In the following essays and addresses written over the past quarter of a century I endeavored to convey my sense of the values of folklore for American cultural and literary history. Recently American historians have begun to turn to folklore as a vital source for black, ethnic, urban, and frontier historical writing. Some of them, such as Joseph Boskin, Lawrence W. Levine, Donald R. McCoy, Gilbert Osofsky, Mario De Pillis, C. L. Sonnichsen, Sterling Stuckey, and Rudolph J. Vecoli, actively encourage the marriage of American history and folklore in a manner I can only find heartwarming after years of frosty indifference.[1] There was the occasion a decade ago at the meeting of the Mississippi Valley Historical Association (now the Organization of American Historians) when one distinguished historian, member of the panel reviewing my plea for attention to ethnic and other tradition-oriented groups, scoffed, "Who cares about a few obscure Indians?" The climate has changed, and obscure Indians, blacks, immigrants and other overlooked Americans now are

receiving attention, an attention that does indeed call for a
merging of historical and folkloric methods.

These essays on theory and research techniques complement my narrative account in *American Folklore* and selection of field materials in *Buying the Wind*. The first essay
looks in a personal way at the scene in folklore studies in the
United States in the past three decades and states the need
for an historical theory. In the next four essays the theory
is set forth. The final seven essays deal with specific research
techniques for implementing the theory in folkloristic approaches to American history and literature.

1. Joseph Boskin, "Sambo: The National Jester in the Popular Culture,"
in Gary Nash and Richard Weiss, eds., *Fear: Race in the Mind of America* (New York: Holt, Rinehart and Winston, 1970), pp. 165–85; Lawrence
W. Levine, "Slave Songs and Slave Consciousness: An Exploration in
Neglected Sources," in *Anonymous Americans: Explorations in Nineteenth Century History*, ed. Tamara Harveven (Englewood Cliffs, N.J.:
Prentice-Hall, 1971); Donald R. McCoy, "Underdeveloped Sources of
Understanding in American History," *Journal of American History* 54
(1967): 255–70; Gilbert Osofsky, "A Note on the Usefulness of Folklore,"
in *Puttin' On Ole Massa* (New York: Harper Torchbooks, 1969), pp.
45–48; Mario S. De Pillis, "Folklore and the American West," *Arizona and
the West* 4 (1963): 291–314; C. L. Sonnichsen, "The Grassroots Historian," *Southwestern Historical Quarterly* 73 (January 1970): 381–92;
Sterling Stuckey, "Through the Prism of Folklore: The Black Ethos in
Slavery," *Massachusetts Review* 9 (Summer 1968): 417–37; Rudolph J.
Vecoli, "Ethnicity: A Neglected Dimension of American History," *American Studies in Scandinavia*, no. 4 (Summer 1970), pp. 5–23.

# Acknowledgments

My chief debt is to the historians who have allowed me to wear the hats of folklore and history simultaneously. I have always taught in history departments, one year at Harvard, twelve years at Michigan State University, and since 1957 at Indiana University. At Indiana I acquired the title of professor of history and folklore, and for many years was the only one in the country; but now three of my doctoral students in folklore have found hospitality in history departments. My fellow historians in Bloomington have been uniformly generous and sympathetic toward my aberrant behavior. I would single out three for specific mention: my two chairmen over the past thirteen years, Robert F. Byrnes and Leo Solt, who have always aided me, and the late Oscar O. Winther, long-time friend and my fellow-organizer of the Yugoslav-American history and folklore seminars at Novi Sad, Yugoslavia, in 1965. The best part of a joint appointment is that you can enjoy your colleagues without having to see too much of them.

Over the years I have also learned a great deal from Dan Boorstin and Jack Garraty.

None of these historians is of course culpable for my sins, nor am I suggesting that they in any way condone my idiosyncrasies.

For permission to reprint the essays in this book I wish to thank the following:

*Journal of American Folklore, Zeitschrift für Volkskunde, Journal of the Folklore Institute,* the Purdue Research Foundation, the University Press of Kentucky, the Detroit Historical Society, and the California Folklore Society.

American Folklore and the Historian

# 1

# Fakelore

All folklorists know that *folklore* was coined in 1846 by William John Thoms, but relatively few know that the present writer has the dubious distinction of coining the word *fakelore* in 1950. Since *Time* magazine and the *Saturday Review* have used *fakelore* in their pages, the term has by now attained national currency. The reasons that led to my contriving this neologism derive directly from the state of American folklore studies in the 1940s, and in a larger sense the state of American mass culture, as I perceived them. The following account is therefore highly subjective and personal.

Folklore as an academic subject was barely lifting its head in the 1940s. At Harvard, where I completed my Ph.D. in 1943, in a new field called History of American Civilization, folklore was almost wholly unrepresented. George Lyman Kittredge, whose eminence as a Shakespearean scholar lent

From *Zeitschrift für Volkskunde*, vol. 65 (1969).

prestige to his studies of balladry, witchcraft, and popular
belief, had retired and left no successor. My own interest in
and awareness of the subject matter of folklore developed ac-
cidentally through an undergraduate paper on Mark Twain's
debt to the oral tall-tale tradition of the frontier. This interest
led to my publishing, in 1939, two years after my graduation,
an edition of almanac tall tales from the 1830s, 40s, and 50s,
under the title *Davy Crockett, American Comic Legend*. As I
had just entered graduate school, I felt keenly the need for
some direction in folklore and learned by chance of the presence on the faculty of one folklore-minded professor, Kenneth
H. Jackson, in the Celtic department; he agreed to give me
a reading course and initiated me into the mysteries of the
Motif-Index. (Professor Jackson shortly after left Harvard to
take the chair he presently occupies at the University of Edinburgh.) My dissertation on "New England Popular Tales and
Legends," completed in 1943 and published in 1946 under the
title *Jonathan Draws the Long Bow,* while it was based entirely on printed sources, did carry me deep into folklore research. Then in 1946, when I had begun teaching at Michigan
State University, I undertook my first expedition into the
field, in the remote and ethnically varied Upper Peninsula
of Michigan. This same year I attended the summer Folklore
Institute at Indiana University that Stith Thompson had
initiated in 1942 on a quadrennial basis as a means of bring-
ing together the relatively few scattered folklorists around
the country.

So much for autobiographical background. The one point
I would underscore is that I stumbled into folklore from a
training in American cultural and intellectual history, and
that no other folklorist at that time had entered our common
field through that particular door. Stith Thompson came to
folklore through English literature, Archer Taylor through
Germanics, Ralph Steele Boggs through Spanish. Consequently
the folklore scholars of the 40s were comparative, or literary,
or ballad, or anthropological folklorists. But they were not
American folklorists; that is, although Americans, they were
not Americanists.

Then in 1944 Benjamin A. Botkin published his *A Treasury of American Folklore*.[1] This fat volume of over six hundred pages, which sold at the time for $3.95 (today it would
sell for at least $12.50), proved an immediate and enormous
success, both commercially and critically. It received feature
reviews in the *New York Times* and *New York Herald Tribune*
weekly book sections and in the *Saturday Review of Literature,* and was adopted by the Book of the Month Club as a
bonus dividend. Millions of Americans came to know the
subject of American folklore through this book and its successors. The first treasury has gone through more than twenty
editions and remains in print up to today. Its popularity led
Mr. Botkin to resign his position as curator of the Archive
of Folksong in the Library of Congress and to become a free-
lance writer and compiler of subsequent treasuries, covering
the geographical regions of the United States. It was directly
as a consequence of these treasuries and their influence that
I publicized the word *fakelore.*

My personal reaction to these treasuries was one of shock,
or actually double shock, first as to the method of their compilation, and second, at the approval they received by professional folklorists. The method, in a word, was that of the
scrapbook. The treasuries were in the most literal sense a
scissors and paste job, with no philosophic unity and a wide
discrepancy of sources. Yet the reviewers in the folklore
journals—Wayland Hand in the *Journal of American Folklore,* Levette J. Davidson in *California Folklore Quarterly,*
and Arthur Palmer Hudson in *Southern Folklore Quarterly*—
uniformly praised *A Treasury of American Folklore.* It is
noteworthy that Hand was a professor of German and Davidson and Hudson were professors of English. But since no
academic specialists in American folklore then existed, these
reviewers were as qualified as any.

These uncritical encomiums seemed to me seriously to
injure the cause of the mature study of American folklore.
It was clearly a commercial rather than an intellectual ven-

1. (New York: Crown, 1944.)

ture, cleverly packaged for the American mass audience: a lot
of book for little money, selections chosen for light bedside
reading and appeal to superficial American nationalism. Furthermore, the *Treasury* brought within its covers a number of
writers who regarded the materials of folklore as subjects for
romantic and sentimental treatments. One can open any of
the Treasuries at random and find a wide disparity of sources,
ranging from purely literary to journalistic to some field texts,
although these latter are a small minority. For instance, in
the section on "Liars" in *A Treasury of American Folklore*
(pages 490–650), there are selections from Mark Twain; the
able collector-retoucher Vance Randolph; memoirs of chatty
Texans; manuscripts of the Federal Writers Project in various
states (a praiseworthy project but untrustworthy in its methods and materials); the rewritten tall tales of Carl Carmer in
*The Hurricane's Children;* the romantic local colorist of the
Southwest J. Frank Dobie; a pre-Civil War North Carolina
humorist; verses about tall tales by Carl Sandburg; jokebooks
and humor anthologies; the somewhat rewritten Florida Negro tale collection of Zora Neale Hurston, *Mules and Men;*
recollections of a circus clown; an overly precious book of
Cape Cod legends by Elizabeth Reynard called *The Narrow
Land;* coy invented tall tales about Paul Bunyan, the pseudohero of northern lumberjacks; and so on. The treasuries are
essentially packages of literary confections. There is little
doubt that the raw field texts would never have commanded
a mass audience.

     My own chance to review Mr. Botkin came with his sec-
ond treasury, *A Treasury of New England Folklore,* which I
was asked to review for the *Saturday Review of Literature.*[2]
In low key I opened with a paragraph of mild praise, and
three columns of softly expressed criticism. A couple of friends
confided to me their view that this criticism was "devastating."
But its effect was nil, and the *Book Review Digest* for 1948
reprinted the entire first paragraph and only one sentence
of the criticism. There was however one unexpected consequence. The editor of the *American Mercury,* Charles Angoff, who had succeeded the celebrated baiter of the American

2. 31 (January 17, 1948): 9–10.

"booboisie," Henry Louis Mencken, saw the review and asked
me to write an article attacking the misrepresenters of folklore. Accordingly I wrote the piece "Folklore and Fake Lore,"
which appeared in the *American Mercury* in March, 1950.[3]
This was the first use of the word and the concept of *fakelore*.
Mr. Angoff arranged for a reply, immediately following my article, by James Stevens, author of *Paul Bunyan* (1925), the
most successful popularization of the Bunyan stories. In his
rebuttal, "Folklore and the Artist," Stevens contended that
he was taking liberties with folk traditions in the manner of
Homer or any man of letters who wrote as an imaginative
author. The trouble with this argument is that Stevens claims,
and the public believes, that they are reading genuine folklore.
(See his Introduction to the second edition of *Paul Bunyan*.)[4]

This article, "Folklore and Fake Lore," kindled a furious
and bitter controversy whose scars still remain. It was at this
point that I decided to abandon efforts at polite and decorous
criticism and resort to forceful language. The word *fakelore*
was conceived in this spirit. By 1950 my thinking had reached
the following position: (1) American mass culture was highly
commercial, blatant, loud, aggressive, and the book industry
partook of these traits; (2) in another age, say Victorian
England, subtle thrusts might be appreciated, but in twentieth-century United States one needed to shout at the top
of his voice; (3) the study of American folklore was being
invaded by commercializers and could not as yet be protected
by scholars, since specialists in American folklore had not yet
been trained; (4) the distinction must be made between the
frivolous and the serious investigation of American folklore;
(5) even some respected scholars of American literature and
American history turned fakelorist when they dabbled with
folklore.

Accordingly in that article I wrote these words:
> In recent years folklore has boomed mightily, and reached
> a wide audience through best-selling books, concert and
> cabaret folksingers, even Walt Disney cartoons. But far
> from fulfilling its high promise, the study has been

3. 70: 335–43.
4. New York, 1928.

falsified, abused and exploited, and the public deluded
with Paul Bunyan nonsense and claptrap collections.
Without stirring from the library, money-writers have
successfully peddled synthetic hero-books and saccharine
folk tales as the stories of the people. Americans may be
insufficiently posted on their history and culture, as the
famous *New York Times* survey indicated, but their
knowledge of these subjects is erudition, compared with
what they know about their own folklore. The saddest
aspect of this fraud is that the spurious article is so dull
and thin, and the genuine material so salty and rich.
These charges I repeated in book reviews in the *Journal
of American Folklore* and in other journals. At that time
only one other critic shared my views, Stanley Edgar Hyman,
who two years earlier had written a vitriolic critique of the
state of American folklore scholarship, which he called "ap-
palling" and "monstrous."[5] Hyman was an extremely gifted
literary critic, a *New Yorker* staff writer, husband of the late
novelist Shirley Jackson, and he brought to his attack on
American folklorists the kind of ferocity which apparently is
needed to gain the attention of apathetic and preconditioned
American readers. However Hyman has for some years ceased
to have any connections with the American folklore movement.
His premises differed completely from mine, as he was firmly,
even fanatically committed to the thesis of myth-ritual origins
of all folk expression, and he clubbed everyone in sight from
Ben Botkin to Stith Thompson. The articles and reviews by
Hyman and myself provoked bitter responses. In the "Editor's
Page" of the *New York Folklore Quarterly*,[6] Harold W.
Thompson, author of a book on New York State folklore,
*Body, Boots, and Britches*[7] and teacher of folklore courses at
Cornell University, referred to "certain neurotics swollen with
envy and arrogance" who were criticizing successful folklorists.
But the recriminations in print were mild compared to those
uttered in living rooms and dark corridors.

5. "Some Bankrupt Treasuries," *Kenyon Review* 10 (1948) : 484–500.
6. Spring, 1952.
7. (New York: J. B. Lippincott, 1940.)

What precisely did I mean by *fakelore?* Fakelore is the presentation of spurious and synthetic writings under the claim that they are genuine folklore. These productions are not collected in the field but are rewritten from earlier literary and journalistic sources in an endless chain of regurgitation, or they may even be made out of whole cloth, as in the case of several of the "folk heroes" written up in the image of Paul Bunyan, who had at least some trickle of oral tradition at the beginning of his literary exploitation. The impulse to present so-called American folklore suddenly developed in the 1920s and 30s in response to the nationalistic mood following World War I and America's new place in the sun. Why should not Americans possess their own folk heroes, folktales, and folksongs, instead of having to depend on imported folklore and mythology from Europe? So a mass market existed, and publishers and writers rushed to supply the need. Hence the great success of Paul Bunyan. Some writers knew better, some did not, but in either case the product they tendered was ersatz.

These rewriters of folklore tailored their writings to their market. They followed the popular stereotypes of myths, legends, and folklore in the mind of the public, and so what they wrote was intended to be quaint, cute, whimsical, syrupy, and childlike. Children as much as adults constituted the market. Out of a thousand examples let me give this one, "How Annie Christmas Mourned for Her Gambling Man," in a book by Carl Carmer, *The Hurricane's Children*,[8] devoted to American hero giants. In his preface Carmer writes, "I owe a great debt to the patient workers in American folklore who have collected these stories." Then he adds that he has set them down "wherever it is possible, as they have been told to me by folks throughout the country. . . ." In the Annie Christmas story, he introduces a giantess supposedly known around the New Orleans waterfront as a fighter and lifter of great weights.

> Annie Christmas could carry three barrels of flour at once, one balanced on her head and one under each

8. (New York and Toronto: Farrar and Rinehart, 1937.)

arm. When the river got high one spring and was about
to flood the country above New Orleans, Annie Christmas
prevented the disaster by throwing up a new and higher
levee all by herself in one day (p. 104).

Now this is double fakelore. In the accounts of Annie
Christmas written by Herbert Asbury and Lyle Saxon, two
popular authors specializing respectively in city underworld
and Louisiana local-color nonfiction, Annie Christmas was a
legendary whore of New Orleans. Naturally Carmer could not
so describe her in a book for children, so he suppressed this
the central element. But in fact there never was any Annie
Christmas. She was completely concocted by Lyle Saxon for a
sensational newspaper feature story. To Mr. Botkin's credit,
he reprints Saxon's disclosure in *A Treasury of Mississippi
River Folklore*.[9] We now know that a number of the alleged
regional demigods brought out in the wake of Paul Bunyan
were similarly contrived by publicists: Old Stormalong, King
of Yankee sailors: Joe Magarac, hero of Pittsburgh steelwork-
ers; Tony Beaver, the West Virginia lumberjack; Bowleg Bill,
the seagoing cowboy of Cape Cod; Febold Feboldson, the
Nebraska plainsman. No oral legends about these figures have
ever been reported, although their promoters, and the assem-
blers of hero tales, all claim them as genuine American folk
heroes. Most of these writers know little or nothing about the
discipline of folklore, and simply jumped on the bandwagon
when these comic demigods became fashionable, turning out
one children's book after another on one pseudohero after
another. You can find these books listed under such authors as
James Cloyd Bowman, Harold Felton, and Irwin Shapiro.
But scholars respected in their own fields also entered this
lucrative market place. Walter Blair, professor of English at
the University of Chicago, who has written excellent studies
of American humor and Mark Twain, committed a juvenile
folkhero volume, *Tall Tale America*, subtitled *A Legendary
History of Our Humorous Heroes*, embodying all the worst
sins of fakelore. The canons of scholarship in other fields were
simply left behind when a literary critic or historian or anthropologist dabbled in folklore. Here is a passage from *Tall*

9. (New York: Crown, 1955.)

*Tale America* about the birth of Johnny Appleseed, the name given John Chapman, who planted apple trees in the Ohio Valley in the early nineteenth century.

> Back there in Massachusetts on the day Johnny was born, there was one of those Massachusetts May storms that rain cats and a fair number of dogs. But along about when Baby Johnny had polished off his first big cry, the sun came out and made a handsome rainbow.
>
> One end of this rainbow was hitched to Monadnock Hill, where the great carbuncle sparkled in the sunshine. From here the rainbow arched up in the grey-blue sky until the other end swooped down right smack into the Chapman dooryard near Ipswich. There, this end of the rainbow got all tangled up in a big Spitzenberger apple tree which was so loaded with blossoms that it looked more or less like a big snowball. Result was the rainbow colored up the blossoms with all the colors you can think of, off hand, at any rate.
>
> The nurse that was taking care of Johnny and his mother claimed that she picked him up and carried him over to the window for a look at the tree.
>
> "You'll never believe the way he carried on," she said. "Why, he humped and gurgled and stuck out his little white paws as if he wanted to pick all those blossoms! And he was only forty minutes old, too!"
>
> Well, frankly, some of us historians *don't* believe this story—sounds fishy to us. But it's a known fact that as long as Johnny was a baby, each spring he'd whoop and squall and holler around, not giving the family a lick of peace, until they handed him a branch of apple blossoms to hang onto. Then he wouldn't bang the petals off, or eat them, like other babies would. Instead, he'd just lie there in his crib, looking at those apple blossoms, sniffing at them now and then, and smiling as happy as an angel plumb full of ice cream.

This gooey fabrication gives a fair idea of the style and mood of ersatz folklore. The few actual oral traditions known about Johnny Appleseed indicate a virile and coarse-grained figure.

Where did the American Folklore Society stand on the fakelore controversy? Here is another element in the situa-

tion that needs explaining. During the early 1940s this Society, although founded back in 1888, was having difficulties
staying afloat. Through the first three decades of the twentieth century it had been maintained by the anthropologists,
with Franz Boas and Ruth Benedict serving as successive
editors of the *Journal of American Folklore* (1908–39). Then
came a vacuum, and MacEdward Leach, professor of English
at the University of Pennsylvania, filled it as long-time sec-
retary-treasurer. During the 1940s, the Society could never
count on continuous attendance at its annual meetings, which
were divided between the Modern Language Association and
the American Anthropological Association. University professors considered themselves first literary scholars or anthropologists, and dropped in on the folklore sessions only if
they happened to be available. In 1946 I attended my first
convention of the American Folklore Society and thereafter
went regularly, but the only other person who also attended
annually was MacEdward Leach. Accordingly the Society
could not count on professional supporters and to remain
solvent depended on a sizable number of amateurs and dilet-
tantes attracted to the entertainment aspects of folklore.
Throughout the 1950s and into the 1960s the Society was
caught between the claims of the "purists" and of the "popularizers," and it polarized further between Indiana University, representing the professionals, and the University of
Pennsylvania, the home base of the Society and hence the
spokesman for dues-paying amateurs. Some of the national
meetings in those years turned into bitter shouting matches.

   The center of the popularizers came to be New York,
both the city and the state. A New York Folklore Society was
organized in 1945 and began issuing the *New York Folklore
Quarterly*, strictly on a lightweight basis. Articles were brief,
chatty, unburdened with documentation. Mr. Botkin contributed an anecdotal news column reiterating his conception
of applied folklore. His close friend Moritz Jagendorf, a
dentist, and a prolific writer of regional folklore for children
in a bouncy style, contributed regularly and served as president. This group deeply resented my use of the word *fakelore* and in a paper presented to the American Folklore Society in 1957, Mr. Jagendorf called it "discourteous," accused

me of envying authors whose books sold widely, and restated
his position that writers were like folk who could change stories
as they pleased. The bitterness of these years came to a climax
in the annual meeting of 1964 held in New York City, when
for the first time in the history of the Society the nominee
for president presented by the nominating committeee—myself—was challenged by a packed business meeting and a substitute elected. I was in England at the time, and received
a host of angry letters from members of the Society resentful
over this affair.

The discussion of *fakelore* has taken a different turn
from what the editors of the *Zeitschrift für Volkskunde,* or I
myself, had anticipated. Instead of defining a term, I have in-
dulged in a personal history of the American folklore scene.
Let me at once add that this *memorat* is written in no spirit
of rancor, that it has a happy ending, and that it does contain a moral. As matters now stand, the battle of fakelore is
largely won, at least within the universities. The American
Folklore Society has met independently for the past two years
(and I was elected president in 1966), with the support of a
substantial number of faculty and graduate students who
now make folklore their chosen careers. The Society is truly
a professional and learned society. Indiana University has
turned out some twenty-five Ph.D.'s in folklore in the past
ten years, who are well established at other universities, and
other folklore Ph.D.'s are beginning to be produced at the
Universities of Pennsylvania, Texas, and California at Los
Angeles. An Indiana doctoral candidate in folklore has been
appointed editor of the *New York Folklore Quarterly.* The
American Folklore Society is prospering financially while
maintaining scholarly standards. True, the public at large
still has little understanding of folklore as a scholarly subject,
and the federal government fails to give the support that folklore enjoys in European countries, in Brazil, and in Canada.
But this too may come.

A final word should be said about Mr. Botkin and his
series of treasuries. In any history of the American folklore
scene Ben Botkin deserves a respected place. His first series
of *Folk-Say* volumes, published annually in Oklahoma from
1929 to 1932, directed general attention to indigenous oral

traditions as a source for regional literature. When as a cal-
low graduate student in 1939 I first met Ben in Washington,
D. C., he showed me every kindness, and he has always gener-
ously assisted younger folklorists. The treasuries made an impact on the public imagination that is in itself a phenomenon
for the folklorist to contemplate, and they do point to sources
that the folklorist can consider and screen. Had they not
received such extravagant praise, no controversy would have
arisen.

The moral of this tale is perhaps now evident. *Fakelore*
was intended as a rallying cry against the distortion of a
serious subject. It seems almost incredible that such elemen-
tary principles as the necessity for fieldwork and the faithful
rendering of texts had to be debated. It all goes back to the
curious lack of specialization in American folklore, which
fell into a no-man's-land between comparative folklorists and
scholars in American Studies. To overcome this lack of any
body of theory fitting the needs of the United States, I presented two lengthy papers to the Society, "A Theory for
American Folklore" (1957) and "A Theory for American
Folklore Reviewed" (1968). In essence, this theory holds
that the folk traditions of countries colonized in modern
times—in North and South America and Australia—must be
correlated with their major historical developments from
colonization to industrialization.

There appears to be no close parallel in other nations to
the fakelore issue in the United States, where popularization, commercialization, and the mass media engulf the culture. *Folklorismus* does not seem to have affected the vigorous
growth of folklore institutes, seminars, archives, and investiga-
tions described in the impressive issue (1969) of the *Journal
of the Folklore Institute* devoted to Germany, Austria, and
Switzerland. Yet it can also be said that the sentimentalizing
and prettifying of folklore materials is preferable to the ideo-
logical manipulation of folklore, a more insidious kind of
fakelore which so far has made little headway in these states.

# 2

# A Theory for
# American Folklore

This first joint meeting between the American Folklore Society and the American Studies Association may occasion
private doubts along with public felicitations. Some cynic
might question the usefulness of two amorphous organizations
joining together to pool their insecurities and inchoate hopes.
In reply I can point to the success of such union already prag-
matically demonstrated in the nuptials between the secretary-
treasurer of the American Folklore Society, MacEdward Leach,
and his charming spouse, a holder of the doctor's degree in
American Civilization from the University of Pennsylvania.
The argument of this paper will be that the child of such
union is the properly reared American folklorist of the next
generation.

This paper was read at a joint meeting of the American Folklore Society
with the American Anthropological Association and the American
Studies Association at Chicago, 27 December 1957. It was printed in the
*Journal of American Folklore,* vol. 72 (1959).

We may begin by considering the likely reactions of a young scholar who visits our Society because he finds himself interested in folk traditions within the United States. He comes here by a devious route, from his doctoral study in English, foreign languages, music, or one of the social sciences, and he seeks guideposts. He observes considerable enthusiasm in the folklore fraternity, evident in national, regional, and state meetings and journals. But it will not take him long to notice a disparity between the professional order of his own field and the helter-skelter domain of folklore. In place of the one established discipline there are transients or refugees like himself from a host. Instead of the one standard vocabulary, the common frame of reference, and the accepted critical or empirical approach within which controversy arises, he witnesses a kaleidoscope of activities and hears a multiplicity of accents. The annual program may cover hot jazz recordings, costumed Indian dances, field reports interspersed with song and tale or demonstrations interspersed with sage commentary, distribution analyses weighted with maps, erudite genealogies of legend or ballad, and advice from writers of children's books who wish to restore folklore to the folk. Our friendly visitor may feel he has wandered into some kind of pedagogical sideshow. Eventually, as he becomes acculturated, he may learn to distinguish type and motif patterns among these variegated folklorists. I should like to classify seven leading types, and comment on their inapplicability to the study of folk traditions in the United States, even though they may admirably serve their own ends.[1]

1. Donald Davidson distinguished between scholarly and participant attitudes toward American folklore in a still timely article, "Current Attitudes Towards Folklore," *Tennessee Folklore Society Bulletin* 6 (1940): 44–51 (reprinted in *Still Rebels, Still Yankees, and Other Essays* [Baton Rouge, La., 1957], pp. 128–36). E. J. Lindgren describes the Finnish, American anthropological, and psychological approaches to folklore in "The Collection and Analysis of Folk-Lore," in the *Study of Society*, ed. F. Bartlett et al. (London, 1939), pp. 238–78, a standard summary that gives no attention to folklore in the United States.

Existing Views

*Comparative Folklorists.* A professionally trained folklorist in the United States today has drunk deep of the Finnish historical-geographical method. Stith Thompson and Archer Taylor brought to America the illustrious tradition of the Grimms, Bolte and Polívka, Kaarle and Julius Krohn and Antti Aarne, and enhanced it with their giant studies of the folktale, riddle, and proverb. The Finns speak about the necessity of gathering all possible variants, comparing them to determine their oldest elements, and so plotting the mystical *Ur*-form from which all subsequent forms have radiated. To assist in the task of working through the labyrinthine mass of variants, Thompson and Taylor have constructed awesome indexes of motifs and riddles. The preparation of these necessary tools of research has almost become an end in itself, obscuring the original theoretical premise, that a complex tale or other folklore item originated at one time in one place and can with infinite pains be traced to its lair.

This scholarship originated in Europe and was designed to fit European conditions. Märchen or animal tales or runesongs will not be traced to Jamestown or Plymouth—save as a port of entry. The Finnish method can be applied within North America, as Stith Thompson has shown with the Star Husband tale, but such a study deals with primitive literature and not with American civilization.[2] The American folklorist wants to know what happens to folk materials in the United States. He is not internationally minded in the Finnish sense, comparing variants wherever they are found, but in the American sense, comparing nationality traditions in the United States with their forms and functions in the lands of their origins. His problem is not to find the *Ur*-type of a given tale, but to contrast Italian-American with Italian folk traditions and folk customs. Kaarle Krohn himself has said that the special national imprints on folklore are fully as

2. "The Star Husband Tale," *Studia Septentrionalia* 4 (1953) : 93–163.

worthy of investigation as the common international aspects.[3]
His statement applies with special force to the United States
with her unique history.

*Cultural Anthropologists.* Recently Bascom has attempted to
close the widening gulf between anthropological and humanistic folklorists in a series of meaty papers.[4] No humanist
has accepted his invitation to respond in kind, and his articles
underscore the difficulty of cross-disciplinary communication.
The tradition of American anthropological friendliness to
folklore goes back to Boas, who edited our journal from 1908
to 1923. Boas demolished the prevailing notions of Daniel
Brinton in the celestial theory of Indian tale origins, through
painstaking fieldwork which demonstrated the cultural in-
dividuality of tribal traditions. Borrowing by culturally similar neighbors explained common tale elements, and not any
psychic unity of mankind. He regarded tribal folktales as a
form of primitive art, reflecting the culture from which they
sprouted. Now every anthropologist who publishes in our
journal makes his obeisance to Boas' *Tsimshian Mythology,*
the classic work that constructed an ethnography from tales.
At the present time, when anthropologists increasingly pass
folklore by for studies in social organization and personality
in culture, it is Herskovits, the student of Boas, and Bascom,
the student of Herskovits, who have principally retained hospitality to folklore. In their addresses we see the Boasian emphases on folklore as a mirror of culture—a mirror that distorts
as well as reflects—and on folktales as a form of art.

Some of their counsel lights up the distance between anthropological and American folklorists. Herskovits recommends
that the humanist distinguish between folk literature and

3. Kaarle Krohn, *Die Folkloristische Arbeitsmethode* (Oslo, 1926), p.
164. The definitive statement of the historical-geographical method is
Antti Aarne, *Vergleichende Märchenforschungen* (Helsingfors, 1907). A
succinct exposition by Stith Thompson is his "Narrative Motif-Analysis
as a Folklore Method," in *Beitrage zur vergleichenden Erzählforschung,*
ed. K. Ranke (Helsinki, 1955), pp. 2–9.
4. William R. Bascom, "Folklore and Anthropology," "Four Functions
of Folklore," and "Verbal Art," *JAF* (*Journal of American Folklore*)
(1953): 283–90; (1954): 333–49; (1955): 245–52. Bascom follows Lindgren's division of folklore "schools" in his discussion.

folk custom, and confine his attention to the former.[5] Bascom proposes that the humanist extend his inquiries from literary and historical to psychological and functional problems, and that he study folklore in its living context of cultural sanctions and conventions and aesthetic satisfactions. He would give the name *verbal art* to this creative folklore.

These proposals serve the cause of the anthropologist who divides his ethnography into convenient categories of culture, but they do not comfort the American folklorist. The anthropologist speaks confidently about culture and folklore. I have heard Bascom say that nothing is so easy to collect as folklore. This may be true in Africa but it is not so in the United States. We are not sure where the folklore is, how to find it, what form it will take, or how viable it is in the community. Nor can we speak with any certainty about "the culture" in dealing with the vast conglomerate society of the United States. The theory of survivals has been discarded as a comprehensive explanation for the appearance of folklore in civilized society, but some manifestations of belief and custom *are* fading survivals; others are, as Herskovits suggests, reinterpretations; others are new growth; others are artificially stimulated from mass media. Prized traditions and folkways lie hidden in the Kentucky Pine Mountain or the Louisiana bayous or the Carolina sea islands. Other folklore flourishes in the midst of American life, among college students and athletic teams. The humanist cannot generalize about American folklore the way the anthropologist does about folklore among the Chaga or Navajo.

So no easy distinction between verbal art and ethnography makes sense to the folklorist.[6] Belief in the devil qualifies as supernatural tradition, but the anthropologist would place this notion under religion. Hunting mushrooms each spring

5. Melville J. Herskovits, "Folklore after a Hundred Years: A Problem in Redefinition," *JAF* 59 (1946) : 89–100. See also his *Man and His Works* (New York, 1948) , ch. 24, "Folklore," pp. 414–26.
6. The basic concern of the folklorist with traditional ideas that may or may not become attached to material objects is well stated by Allan Gomme, "The Folk-Lore Society: Whence and Whither," *Folk-Lore* 63 (1952) : 1–18 (esp. p. 17) ; Samuel P. Bayard, "The Materials of Folklore," *JAF* 66 (1953) : 1–17.

is an Indiana folkway, but the anthropologist sets such a
practice under food gathering. The shivaree or couvade are
neither verbal nor art but they belong to Euro-American
folk tradition.[7]

Our anthropological friends do provide enormously valuable suggestions for the American folklorist. The concept of
culture can be applied regionally to American subcultures,
as a tool for slicing up and making more digestible the forty-
eight contiguous states. Herskovits in advocating attention to
contemporary folk groups like professors in the faculty club
or GIs home from the barracks gives us excellent direction.
Bascom's demands for data about the narrator and his audience and the attitudes in the culture toward tale and song,
proverb and riddle, warn collectors who gather only texts.
Especially should the theoretical field problems posed by anthropologists furnish suggestions to American folklorists. One
thinks of Boas investigating the Tshimshian and the Kwaki-
utl to test the hypothesis that American Indians had crossed
into North America from Siberia, of Herskovits working from
Dahomey to Trinidad and Haiti and Brazil and Surinam to
check African Negro retentions in the New World, of Redfield
comparing four Guatemalan communities ranging from simple village to complex town to sharpen the concept of the
folk society, of Kluckhohn examining the value systems of
five adjacent cultures in western New Mexico (Navajo, Pueblo, Spanish-American, Mormon, Texas homesteader).[8] The
intricate mosaic of American civilization makes possible any

7. Corinne L. Saucier writes, "Parmi les coutumes qui ont subsisté
depuis le début de la colonie française, on compte le charivari [shivaree]"
(Traditions de la paroisse des Avoyelles en Louisiana, MAFS 67, Philadelphia, 1956), p 63. For the couvade see Wayland D. Hand, "American
Analogues of the Couvade," Studies in Folklore, ed. W. E. Richmond
(Bloomington, Ind., 1957) ,,pp. 213–29.
8. Representative theoretical essays are: Franz Boas, "Relationships
between North-west America and North-east Asia," in Race, Language
and Culture (New York, 1948), pp. 344–55; Melville J. Herskovits, "Problem, Method and Theory in Afroamerican Studies," Afroamerica 1
(1945): 5–24; Clyde Kluckhohn, "A Comparative Study of Values in
Five Cultures," in E. Z. Vogt, Navaho Veterans: A Study of Changing Values, Papers of the Peabody Museum of American Archaeology and Ethnol-
ogy, 41, no. 1 (Cambridge, Mass., 1951): vii-ix; Robert Redfield. "The Folk
Society," American Journal of Sociology 52 (1947): 293–308.

number of analogous inquiries which the folklorist can test in the field. But the problems he frames will be based on the folklore of one unique, complex culture.

*Folksong and Folkmusic Specialists.* After attending the meetings and reading the journals, the visitor to our Society—or even the old member—may feel himself overwhelmed by the devotees of folksong and folkmusic. Francis James Child is king here, and Cecil Sharp his high priest. Ballad variants are microscopically scrutinized, their pedigrees exhaustively traced, their music subjected to IBM tests, the liaison of folksong and broadside and recording and art song psychoanalyzed. A new phalanx under the banner of ethnomusicology marches into the hall to the rhythms of African drumbeats and Indian love calls. A bystander gains the impression that America is a land of troubadours whose inhabitants carol before breakfast, woo at luncheon with love lyrics, entertain in the evening with ballad shockers, and retire with gospel hymns—folk of course.

This folksong scholarship represents largely an Anglo-American development. Percy, Ritson, and Scott unearthed the old ballads; Child in America canonized them; Sharp came from England to capture them in the Southern Appalachians; and Belden, Barry, Brown, and a host of others have collected them assiduously ever since. One notices in both countries the cleavage between folksong specialists and other folklorists. The Folk-Lore Society in London and its prime movers, Gomme, Lang, Hartland, Clodd, and Nutt, belong to a separate scholarly tradition from the line that leads through Percy to Cecil Sharp and the formation of the English Folksong and Dance Society. In the United States we recognize how exclusively preoccupied with folksong are Barry and the Lomaxes. The collection and study of folksong texts and tunes appear to the American folklorist as self-contained pursuits. Kaarle Krohn himself suggested that the study of folk music on the one hand and narratives and folk beliefs on the other required different skills and aimed at different goals.[9]

If the American folklorist finds the problems of folksong peripheral to his concerns, he sees in the materials of folk-

9. Krohn, *Die Folkloristische Arbeitsmethode,* p. 18.

song very direct connections. The English and Scottish popular ballads undergo a process of Americanization as they take on the coloring of their new environment. They may shed their tragic elements to reflect the happy-ending compulsions of American life, as Hyman ingeniously suggests.[10] A native balladry arises from the history and occupations of the New World. How successfully folksong may be wedded to its American setting appears in Eckstorm and Smyth's *Minstrelsy of Maine* where an historical division of woods songs is presented, and keen essays comment on their forms and themes, to show, for example, how the modern newspaper crime story displaces the old ballad formulas.[11] In Korson's collections of coal mining lore we see too the links between song, legend, and custom which rise out of a common background.[12] The Fifes declare that folksongs alone can furnish the outlines of Mormon history and theology.[13]

*Special Pleaders.* Occasionally a voice is still heard in strident exposition of one all-embracing interpretation of folk traditions. The plea may be aggressively asserted in behalf of myth-

10. Stanley E. Hyman, "The Child Ballad in America: Some Aesthetic Criteria," *JAF*, 70 (1957) : 235–39. D. K. Wilgus has criticized Hyman for neglecting to note the same degenerative process occurring with Child ballads in England ("Shooting Fish in a Barrel: The Child Ballad in America," *JAF*, 61 [1958]: 161, 164) . But his evidence really complements Hyman's, for with the present hegemony of the United States in the Western world, the American ethos and culture are exported along with Western dollars. Hyman's examples of the happy-ending Child ballads fit into his larger thesis on the denial of the tragic vision in America, e.g., in the case of Freud, whose somber insights into human nature have been perverted into rose-colored prescriptions for personality cures by American psychoanalysts.

11. Fanny H. Eckstorm and Mary W. Smyth, *Minstrelsy of Maine: Folksongs and Ballads of the Woods and the Coast* (Boston and New York, 1927) . For the comparison of headline news stories and balladry see pp. 378–83, "Of Ballads and Ballad-Making." Winifred Johnston has also written on this point, "Newspaper Balladry," *American Speech* 10 (1935) : 119–21.

12. George Korson, *Minstrels of the Mine Patch: Songs and Stories of the Anthracite Industry* (Philadelphia, 1938) , and *Coal Dust on the Fiddle: Songs and Stories of the Bituminous Industry* (Philadelphia, 1943) .

13. Austin and Alta Fife, *Saints of Sage and Saddle* (Bloomington, Ind., 1956) , p. 316.

ritual origins, or sexual symbolism, or the class struggle. Here
are flung the long shadows thrown by Frazer, Freud, and
Marx. Such unitary views belong to Europe in the nineteenth
century, when solar mythologists and cultural evolutionists
interpreted all folklore as myths about the sun or survivals
from savages. Today Hyman quotes Englishmen on the ritual
origins of folklore—Raglan, Weston, Cornford, Cook—and we
strain to see a ritual sacrifice in Mike Fink's shooting of Tal-
bert. In criticizing American folklorists for failure to develop
any theoretical premises, Hyman has performed salutary service.[14] But the student of American folk materials, bewildered
by their variety and number, cannot dally along the garden
paths of the special pleaders even if they appear seductive
—which they don't.

*Regional Collectors.* The four approaches to folklore just
mentioned came to the United States from abroad. Three
others have evolved in this country to deal with purely American materials.

Regional collecting in the United States is motivated chiefly
by convenience and emotional identification with a locality.
Collectors visit "their people": Randolph in the Ozarks, Dobie
in Texas, Chase in the Virginia Appalachians, Henry W.
Shoemaker in central Pennsylvania, Leonard Roberts in the
Kentucky Pine Mountain, Fife in Mormon Utah. So the re-
gionalist becomes identified with the area of his birth or
residence, or at least his summer vacations. Gardner revisited
the Schoharie Hills of New York for six summers to gather
her harvest. Korson has identified himself with the coal miners.
Brewer confines himself to the southern Negro, Saucier to the
Louisiana Cajuns. The collections that result include tech-
nically excellent works and have furnished us with indispensable materials. Nevertheless, even at best they remain on the
level of text-hunting. Eventually, the regional folklorist turns
into a parochial folklorist, ploughing the same field endlessly,

14. His position is stated in Stanley Edgar Hyman, "The Ritual View of
Myth and the Mythic," *JAF* 68 (1955) : 462–72. A more moderate claim
by another American ritualist, Herbert Weisinger, would limit the myth-
ritual theory to Western civilization (*JAF* 59 [1956]: 387–90) .

collecting simply to collect. This may be as large a goal as the
collector wishes to set for himself; Randolph admits his concern begins and ends with the Ozarks, and Dobie considers
the United States an appendage to Texas.[15] But our potential
American folklorist does not intend to be an Ozarkologist
or a Texologist. He is concerned with the whole civilization,
and with all its regions and occupations. Presumably he will
work now with one, now with another body of material, according to the questions he has framed. As does the anthropologist, he will base his expeditions on an hypothesis
and test it in the field with tough empirical data.

County collecting gained headway in England in the
late nineteenth century and produced substantial contributions for Shropshire, Herefordshire, Guernsey, and other
districts. These collectors were seldom theoretical scholars,
while the theorists like Lang and Gomme did no collecting,
but library and field folklorist joined forces in their search for
survivals and were occasionally linked by a dual figure like
Charlotte Burne. American regional collecting can similarly
be tied to theoretical questions. The kind of collecting which
Halpert advocates, by lifetime residents in their own back-
yard, will yield an aimless piling up of folklore bric-a-brac.[16]

*Literary Historians.* In 1931 Constance Rourke wrote a seminal book, *American Humor,* which bore important implica-
tions for folklore and literature. Calling attention to forgotten
sketches, yarns, and farces of the antebellum decades—such as
Meine had reprinted the previous year in his *Tall Tales of
the Southwest*—she declared that this indigenous vein of popular folk humor formed a fertile subsoil for the flowering of
American literature. In the writings of major American

---

15. Randolph told me this himself. See Dorson, "A Visit with Vance
Randolph," *JAF* 67 (1954) : 260. Dobie has written, "I care next to
nothing for the science of folklore . . ." (*Backwoods to Border*, ed. J. Frank
Dobie, Publications of the Texas Folk-Lore Society, 18 [Austin, Texas,
1943]: x) .
16. Herbert Halpert, "Some Undeveloped Areas in American Folklore,"
*JAF* 70 (1957) : 304. Halpert's excellent unpublished doctoral dissertation
is the best refutation of this position ("Folktales and Legends from the
New Jersey Pines: A Collection and Study," Indiana University, 1947) .

authors she traced the forms of lampoon, hoax, comic meta-
phor, burlesque, and hyperbole drawn from folk and popular
sources. Other literary scholars pressed forward into the exciting domain she had surveyed, and the string of small-scale
and full-length studies of folk humor in American literature
has continued unabated to the present day.

While Miss Rourke displayed brilliant insights into
American comic legend, she never engaged in fieldwork and
showed little awareness of the international currents of folklore. Consequently she fails to distinguish sharply between folk
and subliterary traditions. The later literary scholars she has
influenced know little about folklore except what they read in
her *American Humor* and compound her shortcomings. A
now famous source like the New York *Spirit of the Times*
contains a mass of humorous sketches and tales, some of
which can be recognized as folktales, while others represent
autobiographical, semifictional, or fanciful events. In their
anthologies and critical studies the literary scholars never
properly discriminate between these forms, since they lack the
tools of the folklorist to identify traditional motifs and tale-
types. When a praiseworthy article does appear identifying
humorous folktales in pre–Civil War Louisiana newspapers,
we observe that its author, Moore, acknowledges aid from a
professional folklorist, Jansen.[17]

Without such aid, the literary historians fall into egre-
gious error. We see the able excavator of *Native American
Humor (1800-1900)*, and the Mike Fink legends, Walter
Blair, betrayed into a book of spurious folk heroes in *Tall
Tale America*. Writing about tall tales in his study of the
*Spirit of the Times,* Yates conjectures whether the author of
a piece titled "Cut Legs" might have been influenced by Irving's "The Devil and Tom Walker," and wonders if Benet
read "Cut Legs" before writing "The Devil and Daniel
Webster." Yates does not know that "Cut Legs" is a widely
distributed European folktale about the devil, types 1030 and
1036, "The Crop Division," while the other two stories are

---

17. Arthur K. Moore, "Specimens of the Folktales from Some Antebellum
Newspapers of Louisiana," *Louisiana Historical Quarterly* 32 (1949):
723–58.

sophisticated compositions.[18] Of many inadequate articles
that could be cited on folklore in American literature, offering no supporting evidence, a recent one on *Huckleberry Finn*
in the journal *American Literature* can serve as the horrible
example.[19]

The realm of Americana in which oral humor and legend
crisscross with popular culture and creative literature holds
vast riches for students of American civilization. Literary historians have entered this domain from the side of print, in
studies of writers who have assimilated the varied folk traditions of American life into their stories, novels, poems, and
plays. Exciting anthologies and essays came from the original
spadework of Rourke, Meine, Blair, and DeVoto, but the
deeper subsequent scholars dig toward folk roots, the more
unsatisfactory their research appears.

*Popularizers.* Curiously, the one group in the United States
who profess most concern with American folk traditions have
least interest in its serious study. These are the popularizers,
whose organ is the *New York Folklore Quarterly,* whose leading figure is Benjamin A. Botkin, the treasury manufacturer,
and whose shrillest spokesman is Moritz Jagendorf, a writer
of children's books.

Popularization of folklore begins back with the brothers
Grimm, who soon discovered the market appeal of fairy tales.
The issue over tampering with folk materials disturbed even
the great team of English folklorists and led Gomme to chide
Lang for dispensing multihued fairy books. Two prodigiously
prolific Victorian clerics, Baring-Gould and T. F. Thiselton
Dyer, poured out popularized tomes of folklore that now
molder on library shelves. Folklore did not become big business in the United States until the 1940s, when Botkin began
issuing his treasuries, Alan Lomax took to the air, and Burl
Ives hit the night clubs. The cavernous maw of the mass

18. Norris W. Yates, *William T. Porter and the Spirit of the Times*
(Baton Rouge, La., 1957), pp. 160–61.
19. Ray W. Frantz," "The Role of Folklore in *Huckleberry Finn,*" *American Literature* 28 (1956): 314–27. My comments on this article appeared
in "Folklore in American Literature, a Postscript," *JAF* 71 (1958): 157–
59.

media gobbled up endless chunks of folksiness, and a new rationale appeared for the folklorist: his mission is to polish up, overhaul, revamp, and distribute folklore to the American people. This he can do through the writing of juvenile and treasury folk-books, singing and recording of folksongs, and staging of folk festivals.

In our quest for guidelines to a theory of American folklore, we cannot tarry with folklore performers and popularizers. They employ no theoretical premises, and engage in no basic research in the field or in the library. Their aim is to reach the public with any materials at hand, and their methods too often are the methods of fakelore. The American folklorist must take his stand squarely for or against standards and theory. When Tidwell commits himself to Botkin's formula with *A Treasury of American Folk Humor,* he must expect criticism for rehashing old jokebooks. My quarrel is less with Botkin than with folklorists who praise his patchworks as models of research. One notes that the eulogistic reviewers in the folklore journals of his first treasury possessed little or no background in American Studies.[20]

*Conclusion.* This then is the current brew of folklorist traditions: a blend of Thompson's *The Folktale,* Boas' *Tsimshian Mythology,* Sharp's *English Folksongs of the Southern Appalachians,* Raglan's *The Hero* cum Hyman, Randolph's Ozarkadia, Rourke's *American Humor,* and Botkin's *A Treasury of American Folklore.* From some or all of them the American folklorist may gain inspiration and fruitful concepts, but none fits his needs entirely. He must fashion his own platform and

20. Halpert has chosen to champion Botkin in his presidential address, *JAF* 70 (1957) : 300–301. My criticisms of Botkin's treasuries are given in the following reviews: *A Treasury of New England Folklore,* in *Saturday Review of Literature* 31 (1948) : 9–10, and another in *American Literature* 20 (1948) : 76–78; *A Treasury of Southern Folklore,* in *Mississippi Valley Historical Review* 37 (1950) : 354–55; and another in *JAF,* 63 (1950) : 480–82; *A Treasury of Mississippi River Folklore,* in *Minnesota History* 35 (1956) : 39–41. One folklore popularizer with a background in American studies but an innocence in folklore matters is Marshall Fishwick, who climaxed a series of inept articles on American folk heroes with a book, *American Heroes. Myth and Reality* (Washington, D. C., 1954) . My criticisms are registered in *Minnesota History* 34 (1955) : 261–62.

define his own targets. An occasional article like Bayard's attempt to pin down the elusive nature of folk matter, or earlier
symposia that have appeared in our journal, merely emphasize
the absence of continuity and common terms and agreed
goals for American folklorists.[21]

## Folklore and American Civilization

Existing folklore theories and philosophies bear little relevance to the American situation because American civilization
is the product of special historical conditions which in turn
breed special folklore problems. American history begins in
the seventeenth century. It looks back to no ancient racial
stock, no medieval heritage, no lineage of traditions shrouded
in a dim and remote past. The American folklorist must face
a question that few of his colleagues anywhere in the world
need ask, namely, what is his own folklore? Even in those
countries whose history is most analogous to our own, the
Latin American republics, Australia, or Canada, a far simpler
situation exists; the folklorist deals with transplanted Englishmen, Frenchmen, Spaniards, Portuguese, or with a fusion between a distinct European and a tenacious Indian inheritance.
In the United States the tower of Babel has been re-erected.
Those countries where folklore science has flourished most
vigorously, England, Germany, Finland, Ireland, Sweden,
Japan, possess the tidiest of cultural histories. But what are
the common traditions of Yankee and immigrant, of Negro
and Indian?

We may look for them in the great dramatic movements
of American history: exploration and colonization, Revolution and the establishment of a democratic republic, the westward surge, the tides of immigration, the slavery debate that
erupted in Civil War, and the triumph of technology and
industrialization. This is the framework of the traditions and
institutions that have shaped the American character. They
need to be taken into account in the history of American liter-

21. Bayard, "The Materials of Folklore"; "Conference on the Character
and State of Studies in Folklore," *JAF* 59 (1946) : 495–527; "Folklore Research in North America," *JAF* 60 (1947) : 350–416.

ature, philosophy, religion, economics, politics—and folklore. These forces have affected the folk traditions brought into the United States from Europe, Africa, and Asia, and they have shaped and created new folklore, or new adaptations of old folklore themes. The facts of American history create problems for the American folklorist—for instance, in the study of immigrant folk materials—which are central to his concern but peripheral or nonexistent for the comparative folklorist. Hence the American folklorist should be trained in American history and civilization as well as in folklore. Conversely, scholars trained in American Studies or in American literature should be schooled in folklore if they intend to deal with folkloristic, subliterary, and popular materials of American culture.

In this paper one may merely suggest problems and inquiries the American folklorist will be equipped to undertake.

*Colonization.* The colonial period is the breeding ground and nursery of American folklore. Where the comparative folklorist searches for the elusive *Ur*-form in the steppes of Siberia or a village by the Ganges, the American folklorist takes his point of departure with the settlements of the seventeenth century. Here is the historic moment when European traditions crossed the Atlantic and took root in the wilderness environments. Here English and Indian supernaturalism mingled, and here the giant tasks of taming a new world inspired a new growth of legend. One can even discern the first shoots of a humor that in time becomes distinctively American. The seventeenth century especially is permeated from top to bottom of society with respect for the supernatural, since rationalism had not yet driven its wedge between the intellectual and the folk.

A surprisingly full body of colonial writings is available to the folklorist. The colonists poured their literary energies into accounts of voyages and explorations, promotional tracts, diaries and journals, providential histories, lurid Indian captivities, and descriptions of the savages and denizens of the New World. Early in the eighteenth century newspapers and almanacs and broadside ballads appear. Since the lives of the colonists were intimately connected with supernatural beliefs and wonders, folklore abounds in these productions, in the form of English witchcraft, Indian shamanism, travelers' chimeras, Puritan providences. Such works as the *Account of Two-Voyages to New England* by John Josselyn, which appeared in 1675, or the *General History of Connecticut*, which Samuel Peters published in 1781, are strewn with colonial marvels and prodigies. Kittredge found abundance of transplanted English folk notions in the Massachusetts almanacs of Robert B. Thomas.[22] From the reports of early travelers Masterson assembled natural history tales, the narrative blend of bestiary lore, exaggeration, and misconception which formed so appetizing a fare for English readers of American wilderness adventures.[23] But for the most part colonial folklore is virgin territory.

Let me give one example of research possibilities. The American folklorist can find in the seventeenth century a wealth of remarkable providences. These are customarily discussed by American intellectual and literary historians in their treatment of Puritanism and the Mathers. Increase and his son Cotton compiled a splendid assortment of marvelous happenings to illustrate the wonderful workings of God in the New World. Since the Puritans regarded themselves as God's elect, and since they had voyaged to Massachusetts to establish a holy commonwealth dedicated to His Revealed Word, and since furthermore God communicated to his saints by direct intervention into the natural world, the people of Massachusetts Bay scrutinized fearfully and hopefully every providential manifestation of the divine will. Through providences they could check the course of their personal roads to salvation, and of their corporate cause for a Bible commonwealth. By definition the providence embraced the extraordinary, untoward occurrence. Increase Mather, as the foremost minister of the Bay Colony, set about collecting all examples of providences throughout the Puritan communities, and his fellow ministers zealously abetted the work; his indefatigable

22. George Lyman Kittredge, *The Old Farmer and His Almanack* (Cambridge, Mass., 1904, 4th impression, 1924). The first Thomas Almanac appeared in 1793.

23. James R. Masterson, "Travelers' Tales of Colonial Natural History," *JAF* 59 (1946) : 51–67, 174–88.

son Cotton continued the hunt. Folk beliefs that had taken
root in the rocky New England soil and twined around the
lives of the colonists are brought to light in the providences.
Calamitous events that lingered on in the memories of later
generations are written down as providences. The providences,
in short, were based on supernatural motifs and floating
legends.[24]

In June of 1648 a crowd of people in New Haven harbor
saw a brave ship sail through the air and vanish in a smoky
cloud, immediately upon a thunderstorm. Their minister, Mr.
Davenport, declared in public that God had condescended to
quiet the afflicted spirits of his people who were troubled at
the fate of their kinsmen, by sending them this account of his
sovereign disposal of their lives. Half a century later, when
Cotton Mather assembled his *Magnalia Christi Americana,*
this spectral sight was still the subject of marveling talk.
Similar reports of phantom ships circulated through the
colonies.[25]

When the prospects of the Bible commonweath reached
low ebb, and grumblers and fainthearted retreated to the
mother country, and cynics sneered at the Congregational
churches, Governor John Winthrop dramatically recounted
God's providential judgments on these sinners. A ship had
blown up in Boston harbor with scoffers on board; others had
miserably lost family and fortune.[26] This same motif of ven-
geance by the gods recurs throughout Puritan literature, lend-
ing special strength to the Puritan conviction that God

24. Increase Mather's *An Essay for the Recording of Illustrious Providences*
(Boston, 1684) was expanded by Cotton Mather in book 6 of the *Magnalia Christi Americana* (London, 1702). William Turner included many
American providences in his *A Compleat History of the Most Remarkable
Providences* (London, 1697). I have reprinted a number of Puritan "Remarkable Providences" in section 3 of my *America Begins* (New York,
1950), pp. 115–66.
25. The accounts of the New Haven specter ship are reprinted from
John Winthrop's journal and Cotton Mather's *Magnalia Christi Americana* in my *America Begins,* pp. 159–60, and two other seventeenth-
century reports of ghost vessels are given on pp. 158–59.
26. John Winthrop, *Journal "History of New England" 1630-1649,* ed. J.
K. Hosmer (New York, 1908), 2: 9–12, 82–83, reprinted in *America Begins,* pp. 133–37. See the motifs under C50, "Tabu: offending the gods."

championed his elect in the ceaseless battle against sinners and
Satan. Hence Quakers, antinomians, savages, perverts all met
with shocking fates, while saints escaped the terrors of the
deep and the wilderness through providential deliverances.
The reservoir of traditional folklore motifs supplied Puritan
ministers and their congregations with abundant themes for
their marvels and prodigies. Yet none of the splendid studies
by Miller, Murdock, Wertenbaker, Winslow, Simpson, considers this Puritan debt.[27] The providences are but one point
where colonial folklore and history intersect.

*The Westward Movement.* Seaboard settlers early began
pushing inland across the Appalachians toward the Pacific,
in an historic trek that lasted until the end of the nineteenth
century. Frederick Jackson Turner dramatized the role of the
continuous frontier in determining the course of American
history and the shape of the American character, and folklorists can supply a corollary to his thesis. The frontier bred
not only new species of men and new institutions remote from
European influences, but it cradled folk-heroes and released
a flood of legends. Literary historians like Rourke have over-
stated the American and Western uniqueness of these strong
heroes and tall tales, which have their counterparts in the
East, in Europe, and throughout the world, but the frontier
did indeed provide favorable conditions for the propagation
of heroic story. Ancient tales and formulas crept into campfire circles and hunters' cabins, to take on half-horse half-
alligator coloring. Frontier society approximated the Heroic
Age level of culture depicted by the Chadwicks, with the same
devotion to fighting, hunting, drinking, and sporting, and the
same seminomadic, individualistic heroes. The legends of
Davy Crockett and the process of their growth show astonishing resemblances to those of the folk-epic heroes of other

27. Perry Miller, *The New England Mind: The Seventeenth Century* (New
York, 1939) , and *The New England Mind, from Colony to Province* (Cam-
bridge, 1953) ; Kenneth B. Murdock, *Literature and Theology in Colonial
New England* (Cambridge, 1949) ; Thomas J. Wertenbaker, *The Puritan
Oligarchy* (New York and London, 1947) ; Ola E. Winslow, *Meetinghouse
Hill, 1630–1783* (New York, 1952) ; Alan Simpson, *Puritanism in Old and
New England* (Chicago, 1955) .

countries. A narrow biographer like James Shackford has no
tools to comprehend this cultural process of legendary creation, even though he subtitles his book on David Crockett
*The Man and the Legend.* Heroic Age epics grow through
cross-fertilization between oral tradition and popular literature, and so the case of Crockett requires the perspective both
of folklore and of American civilization.[28]

Other heroic patterns germinate along the moving frontier.
The disintegration of the leatherstocking hero-figure from
Cooper to the Beadle dime novels and Wild West movies is
skillfully pursued, on the level of print, by Henry Nash
Smith in *Virgin Land.* The outlaws best symbolized by Jesse
James, Sam Bass, and Billy the Kid all share certain features of
badmen folk-biography, which their historical biographers
rarely appreciate. Most of the books on Jesse James are based
on literary sources, with one notable exception, *Jesse James
Was My Neighbor,* by Homer Croy, who gathered many oral
traditions about Jesse, some of which fall squarely into the patterns of folktale. Yet Croy declares that his book eschews all
legend and folklore and can be trusted as accurate history.[29]
The American folklorist can still tap streams of legend flowing
from frontier days. There has just come to light the full saga
of Liver-Eating Johnson, a saturnine mountain man who ate
the livers of Crow Indians he relentlessly killed and scalped—
according to the hitherto unrevealed reminiscences of White-
Eye Anderson, who heard the grisly account from Del Gue,
who partnered with the Liver-Eater.[30]

28. My article, "Davy Crockett and the Heroic Age," *Southern Folklore
Quarterly* 6 (1942) : 95–102, applies to the Crockett legends the principles
of folk-epic development elaborated by H. M. and N. K. Chadwick in
*The Growth of Literature,* 3 vols. (Cambridge, England, 1932–40) . Since
then C. M. Bowra has supplemented their work with *Heroic Poetry* (London, 1952) . The biography alluded to is James A. Shackford, *David
Crockett, the Man and the Legend* (Chapel Hill, 1956) .
29. Homer Croy, *Jesse James Was My Neighbor* (New York, 1949) , p. 12:
"I am not putting in this book any legends or folktales."
30. *Crow Killer,* the legendary life of Liver-Eating Johnson, was written
by Raymond W. Thorp and Robert Bunker (Bloomington, Ind., 1958) .
See the pithy remarks of Bernard DeVoto on mountainman yarning in
*Across the Wide Missouri* (Boston, 1947) , pp. 44–45.

Fabulous myth as well as heroic legend flourished on the frontier. The travelers' tales of natural wonders which amazed Europeans in the seventeenth century find their counterpart in the exaggerations about the agricultural paradise and the uninhabitable desert. Henry Nash Smith has brillantly sketched these myth pictures from documentary sources, but they appear in oral tales too.[31] "Oregon" Smith, one tall-tale hero in the United States who has been adequately studied, derived his name from marvelous accounts of the Oregon territory he brought back to Indiana and Illinois in the 1850s. These tales were not idle whoppers, for in the emigrant guides of the period we find reports of Oregon which rivalled those of California, and pictured an earthly paradise that stimulated emigration.[32] Such emigrant guides doubtless influenced frontier traditions, along with other cheap printed articles like recipe books, almanacs, and songsters—a point recently made by Louis Jones in advocating cooperation between local historian and folklorist.[33]

Some frontier historians have utilized folklore materials. The studies of frontier social life and institutions by Everett Dick rely on personal interviews with old settlers as well as documentary sources. Especially has Theodore Blegen sharpened the concept of grass roots history in his sensitive essays on pioneer folk-culture of the high Midwest.[34] The frontier culture complex, lacking the intellectual instruments of Eastern culture like cities, schools, libraries, and courts of law, contains many elements of folk custom which can be given his-

31. Henry Nash Smith, *Virgin Land: The American West as Symbol and Myth* (Cambridge, 1950), ch. 11, "The Garden of the World and American Agrarianism," and ch. 16, "The Garden and the Desert."

32. Wm. Hugh Jansen has written a doctoral dissertation on "Abraham 'Oregon Smith: Pioneer Folk Hero, and Tale-Teller," Indiana University, 1949. A good example of an Oregon trail narrative and emigrant guide is Joel Palmer, *Journal of Travels over the Rocky Mountains, to the Mouth of the Columbia River; Made During the Years 1845–1846* (Cincinnati, 1847).

33. "Three Eyes on the Past: A New Triangulation for Local Studies," *New York Folklore Quarterly* 12 (1956): 5–6.

34. Everett Dick, *The Sod-House Frontier 1854–1890* (New York, 1938), and *Vanguards of the Frontier* (New York, 1941); and Theodore C. Blegen, *Grass Roots History* (Minneapolis, 1947), and *The Land Lies Open* (Minneapolis, 1949).

torical and comparative treatment. As frontiersmen adapted
themselves to shifting environments from trans-Appalachia
to the Great Plains, so presumably did they adjust their folkways.

*Immigration.* While one stream of Americans poured westward to reach the Pacific, an incoming flood of Europeans
crossed the Atlantic to become Americans. Historians of American civilization have recognized the distinctive and prominent
role played by immigrant groups, but the full story of transplantation and acculturation can never be told without
considering immigrant folk traditions.[35] The ethnic inheritance which European and Asiatic newcomers brought with
them consisted in good part of traditional observances, cuisine,
demonology, remedies, entertainments. What happened to
these folkways and folk beliefs after their possessors came to
the United States? By examining their tenacity, deterioration,
or compromises with the new culture, we see how different
hyphenate groups responded to and acted upon existing American institutions. Yet the only full-length study of this sort,
*South Italian Folkways in Europe and America,* by Phyllis Williams, was undertaken as a handbook for social workers.

The linguist Einar Haugen in his massive study of the
*Norwegian Language in America* drops many fruitful hints
for the American folklorist. He points out that American
culture patterns which vary from those in England often
come from immigrants, and he richly documents the statement
through linguistic evidence. Some words soon dropped from
the vocabulary of Norwegian immigrants, yielding to American terms, but others hung on durably, according to the dis-
appearance or retention of culture traits. By this reckoning
the church and home proved the most conservative Norwegian
institutions, and the store, the farm, and the polling booth
the most intrusive American ones.[36] Folk materials can be
similarly analyzed, to see which survive the ocean crossing.

35. A stimulating set of essays is Marcus L. Hansen, *The Immigrant in
American History* (Cambridge, 1940), particularly ch. 9, "Immigration
as a Field for Historical Research," but it makes no mention of folklore.
36. Einar Haugen, *The Norwegian Language in America* (Philadelphia
1953), vol. I, ch. 5, "The Great Vocabulary Shift."

One question that has always intrigued me is what happens to demonic beings when immigrants move from their homelands. Irish-Americans remember the fairies, Norwegian-Americans the *nisser*, Greek-Americans the *vrykólakas*, but only in relation to events remembered in the Old Country. When I once asked why such demons are not seen in America, my informants giggled confusedly and said, "They're scared to pass the ocean, it's too far," pointing out that Christ and the Apostles never came to America. Apparently the ethnic supernatural figures are too closely associated with the culture and geography of the Old Country to migrate. But shamanistic and magical beliefs easily span the waves: beliefs in bloodstopping, the evil eye, second sight. A tavern keeper in Hurley, Wisconsin, Sam Colasacco, graphically described to me the *fattura* that occurred in the village of his birth near Rome, where a spell-caster rendered a bridegroom impotent. On finding the account, Sam declared that a similar spell had been perpetrated by an Italian in Iron Mountain, Michigan, on his own son.

We know little about the vitality of these beliefs in the new context of American civilization. Marvin Opler studied Japanese-Americans relocated at Tule Lake, California, and reports that the artificial confinement of many Issei and Nisei families regenerated Old Country supernaturalism, which lapsed again after the dispersal of the camps.[37] Yet we may well be mistaken in presuming that Old Country folk beliefs disintegrate under the impact of American life. In one day's field recording from the only Greek family in Iron Mountain, Michigan, I secured some 12,000 words of traditional texts testifying to their vigorous retention of Old Country folk ideas. These five isolated Greek-Americans maintained a close relationship with the mother country. George Corombos had revisited Greece several times and brought back a bride from one trip. The Coromboses still owned their home in Bambakou, and rented it out. Their pride in the beauty of Ban-

37. Marvin K. Opler, "Japanese Folk Beliefs and Practices, Tule Lake, California," *JAF* 63 (1950): 385–97. An earlier article, by Opler and F. Obayashi, "Senryu Poetry as Folk and Community Expression," *JAF* 58 (1945): 1–11, dealt with a folk type of poetry that blossomed at Tule Lake.

bakou and the achievements of her citizens blended with their veneration for Haralampos, the patron saint of Bambakou, and Janaikis, their legendary Turk-destroying ancestor. As Bambakou, and Greece, remained alive in their minds, so did the memory of the *vrykólakas* and the *nereidos* and the *mati*, of saints' miracles and magicians' sorcery. They had never seen the ghoulish *vrykólakas* in America, but the *mati*, or evil eye, still operated in the New World. In fact Ted, my student, and the only American born Corombos, had been victimized by the *mati* as a baby, and was saved by his grandmother, wise in Old Country ways, who undid the dread spell, divining Ted's admirer with charcoal and cloves.[38]

The three generations of Coromboses provided in themselves a study in folk attitudes. The grandmother, no longer living, was referred to as a sage with special, almost shamanistic wisdom in occult matters. Her sons had adapted themselves successfully to American business life, becoming restaurant owners in the familiar Greek-American pattern. While retaining firm allegiance to their folk culture, they had acquired some environmental coloring. So when George Corombos related a tale of the young hero outwitting the stupid giants, he named the story "How the Game of Baseball was Invented in Greece Two Thousand Years Ago," and called the ogrish giants, swinging axes rather than bats, the predecessors of the New York (now California) ball club.[39] The grandson, Ted, alone speaking English perfectly, was fluent in Greek and had absorbed the traditions of the Coromboses, of Bambakou, and of Greece, from his grandmother and father. But he had become aware of the existence of other folk traditions, and was on the point of leaving the folk and becoming a folklorist. A distinction could be made between the sexes as well as the generations; the wives of John and George seemed barely to have touched America, spoke halting English, and unhesitantly admitted their belief in saints' legends and black magic.

38. These texts are published in *Fabula* 1 (1957): 114–43, under the title, "Tales of a Greek-American Family on Tape."

39. Ibid., 132–34. Two European tales, Type 1070, "Wrestling Contest," and Type 1115, "Attempted Murder with Hatchet," have been Americanized here.

The immigrant not only brings in old lore, but he contributes to new lore. Each wave of immigration leaves comic
stereotypes in its wake, and we can still see ripples from the
great Irish influx of the mid-nineteenth century, which produced the stage Irishman and the spate of Irish brogue jokes
that linger with astonishing persistence in pockets of the
land.[40] Today we can observe and collect the comic narratives
that swirl around later incoming groups. Pat and Mike are
matched by Eino and Weino in Finnish dialect stories, by
Yon and Ole in Swedish, by Jan and Bill in Cornish. Each
dialect reproduces the special malapropisms and intonations
that occur when the adult immigrant changes from his own
tongue to English, and mirrors the cultural shock and comic
mishaps of the newcomer in America. The visit to the baseball game is a favorite misadventure in French, Finnish, and
Italian dialect.[41] Jewish dialect folk jests reveal a surprising
reaction by Jewish-American humorists, who poke fun at the
oversensitivity to anti-Semitism of their Yiddish-speaking
fathers.[42] These dialect stories deal with the linguistic and
cultural confusion of immigrant groups but are rendered by
their American-born children and neighbors. There may well
be other forms of folk tradition springing from the impact
of the immigrant.

*Aborigines and Slaves.* American history bears the massive
imprint of two ethnic groups besides the immigrants: the West
African slaves brought into the South to plant and pick cotton, and the Indian tribes relentlessly driven back by the
frontier surge. The American folklorist will concentrate on the
folk materials of Negro and Indian that reflect cultural col-

40. Irish jokes survive among southern Negroes, Kentucky mountaineers,
raftsmen and lumbermen in the Catskills. See Dorson, *Negro Folktales in
Michigan* (Cambridge, 1946), pp. 182–85, and note 147 on pp. 229–30.
Carl Wittke in *The Irish in America* (Baton Rouge, La., 1956), speaks of
Paddy "In Song and Story" (ch. 22) and of "The Stage Irishman" (ch.
23), but says nothing of the Irishman in American folklore.
41. Dorson, "Dialect Stories of the Upper Peninsula," *JAF* 61 (1948):
113–50, gives 84 texts.
42. "Jewish-American Dialect Stories on Tape," 81 texts I collected, in
*Studies in Biblical and Jewish Folklore,* ed. D. Noy, R. Patai, and F. L.
Utley (Bloomington, Ind., 1960), pp. 111–74.

lision and exchange with general American civilization.

The Indian has exerted a powerful influence on the American mind quite disproportionate to his numbers. Hallowell is to be congratulated for eying his role in shaping American ideas and images.[43] White men have spun a kind of bastard folklore about the romanticized redskin, symbolized in the Lovers' Leap legend, but this synthetic folklore has become traditional and merits analysis.[44] Indians in their turn recognized the white men folkloristically, by incorporating European Märchen from the Frenchmen and Spaniards into their repertoires, as Stith Thompson has demonstrated; by sharing folk beliefs, for instance in bloodstoppers and love powders; by elaborating tribal histories in which the white man is the dupe or villain; and by weaving jests that puncture the arrogance of the overweaning paleface.[45] An Ojibwa, John Lufkins, told me in Brimley, Michigan, the anecdote about the Episcopalian minister visiting a Sioux reservation, who asked if his gifts would be safe in the tepee; the Indian chief assured him they would be, since no white man lived within fifty miles. A parallel cycle among white men depicts a stereotyped, laconic Indian who comments monosyllabically on the idiosyncrasies of the white man's culture. Thus, when taken for his first toboggan ride, and asked what he thought about it, the Indian says: "Whoosh. Walk a mile." The evolution of

43. A. Irving Hallowell, "The Impact of the American Indian on American Culture," *American Anthropologist* 61 (1957) : 201–17; and "The Backwash of the Frontier: The Impact of the Indian on American Culture," in *The Frontier in Perspective,* ed. W. D. Wyman and C. B. Kroeber (Madison, Wisconsin. 1957), pp. 230–58. Indian oratory for instance, in speeches and treaty-making, has entered white tradition. See Edward D. Seeber, "Critical Views on Logan's Speech," *JAF* 60 (1947) : 130–46; and Constance Rourke, *The Roots of American Culture* (New York, 1942), pp. 60–75.

44. Louise Pound doubts any Indian contribution to such legends: "Nebraska Legends of Lovers' Leaps," *Western Folklore* 8 (1949) : 304–13. References to numerous New England romantic Indian legends can be found in my *Jonathan Draws the Long Bow* (Cambridge, 1946), pp. 138–56.

45. Stith Thompson, *European Tales Among the North American Indians* (Colorado Springs, Col., 1919), deals with Märchen. Examples of white elements in Ojibwa narratives, from my own fieldwork, appear in Dorson, *Bloodstoppers and Bearwalkers* (Cambridge, 1952), pp. 34–40.

these biracial jests can be traced historically.[46] Still another folklore link between the white and red man lies in Anglo-American and French-Canadian folksongs stereotyping the cruel redskin and the noble savage, as Fife and Redden convincingly demonstrate.[47]

The Negro lives within American civilization rather than on its borders as does the Indian, and yet his fertile and abundant folklore is often treated as a thing apart. The emphasis on animal tales, presumably originating in Africa, and the concentration on Gullah Negroes of the Carolina and Georgia coast, where African retentions are highest, distort the picture. Most of the Brer Rabbit tales come from Europe and many Negro beliefs are pure British. A whole body of traditions has grown up on American soil. Slave songs reflect successive historical periods, as Miles Mark Fisher has shown, even if he strains his evidence.[48] Slave tales in the Old Marster and John cycle, only recently noticed by collectors, come from the heart of the plantation culture, although their parts and formulas can be traced to far continents. Since the Civil War Old Marster has partially been replaced by Boss-man, in tartly comic narratives of race relations.[49] A corpus of Negro protest tales revolving around Jim Crowism exists, though it has not yet received the attention of folklorists. Nor are such tales the exclusive property of Negroes, any more than Jewish dialect jests are restricted to Jews. A white man in Alabama told me this one about a Negro who went North and allegedly

46. Dorson, "Comic Indian Anecdotes," *Southern Folklore Quarterly* 10 (1946) : 113–28.

47. Austin E. Fife and Francesca Redden, "The Pseudo-Indian Folksongs of the Anglo-American and French-Canadian," *JAF* 67 (1954) : 239–52, 379–94. They conclude that "songs about historical events, including songs about dramatic episodes in the relationships of Indians and Whites, have been sung regularly since the earliest days of colonization and have faithfully reflected the changing relationships between the two cultures. . . ."

48. Miles M. Fisher, *Negro Slave Songs in the United States* (Ithaca, N. Y., 1953) .

49. See ch. 4, "Old Marster and John," in my *Negro Folktales in Michigan*, pp. 51–74; J. Mason Brewer, "Juneteenth," in *Tone the Bell Easy*, ed. J. F. Dobie, *PTFS* (*Publications of the Texas Folklore Society*) 10 (1932) : 9–54; and "John Tales" in *Mexican Border Ballads and Other Lore*, ed. M. C. Boatright, *PTFS* 21 (1946) : 81–104.

married a white woman. On his return his boss-man asked
him menacingly if this were true. "No suh, Boss," he answered,
"she's half colored and half Yankee." Anecdotes such as these
can be found in profusion, and their nature restricts them to
oral circulation. They plumb deeply into the troubled currents of our culture. But their attitudes and messages vary
and will repay scrutiny.[50]

*Regionalism.* Colonial settlement, the westward drive, slavery
and sectional conflict, immigration, economic resources, and
geography have combined to create distinctive regional subcultures. The problem of regionalism has attracted the attention of sociologists, historians, and geographers among others,
who joined in a provocative symposium, published in 1952
under the title *Regionalism in America.* Especially suggestive
for the folklorist is the exciting essay by Rupert Vance, "The
Concept of Regionalism as a Tool for Social Research." Vance
outlines four levels of regional research. He begins with regional analysis by single traits, giving for an example a
regional study of rural house types constructed by folk carpenters, and increases the number of component factors in
the second and third stages. At the "highest level of integra-
tion," Vance speaks of interregional relations and ·compari-
sons. His reminder that regions are dynamic not static cau-
tions the folklorist that regional folk culture is not a simple
tableau but must be studied in depth and in process. Other
suggestive ideas come from the historian Pollard, who proposes that kinship areas based on community of work and
thought determine regional boundaries, rather than statistical
indices of agricultural production, while his colleague Hessel-
tine recommends attention to smaller-than-regional units,
perhaps subregions or districts.[51]

The regional folk-culture complex offers the American
folklorist one of his most inviting targets. A spectacular var-

50. Sections on Negro protest tales appear in my *Negro Tales from Pine
Bluff, Arkansas, and Calvin, Michigan* (Bloomington, Ind., 1958) , pp.
108–28, 228–38.
51. *Regionalism in America,* ed. Merrill Jensen (Madison, Wis., 1952)
pp. 119–206, 145.

iety of regional folk cultures confronts the American folklorist. He thinks at once of German Pennsylvania, the bayou
country of the Louisiana Cajuns, the Spanish-Mexican Southwest, Mormon Utah, Michigan's Upper Peninsula, the Yankee coast of Maine, the Ozarks and the Southern Appalachians. But of uncollected and undefined regions, subregions,
and pockets we can only guess. The publishing house of
Duell, Sloan, and Pearce carved out a number of zones for
their popular series on American Folkways. We would like
to recognize, define and bound such regional zones. Here the
Linguistic Atlas isoglosses constructed by Hans Kurath and
his associates may serve as models.[52] If boundaries for relic
areas of folk speech may be plotted, conceivably the extent of
distinctive features in the regional folk culture may be traced:
say Pennsylvania Dutch *fraktur*, the passion play of *Los Pastores*, the Mormon legend of the "Three Nephites," the comic
dialect story of immigrant groups. But more important even
than establishing the boundaries will be ascertaining the centers and strongholds of the folklore region. Anthropological
concepts of cultural focus, drift, and conservatism can serve
these ends.[53] The fieldwork will require collection on many
fronts rather than along specialized forms of folktale or folksong, and will be complemented by documentary study of
population movements and historical and economic forces.
Beck's *The Folklore of Maine*, although regrettably lacking in
source information, does bind together the occupational background of Maine sailing and fishing with the folkways and
oral traditions of the coastal sea.

52. Kurath contributed an essay on "Linguistic Regionalism" to *Regionalism in America*, pp. 297–310. He is the chief author of the *Linguistic
Atlas of New England*, 3 vols. (Providence, R. I., 1939–43), and of the
*Handbook of the Linguistic Geography of New England* (Providence,
1939), which apply his techniques.
53. These concepts are discussed by Herskovits in *Man and His Works*,
chs. 28, 32, 34: "Conservatism and Change in Culture," "Cultural Focus
and Reinterpretation," "Cultural Drift and Historic Accident." They
might be employed, for example, in discussing folk religion as the focus
of Pennsylvania German folk culture or Ozark folk medicine as a con-
serving force opposed to medical science or dialect folktales of the Upper
Peninsula as an instance of cultural drift.

From my own fieldwork I can suggest some generalizations about the folk-culture complex of the Upper Peninsula. The boundaries are fairly well fixed by the geographical encirclement of the Great Lakes on all sides save the Wisconsin border, and apparently the complex extends through the similar cultural and demographic area of northern Wisconsin and Minnesota. The Peninsula is compounded of occupational groups—the lumberjacks, iron and copper miners, and Great Lakes sailors; immigrant groups—the Finns, French-Canadians, and Cornishmen primarily, with a sprinkling of most European nationalities; and the Ojibwa Indians scattered on small reservations. A free and easy spirit reminiscent of the frontier pervades the fraternal towns, and there is much talk of "whiskey-fighting men" and epic feats of stamina. The complex contains a series of parallel traditions, ethnic and occupational and local-historical, which never cross; the lore of the Indian and the Finn and the lumberjack remain in separate compartments, although one individual may belong to two or three folk groups (like a Finnish lumberjack) and know both an occupational and an immigrant tradition. The younger generation has developed an indigenous folktale form in the dialect story based on speech and behavior of the immigrants.[54]

By contrast, Jonesport on the Maine coast presents a completely homogeneous folk-culture composed of a single Yankee stock, descended from East Anglian settlers, and a single occupation, fishing in the coastal waters. Its tight, static society lives on the offshore islands or along the coast, spending much time in small boats or on beaches, lobstering, clamming, sardining. On shore the people shuck clams, mend twine, and can sardines. Currents of folklore sweep through their lives. They speak of calling the spirits to detect thieves, tell sea legends about buying the wind, revere a giant lobsterman named Barney Beal, dig for treasure guided by wands, and

54. The evidence for these generalizations is in my *Bloodstoppers and Bearwalkers*.

spin comic anecdotes and rhymes about local characters. All the people share the same folk tradition.[55]

Such regions and pockets stand in contrast to the general American mass culture of urbanization, industrialization, and other-direction. The folklorist is particularly qualified to investigate these shadowy corners of American life.

*Patriotism and Democracy.* American history can be viewed in a mythical as well as a factual light. The story of the democratic experiment in the garden of plenty takes on large romantic outlines in Fourth of July orations, promotional tracts, emigrant guides, and election speeches. Puritanism supplied the providential interpretation of the American mission, the Revolution hallowed the cause of democracy, Manifest Destiny blazed the trail to the Pacific. Some of these myths of democratic patriotism are studied in Gabriel's *The Course of American Democratic Thought,* Smith's *Virgin Land,* Weinberg's *Manifest Destiny,* and Curti's *The Roots of American Loyalty.* No one has considered the folk versions of American history where the patriots, the trailblazers, the political saviors, the industrial tycoons, and the labor leaders are deified —or vilified—according to the section and the society. Some glimpses into this folk history can be seen in Dixon Wecter's penetrating look at *The Hero in America,* which throws into relief the lights and shadows of reputations belonging to glamorous political and historical personalities.

These works draw from popular and documentary sources. and can be complemented by field reports from oral tradition. Which of America's great names have passed into folklore? Legends have attached to Lincoln, and a revealing field study would compare Southern traditions of Lincoln the mulatto with Northern legends of the savior.[56] A flood of jests about

---

55. My field trip to Jonesport is reported in the *Proceedings of the American Philosophical Society* 101 (1957) : 270–89, under the title, "Collecting Folklore in Jonesport, Maine."

56. There are materials for the folklorist in Lloyd Lewis, *Myths After Lincoln* (New York, 1929, reprinted 1941) ; Montgomery S. Lewis, *Legends that Libel Lincoln* (New York and Toronto, 1946) ; and Dixon Wecter, "Lincoln: the Democrat as Hero," in his *The Hero in America* (New York, 1941) , ch. 10, pp. 222–72.

Henry Ford still circulate, and we may find considerably more industrial folkstuff than Kenneth Porter was able to uncover when he wrote "The Business Man in American Folklore."[57] Our wars for democratic survival are breeders of tradition, still largely uncollected. Recently two active younger folklorists told me about their collecting experiences along this line; one found Civil War legends rife in central Pennsylvania, the other found Revolutionary reminiscences strong on the Northeastern seaboard, and both reported much folk manipulation and reconstruction of history.[58] I recorded two Revolutionary oral legends in central Maine in July 1956; in one the British fire on and put to rout a ragged band of Americans at the battle of Camden, and then gallantly loan their doctor to the rebels to patch up a warrior's broken leg. Patriotic ballads retell American history in accord with romantic democracy and sectional pride, and for these we can look to old compilations of Revolutionary, War of 1812, and Civil War ballads no longer sung, and hence disregarded by folksong collectors.[59]

*Mass Culture.* Our American civilization has culminated in a mass culture which seems destructive of folklore. The mass media of communication and entertainment fill up the wells of folk tradition with the slag and refuse of gag writers, tunesmiths, Madison Avenue admen, and all the other hucksters in our midst.

This is not a sad state of affairs. I do not propose to tilt at the windmills of our culture to restore pure, unpolluted folk-

57. *Bulletin of the Business Historical Society* 18 (1944) : 113–30.
58. Kenneth Goldstein of Hatboro, Pennsylvania, and Frank A. Hoffmann of Bloomington, Indiana.
59. G. Malcolm Laws says that many once-popular American historical ballads are now found only in collections of old broadsides like *American Naval Songs and Ballads* by Robert Neeser (New Haven, 1938). War songs survive better than ballads (Laws, *Native American Balladry* [Philadelphia, 1950], p. 16). A good early collection is Frank Moore, *Songs and Ballads of the American Revolution* (New York, 1856). An older discussion of an historical ballad is Charles B. Galbreath, "The Battle of Lake Erie in Ballad and History," *Ohio Archaeological and Historical Publication* 20 (1911) : 415–56; and a recent model study is by Austin E. Fife, "A Ballad of the Mountain Meadows Massacre," *Western Folklore* 12 (1953) : 229–41.

lore. Rather I suggest that the American folklorist consider
the relationships between mass culture and folklore patterns.
Paul Bunyan as a folk hero is thin and disappointing, but as
a manufactured production catering to the needs of children,
resort promoters, advertising agencies, journalists, and artists
he offers ample nourishment. In an age of nylon, orlon, and
dacron, why not synthetic folk heroes? Our American folklorist
will interest himself in the process that has molded Paul
Bunyan, Pecos Bill, Joe Magarac in the image of bigness,
power, efficiency. The numerous references to Bunyan in the
nation's press show a surprising variety of attitudes toward
the fabricated behemoth. Instead of a monolithic figure we
find a paradoxical one, who can be invoked by lumber cor-
porations and by the *Daily Worker,* who is regarded as one
hundred per cent American and as a copy of Hercules and
Thor, who is reduced to the understanding of children and
exalted for the taste of operetta, symphony, and ballet audiences.[60]

Besides the creation of artificial folk heroes, or the Bun-
yanizing of genuine ones, mass culture breeds its own special
varieties of folklore. If tradition-directed pockets have their
Märchen and Child ballads, and inner-directed societies their
providences and wonders, the other-directed groups that
dominate contemporary American life, particularly the teen-
age advance guard, possess their jive talk, droodles, parodies,
and parlor puzzles.[61] The teeming high schools and college
campuses, the summer camps and youth organizations, provide the setting for other-directed fun and games, which possess traditional elements.[62] A vast new army, navy, marine
corps, and air force of young men have come into being in
our time and generated a volume of GI jests, pranks, jinxes,

60. Dorson, "Paul Bunyan in the News, 1939–1941," *Western Folklore* 15
(1956) : 26–39, 179–93, 247–61.
61. There is much for the American folklorist to ponder over in David
Riesman's *The Lonely Crowd* (New Haven, 1950). He has pertinent remarks on the vitiation of oral tradition by modern culture in "The
Oral and Written Traditions," *Explorations Six* (Toronto, 1956), 22–28.
62. See Dorson, "The Folklore of Colleges," *American Mercury* 68 (1949) :
671–77, which samples a much larger body of material in the Indiana
University (formerly Michigan State University) Folklore Archives.

bawdy songs, battle legends, and overseas anecdotes.[63] In the white-collar world, salesmen soften their clients and sales executives toughen their staffs with brief pointed stories, the emblems of our high-tempoed culture.[64] Ours is an age of public speakers, and all of them, college presidents or ministers or politicians or conference leaders or professors, rely on the apt anecdote to make their point and retain their audience. When youths gather in groups, they entertain themselves with anal and genital humor, which, as Waterman has shown, can be studied in terms of psychocultural attitudes.[65] These masses of oral materials floating in contemporary American culture merit the attention of folklorists, who may find in them motifs of unsuspected antiquity, clothed in new dress to suit modern times.

This paper has maintained that students of American folklore must find common theoretical ground if they aspire to be more than random collectors or public entertainers. To reach such ground they will need training equally in the science of folklore and in the history of American civilization. This can be done if programs in American Studies provide for instruction in the collecting and analytical techniques of folklore, and if our few advanced programs in folklore include work in American social and cultural history.[66] Each contribution by these American folklorists, whether in terms of immigrant acculturation or the regional complex or mass-culture traditions, then becomes part of a cooperative inquiry into the behavior of folklore within the American environment. Ultimately American folklore will take its place alongside American literature, American politics, the history of

63. The Indiana University Folklore Archives contains 85 folders of GI folklore.

64. I have tape-recorded such tales from Norman Johnson, who used them frequently as national sales-promotion manager of Chevrolet.

65. Richard A. Waterman, "The Role of Obscenity in the Folk Tales of the 'Intellectual' Stratum of Our Society," *JAF* 62 (1949) : 162–65.

66. Tremaine McDowell gives a paragraph to folklore in his *American Studies* (Minneapolis, 1948) , p. 61, but see his sympathetic note, "Folklore and American Studies," *American Heritage* 2 (1948) : 44–47.

American ideas, and other studies that illuminate the American mind.[67]

67. The argument of this paper will be strengthened with the appearance of Daniel J. Boorstin's three volume history of American culture. Boorstin asserts that American civilization differs so widely from European that it must be studied through new categories. See his preliminary paper, "The Place of Thought in American Life," *American Scholar* 25 (1959) : 137–50; and his first volume, *The Americans: The Colonial Experience* (New York, 1958) .

# 3

# A Theory for
# American Folklore Reviewed

Folklorists in the United States have puzzled over the content of American folklore ever since our subject took shape. Can a young nation have any traditions to call its own? Can it claim the traditions brought to its shores from the Old World? In so mobile and commercialized a society, what role can folklore play anyway? To attempt answers to these questions, I presented to the American Folklore Society in 1957 a paper, subsequently printed in the *Journal of American Folklore* along with commentaries by panelists and floor speakers, titled "A Theory for American Folklore."[1] This theory provided the conceptual basis for my book *American Folklore* (Chicago, 1959). Eleven years later I should like to reassess the

This paper was delivered as the presidential address at the American Folklore Society annual meeting held in Bloomington, Indiana, 9 November 1968. It was printed in the *Journal of American Folklore,* vol. 82 (1969).
1. *Journal of American Folklore* 72 (1959) : 197–242.

theory in the light of intervening criticisms and new publications that may challenge, strengthen, or alter certain of the contentions.

The "Theory" was originally divided into two parts; a review of existing approaches to American folklore, of which seven were identified and considered oblique or limited in their premises; and the formulation of a new approach especially designed to grapple with the kinds of folk traditions present in the United States. The idea was to begin with American conditions and evolve a folkloristic perspective, rather than to begin with a priori conceptions from ballad theory or European or anthropological or literary scholarship and wrench them in an effort to meet the American situation. Which areas of American life and history seemed particularly productive of folklore? Again the magic number seven emerged, in a list of historical topics considered most fruitful for the folklorist: colonization, the westward movement, Negro slavery, regionalism, immigration, democracy, and mass culture. Instead of commencing with the genres of folklore and looking for them in the fifty states, the "Theory" proceeded from likely vantage points of American civilization to the categories of folklore. The particular assumption and the fond hope behind the "Theory" are that it will illuminate darkened corridors of American history and contemporary society hidden from the view of historians, sociologists, political scientists, and their academic brethren.

The recently published and admirably presented work of Jan H. Brunvand, *The Study of American Folklore: An Introduction* (New York, 1968), explicitly concentrates on genres. It is not a book of theory but rather a book of definitions, the necessary precursor to any theory, and it fills a large vacuum in the resources of folklore teachers. The examples are selected from Anglo-American traditions, since these are most available to the folklorist in this country. But folklorists in other countries could, and have, constructed conceptually similar volumes, with illustrations of the genres most familiar to them. A book based on the "Theory for American Folklore" could not, so is my contention, be duplicated in another nation. Folktales, folksongs, proverbs, beliefs, folk art are universal; the drama of colonizing, the march across a continent, the institution of slavery, the phenomenon of mass immigration, the platform of democracy, the pervasiveness of technology—none of these are cultural universals, and nowhere have they occurred together save in the United States.

I

A speculative theory needs testing and blooding. At its initial unveiling my "Theory" received a depth examination by five panelists and several floor commentators. And there, to all intents and purposes, the matter rested. American folklore studies continued along their merry separate ways, and the seven sinful schools kept on sinning with increased vigor. The "Theory" created about as much impact as a cherry blossom dropped from the summit of Mount Fuji onto a snowbank at the foot.

In my heart of hearts, perhaps, I yearned for a caustic critic—an Andrew Lang tilting at Max Müller or a Joseph Jacobs in turn jabbing at Lang, men who held the British public spellbound for four decades with the virtuosity of their debating skills. But this Walter Mitty fantasy disintegrated swiftly in the cavern of American scholarship. Our hopeful theorist, if he does not belong to a modish cult—say of symbolic structuralism, or sociopsychodynamics, or linguistic folklife, or computerized mythology—is either summarily clubbed or blithely ignored. There were some cavalier reviews of *American Folklore,* for instance by Kenneth Lynn in the New York *Herald Tribune* and by Ann Chowning in the *American Anthropologist,* but these were barbs of nonfolklorists not knowing even the terms of the subject. There were the sweeping denouncements of folklore in the *Wall Street Journal* and the *Congressional Record* in reaction to small grants given folklore programs under the National Defense Education Act. The resulting attempt to educate congressmen and senators as to the serious values of folklore studies could not be called a dialogue of high philosophical tenor.

Yet the "Theory" did receive three searching analyses from unexpected quarters: a teacher of social sciences in Pennsylvania, a historian at the University of Massachusetts, and a female but not very ladylike Soviet ethnologist. None

were personally known to me, and it is a curious commentary
on American scholarly communications that the lengthy article by the historian Mario De Pillis, devoted entirely to a
review of my ideas, escaped my attention for four years until
Bruce Buckley mentioned it parenthetically during a long-
distance telephone call. It appeared in *Arizona and the West*
under the deceptive title "Folklore and the American West."[2]
In any event these three critiques can serve to sharpen, if they
do not dismember, the "Theory."

The first critique took the form of a sequence of forty-
four pointed questions that Phil R. Jack addressed to the
"Theory." These were printed in the *Journal of American
Folklore* and were followed by my answers, keyed to the page
numbers and topics listed in the questions.[3] Jack probed and
poked at most of the main assumptions of the "Theory":
the alleged uniqueness of American historical conditions as
folklore-generating factors; the downgrading of the regional
method as parochial; the rejection of alternate approaches to
American folklore other than the whole-civilization approach.
He questioned the validity of the whole-civilization approach
itself, since fakeloristic writings had been issued in its name.
These well-couched, darting queries, one leading skillfully
into another, certainly subjected the "Theory" to rigorous
scrutiny, but they only served to reinforce my confidence in
the general thesis, for the questions could be readily met.
First, the regional approach as such was not denigrated; regionalism was presented as one of the special shaping forces
of American civilization rich in folklore dividends. Objection
was made not to the efforts of the single-minded regional collector, for on them depends any larger synthesis, but rather
to the limits of his horizon. The "Theory" calls for cross-
regional comparisons. Second, as for alternative approaches,
the "Theory" is indeed dogmatic in insisting on the priority
of its principles over the casual flirtations with American
folk traditions characteristic of the available systems. In the

2. 4 (1963) : 291–314.

3. Phil R. Jack, "Questions on 'A Theory for American Folklore'," and
Richard M. Dorson, "Replies to Questions on 'A Theory for American
Folklore'," *Journal of American Folklore* 73 (1960) : 325–30.

original floor discussion George Herzog inquired whether an ethnomusicologist was disqualified by his training from studying folk and Indian music in the United States. The answer is that any specialist has of course perfect license to pursue his interests without fear of apprehension by a Dorson undercover agent or brainwashed student, but the specialist in ballads or literature or other subject matter is simply not dealing with the full American context of his genre. Finally, what then about the popularizers, who alone of the extant groups of folklorists do employ the whole-civilization approach? Would not their shortcomings invalidate the approach? The response here is that the term *whole-civilization,* which Jack has foisted upon the "Theory," is misleading, since the "Theory" cannot be applied to anyone who assembles a package of folk materials with "American" in the title. In fact, the nontheoretical popularization of American folklore was one of the stimuli for the construction of the "Theory."

In "Folklore and the American West," De Pillis devoted most of his twenty-three-page article to a close testing of the "Theory" and related writings of mine. One block of seven pages turns aside to examine two collections of state folklore for Kansas and Wisconsin, because "the best way to assess Dorson's theory is to see how the procedures have been working."[4] Since the "Theory" never advocated a state basis for collecting but rather rejected it for the regional concept, this interpolation is irrelevant, except perhaps to justify admission of De Pillis' article into a western journal. In the course of his article De Pillis mentions Dorson eighty times, a compliment I cannot match in the present paper, much as I would like to deal with all his points. In summary they seem to boil down to this: Dorson is waging a "lonely, bitter" fight for the cause of scientific folklore and the marriage of folklore and history; in spite of his advocacy of theory and discussion of ideas he is hostile to all extant theories and to theory in general; he neglects the interpretations through myth and symbol, say, of Mircea Eliade or of American cultural historians like Marvin Meyers and Henry Nash Smith, who actually

4. De Pillis, "Folklore and the American West," 294–301.

employ methods and concepts very close to Dorson's position
on scientific folklore; he poses a surprisingly pedestrian definition of *folklore* as collecting oral facts for no particular purpose other than to express sympathy with the hidden, anonymous millions after the fashion of nineteenth-century
romantics; his evidence of mass-culture folklore is thin and
insignificant.

This summary is unfair to De Pillis in the sense that his
eighty references include some generous sentiments, but my
concern here is with his criticisms.

First, on the use of myth as an analytic tool in folklore
studies and American studies: In an article on "Oral Tradition and Written History: The Case for the United States,"
printed in the *Journal of the Folklore Institute* (December,
1964), I contended for just that point. (See pp. 129–44.) One
of the subheadings used to suggest the benefits accruing to
the historian partial to folklore was titled "Strengthening the
Concepts of Myth, Symbol, and Image," and Henry Nash
Smith's *Virgin Land: The West as Symbol and Myth* (Cambridge, Mass., 1950) was acclaimed, with the reservation that
it does not dip below subliterature into oral tradition. Unfortunately the one full-scale attempt to join American history and folklore with the glue of myth and symbol, Frank R.
Kramer's *Voices in the Valley* (Madison, Wis., 1964), so over-
played its hand as to discredit the method. But the method
has value, and can fit into the "Theory," and De Pillis, in attacking what he calls Dorson's "hostility to symbolic interpretation," has registered a hit that I immediately concede. I
refer to his quotation from a statement of mine that some
topics in American history, such as the emergence of the
Mormons, lend themselves readily to folklore treatment, while
others, such as currency reform and Jackson's veto in 1832
of the bill to recharter the Bank of the United States, are
far removed from folklore. De Pillis counters, "It is quite
evident to any American historian that the Bank War can be,
and has been, symbolically interpreted."[5]

The special work that De Pillis cites in behalf of this assertion is Marvin Meyers' *The Jacksonian Persuasion: Politics*

5. Ibid., 303.

*and Belief* (Palo Alto, Cal., 1957; Vintage ed., 1960). De Pillis declares that Meyers' use of "persuasion" is equivalent to Dorson's definition of the "central value of folklore." The two terms alike apply to beliefs, values, attitudes, outlooks, and prejudices of the anonymous millions. Historian and folklorist each look for these revelations in a mass of primary sources, and in claiming uniqueness for his method Dorson is actually robbing history to pay folklore. The cultural historians have been doing this all along, says De Pillis, at least since the publication of *Virgin Land* in 1950.

Money and the emotional legislation it has engendered throughout American history can indeed be interpreted symbolically. The money issue, conceived of as gold versus silver, or specie versus paper currency, or the Bank of the United States versus the people, or Wall Street versus the common man, fits snugly into Parrington's conception of the intellectual tides of American history. Hamilton, the arch-conservative, distrustful of the people, sought to bind big business and big government together through his fiscal policies: establishment of a national bank, assumption of state debts by the federal government, imposition of a protective tariff to aid infant industries. Jefferson construed his election in 1800 as a mandate to save the country from crime-racked cities and greedy industrialism and to restore the republic to its proper base of virtuous citizen-farmers. In the Era of Good Feeling, the demon of Hamiltonian federalism reemerged in the Whiggism of Clay and Webster, to be challenged by a new Galahad called Old Hickory. In his presidential address of 1832 Andrew Jackson reviled the Monster Bank—a phrase used repeatedly by Meyers—as un-American, undemocratic, and unconstitutional. These emotional terms laid low a salutary mechanism of monetary stability and doomed a national bank forever. The stigma of monopoly became attached to trusts and corporate enterprises and has persisted to the present day, reinforced by the trust-busting of Teddy Roosevelt and the muckraking of the Progressive reformers.

The passionate reactions to currency legislation are seen again in the post-Civil War debate over the free and unlimited coinage of silver. When free silver was denied, miners and farmers branded the Coinage Act that limited legal tender to

gold as the Crime of 1873. One of the pivotal issues behind
the Populist movement was the desire of debtor classes for a
softer currency, whether in the form of greenbacks or bimetal-
lism. William Hope "Coin" Harvey wrote a series of best-
selling and bitterly attacked books explaining the intricacies
of the money question in simple terms. In *Coin's Financial
School* (Chicago, 1894), he placed these words in the mouth
of Coin, a youthful Chicago financier turned teacher: "Our
forefathers . . . were led to adopt silver because it was the
most reliable. It was the most favored as money by the people.
. . . It was so much handled by the people and preferred by
them, that it was called the people's money. Gold was considered the money of the rich. It was owned principally by
that class of people, and the poor people seldom handled it,
and the very poor people seldom ever saw any of it."[6]

When the Democrats preempted the Populist program
in the election of 1896, William Jennings Bryan declaimed
memorably for the people and against the Wall Street money
changers with the peroration, "You shall not crucify mankind
upon a Cross of Gold!" In the twentieth century the evil
symbolism of gold has extended to corporate giants and trust
ogres. The celebrated report of the Pujo Committee of the
House of Representatives in 1913 uncovered the wide network
of banker-directors linking financial and industrial institutions. In *Other People's Money* (New York, 1914), Louis D.
Brandeis, later to become a Supreme Court justice, attacked
what he called the "money trust" and in a chapter titled "Our
Financial Oligarchy" used these words to show that the gold
of the bankers was actually the money of the people.

> The goose that lays golden eggs has been considered a
> most valuable possession. But even more profitable is the
> privilege of taking the golden eggs laid by somebody
> else's goose. The investment bankers and their associates
> now enjoy that privilege. They control the people
> through the people's own money. If the bankers' power
> were commensurate only with their wealth, they would
> have relatively little influence on American business.

6. Richard N. Current and John A. Garraty, eds., *Words That Made History: The 1870's to the Present* (Boston and Toronto, 1962), pp. 114–15.

Vast fortunes like those of the Astors are no doubt regret-
table. They are inconsistent with democracy. They are
unsocial. And they seem peculiarly unjust when they
represent largely unearned increment. But the wealth of
the Astors does not endanger political or industrial liberty. . . . The Astor wealth is static. The wealth of the
Morgan associates is dynamic. The power and the growth
of power of our financial oligarchs comes from wielding
the savings and quick capital of others. In two of the
three great life insurance companies the influence of J.
P. Morgan & Co. and their associates is exerted without
any individual investment by them whatsoever. . . . The
fetters which bind the people are forged from the people's own gold.[7]

The reforms of the New Deal as applied to the concentration of financial power followed the thinking and analysis
of Brandeis. Franklin Roosevelt and Truman abetted the
"forgotten man" against the "special interests."

The point is yielded. Monetary legislation can indeed be
treated symbolically by the historian of American ideas. But
De Pillis has made an unwarranted jump from symbolism to
folklore. His syllogism goes like this: Dorson contends that
scientific folklore uniquely taps the thought of the anonymous, inarticulate millions: Meyers and Smith employ the
method of the intellectual or cultural historian to plumb the
emotional attitudes of the masses expressed in rhetorical symbols; hence the methods are virtually the same. Well, they are
not the same. The folklorist goes to folk sources, to word-of-
mouth utterances, to people in their homes or business places
or leisure spots. The cultural historian goes to the library, to
books and periodicals and newspapers, and invariably he goes
to the writings of intellectuals. Even when Henry Nash Smith
plows through hundreds of dime novels to extract popular
conceptions of Western heroes, he is reading the productions
of professional writers, of intellectuals. The people who write
for the folk are not the folk. The politicians who woo the
folk are not of the folk, although they may take on folksy
mannerisms. Marvin Meyers has recourse to Tocqueville,

7. Ibid., 229–30.

James Fenimore Cooper, Andrew Jackson, Martin Van Buren; to writers on economic issues like Theodore Sedgewick and William Leggett; to Robert Rantoul, a lawyer, legislator, and business promoter. Political speeches and writings, and the memoirs of sophisticated travelers and observers, provide the materials for his reconstruction of the Jacksonian persuasion.

Sometimes the intellectuals may catch and convey popular sentiments, but their declamations and polemics have little in common with the idiom of the folk, and where the expression is so different, we cannot assume that the ideas are the same. A vast gulf divides intellectuals from folk and writing from speech. The technique that the folklorist possesses, which the historian, even the new species of oral historian, does not comprehend, is the ability to converse with people of completely different backgrounds along lines of common interest, found in the genres of folklore. In *The Heavenly City of the Eighteenth Century Philosophers* (New Haven, Conn., 1932), Carl Becker has amusingly pictured the attempt of a modern intellectual to converse with a medieval schoolman, and a comparable conversational gulf divides the intellectual from his own less tutored but perhaps more knowing contemporaries. What would Henry Adams have to say to Malcolm X? The chasm between the written and spoken word, even words written for grass-roots consumption, is always underestimated and misunderstood. Albert Lord has stated this sharp distinction, in terms of the Homeric question, as forcefully as anyone.

When all this is said, I believe nevertheless that the division between oral folklore and the literary-rhetorical expression of myths and symbols can be bridged. If the folklorist moves outside genre collecting and the oral historian moves beyond interviews with the political and business elite, the two can meet in the recording of folk prejudices, rumors, biases, awes, hatreds, loyalties, phobias, stereotypes, obsessions, and fantasies. Often one sees these traditional attitudes displayed in letters to the editor columns in the daily newspaper; they are on evidence every day in the *Indianapolis Star*. Surely these deeply felt "persuasions," if we accept Meyers' term, can be collected as readily as tales and songs. To some extent Samuel Lubell has done this in his political interviewing of voter blocs across the country. The one shining example of a grass-roots interviewer taking his tape recorder to the populace is Studs Terkel, who in *Division Street: America* (New York, 1967), laid open the traditional-bound hopes and fears of seventy-one uncelebrated Chicagoans.

As we leave the firm territory of the genres for the terra incognita of group emotions, we will need new labels. *Time* magazine, as I write this, quotes columnist Joseph Kraft on a wave of "folk malevolence" coming from the mass of ordinary Americans fed up with demonstrations, crime in the streets, and inflation.[8] On a field trip to Gary and East Chicago, Indiana, this past February, I was struck by the relative paucity of conventional folklore genres and the volume of talk—folk-talk if you will—that can be translated into traditional prejudices and convictions. Take the "Syndicate," for instance. References to the Syndicate continually bob up in the course of conversation; the Syndicate is supposed to control the second largest business operation in Gary, next to steel, drawing out a million dollars a week to the headquarters in Chicago. But who runs the Syndicate and how it works are very vague matters; the Syndicate is the symbol for organized crime, sometimes equated with the Mafia, as powerful as the government itself, with whom it is locked in a continuous struggle that has little bearing on the lives of the common man, who is trampled on by both monsters. On the positive side, there are traditional qualities, sometimes named, like the Mexican *machismo,* discussed by Américo Paredes, or the Finnish *sisu,* that sustain a people and express themselves in specific actions.

To turn to a related question, the view of the folk De Pillis imputes to me and to the "Theory," namely that of Herder's romantic peasantry exuding the spirit of the soil: De Pillis reads this sense into my phrase "the anonymous, inarticulate millions," but these words do not imply a monolithic, homogenized peasant class, which has never existed anywhere in the United States. The American folk, whoever they are—and intellectuals are sometimes folk in parts of their lives—cover a whole spectrum of world views. Even within a seemingly tight-knit ethnic, regional, or occupational group,

8. September 20, 1968, p. 51, col. 3.

the individual members reveal unpredictable variations of behavior and belief. This easily proven fact is especially true for
the United States, where the mixing of many peoples and
the high degree of mobility and technological change have
shaken loose or recombined traditional mores. The folk group
is composed not of interchangeable units but of distinct individuals who share tradition yet act and think in unpredictable ways.

For example, there was the Mexican-American *curandera*
in East Chicago, seventy-five years old, speaking no English,
who recited examples of her traditional cures for *susto;* but
instead of going to the Old Roman Catholic church next
door, as did her foster son, she went to the Mormon church
in the next town. A liberal leader of the Negro community
in East Chicago, a doctor living in a splendid home, turned
out to have been a native of British Guiana raised on a plantation with East Indian servants and identifying with the
British administrators; when he came to the United States,
he was shocked to see that blacks were treated as Indians had
been back home. In Oakland, California, a courtly Serb
related to me grim accounts of Ustashi atrocities and pungent
jokes of Lala and Sosa, but he had broken with Serbian
mores in remarrying a beautiful, very American fourth-gener-
ation California girl; he had met her when, walking alone,
friendless and penniless down a San Francisco street, he had
heard a recording of Yugoslav music at a party in an upstairs
apartment, entered, and found Susan, who spoke no Serbian,
and he no English. The wife of a retired grocer in Oakland
poured forth a stream of Portuguese lore about *futsadas,* or
witchlike people she had known, victims afflicted with
*cubronte,* the evil eye, and saints' miracles, though she had
never been to Portugal. She learned her Portuguese language
and legends in Honolulu. In Gary, a Negro minister at a
Primitive Baptist church, athletic and handsome, explained
to me that he had received the call as a youngster of five in
Arkansas, gone to Ball State College on a football scholarship,
and now made thirty-five dollars a day in the steel mills as a
crane-operator instructor, although he had never learned to
read; the learned references in his sermons came from books
his wife read to him. In San Francisco, a retired Chinese

career diplomat, with an A.B. and LL.D. from Harvard, recited to me sayings—writing down their Chinese characters—
spirit beliefs, and anecdotal tales recalled from his youth in
China; the day before he had used a special Chinese proverb
to cheer a sick friend bedridden in the hospital: "No flower
blooms a thousand days."

These sagas are not exceptional but typical, and every
American collector can match them and must pay heed to the
unexpected twists and turns of the human spirit they
illustrate.

De Pillis charges that I am hostile to theory. This is a
curious assertion in the face of my proposed "Theory for
American Folklore." My objections are to irrelevant theories
that do not fit the American case. Eliade has nothing to say
about American historical myths, as do R. W. B. Lewis in
*The American Adam* (Chicago, 1955) and Leo Marx in
*The Machine in the Garden* (New York, 1964). As for
the end results of the "Theory," and the purpose for the
collecting of folklore facts, they are the same as for history
and anthropology and other ways of studying man. The
"Theory" proposes to inform us about the cultural behavior
of people in these United States and to offer information quite
outside the provinces of history, anthropology, or literature.
Today one hears everywhere talk about the necessity to introduce courses in the university on Negro or black history and
culture. Books are hastily being patched together, and American historians are desperately retooling to service these courses.
They would be well advised to do some retooling in folklore,
because the culture of the American Negro is primarily a folk
culture. Two dissertations in folklore at Indiana University—
by Lynwood Montell on the Coe Ridge Negro community in
Kentucky and by Gladys Fry on social controls of the antebellum Negro—reconstruct hidden areas of Negro history with
the aid of orally recorded traditions. What meatier source
exists for the penetration of the southern Negro mind than
Newbell Puckett's *Folk Beliefs of the Southern Negro* (Chapel
Hill, N. C., 1926)? And now we have two sterling studies of
the northern Negro in Roger D. Abrahams' *Deep Down in
the Jungle* (Hatboro, Pa., 1964) and Charles Keil's *Urban
Blues* (Chicago, 1966).

A third critique of the "Theory" and its elaboration in the book *American Folklore* comes from the Soviet Union, in a 1962 article by Madam L. M. Zemljanova in *Soviet Ethnography,* titled, in English translation, "The Struggle between the Reactionary and the Progressive Forces in Contemporary American Folkloristics."[9] Zemljanova shows herself rather well acquainted with personalities in American folklore, and she singles out some for censure as reactionaries and others for praise as progressives who interpret folk traditions in terms of the class struggle. The present speaker is her particular bête noire, and while she does not match De Pillis' record, she mentions the name of Dorson twenty times, always, unlike De Pillis, with unconcealed displeasure. Attacking *pragmatism* and its principle of extreme relativity as a rising influence in "the contemporary bourgeois folkloristics of the United States," she announces that the "true character of pragmatic historicism can be seen in the works of Richard Dorson." Pragmatic historicism "declares objective truth to be nonexistent," contrary to Marxian dialectic.

Summarizing the "Theory for American Folklore," Zemljanova finds that it fails to live up to its pronouncements because "Dorson, like all historians of the pragmatic school, denies the leading role of the masses in the history of society and culture." Her main criticisms are that Dorson relies on the reactionary historic-geographic method of motif analysis in commenting on European immigrant and American Negro folklore; that he accepts false bourgeois "folk heroes" like Henry Ford and casts doubt on genuine working-class folk heroes like Paul Bunyan; that he omits the protest folk expression of the Negro, and of the worker in general; that he emphasizes secondary features of folklore, such as orality, traditionality, longevity—a sin in which Dorson is paired with Benjamin Botkin; that he invariably associates folklore with the indecent; that in actuality he is espousing the official ideology of conformism and pacification of citizens who are taught that folklore is harmless amusement divorced from social and political realities.

9. *Journal of the Folklore Institute* 1 (1964) : 130–44.

Let me try to answer Madam Zemljanova in her own terms. There is protest folklore in America. In fact, I have used the label *protest tales,* following John Greenway's *protest folksongs,* to designate Negro stories overtly or covertly based on the sense of racial injustice. This is a vigorous body of oral narratives, but it is only one of a dozen major strands in the Negro repertory, and a given protest tale, say one aimed at Jim Crowism in the South, may be balanced by another showing how colored people are better treated down South than up North. The fame of Paul Bunyan rests not upon lumberjacks but on a profit-motivated advertising agent of a lumber company. Henry Ford is nobody's folk hero, although he is the butt of a joke cycle. There is no solidarity whatsoever in American history between urban factory workers and individualistic farmers, cowhands, lumberjacks, as the failure of the Populist movement testifies. There is no solidarity between urban Negroes and immigrant whites or transplanted Mexicans and Puerto Ricans, but flaring hostilities, reflected in ethnic slurs and the *blason populaire.*

As for the method of motif analysis, this is a convenient way of identifying some but certainly not all kinds of folk materials. Here is where the folklife buffs can make a contribution. Descriptions and photographs of Pennsylvania German cooky cutters or decorated privies may please the folklifists as evidence of their broad horizons, but the historian of American ideas will ask for some meaningful correlation of artifact and historical movement. An exemplary essay accomplishing just that is E. McClung Fleming's "Symbols of the United States: From Indian Queen to Uncle Sam."[10] Fleming identifies six images used widely from 1755 to 1850 in all kinds of artistic devices, from sculptures to wallpaper designs and political cartoons, that symbolized the spirit of America. One image succeeded another in popularity, each having its chronological peak when it represented most persuasively American themes and the American character. The folklorist is especially interested to see the shift that occurs in this iconographic symbolism in the decades between the

10. In *Frontiers of American Culture,* ed. Ray B. Browne and others (Lafayette, Ind., 1968), pp. 1–24.

War of 1812 and the Civil War, when the popular and vernacular tradition overtakes the genteel and cultured tradition.
From the mid-eighteenth century into the first decade of the
nineteenth century, a series of decorous females depicted the
American genius: first the Indian princess; then her Greco-
Roman counterpart, the Neoclassic Plumed Goddess; then a
republican goddess referred to as the American Liberty; and
finally a synthesis of all these in the regal, ceremonial Columbia. What a contrast to the cocky Yankee rustic of Brother
Jonathan and Uncle Sam, who displaced these chaste ladies
in the popular imagination and in popular art! In the twen-
ties and thirties the folk Yankee had begun to make his appearance in stage plays, tavern yarns, newspaper and almanac
stories, comic songs and doggerel, and also, as Fleming shows
us, in the graphic arts. The rise of the Yankee to national
prominence cannot under any circumstance be interpreted
as a liberation movement of the proletariat.

As for Zemljanova's dismissal of the oral, traditional, and
longevity aspects of folklore, if we have to start all over again
on basic definition there is perhaps little point in trying to
communicate. My own view of the subject matter of the folklorist has shifted somewhat from the established genres to
what might be called the unofficial culture.

# II

The best support for the "Theory" may lie not so much in
polemical rejoinders as in fresh and exciting works of scholarship appearing in the past decade, which relate folklore to
central themes in American history, and as it happens, to
themes enumerated in the "Theory."

*Colonization.* An entertaining study of special pertinence is
Percy G. Adams' *Travelers and Travel Liars 1660–1800*
(Berkeley, Cal., 1962). According to the "Theory," the colonial period generated an abundance of nature myths and fabulous reports in consequence of the strange flora and fauna and
the whole hairraising atmosphere of settling in a wilderness.
Adams documents this assertion to the hilt with his genealogies
of the travel lie, the part-folk part-literary genre that embroi-

dered so many travelers' narratives during the expansion of
Europe. A travel lie, according to Adams, "may be defined as
a tale told by a traveler or pseudo traveler with intent to de-
ceive" (page 1). The North American continent came in for a
lion's share of these chimeras that enthralled readers and helped
shape the images of the New World as alternately a land of
wonders and a land of horrors. Adams probably overstates the
case when he says the travel lie was always a deliberate falsehood, for many marvels were generally accepted and became
traditional. He maintains that travelers "invented or changed
geography, and animals, and plants. One fabricated a tale
of a fabulous river—not the Missouri—that connected the
Rockies with the Mississippi . . . another advertised a Louisiana plant, the juice of which . . . made Indians live over a
hundred years" (page 11). The terms *invention* and *fabrication* seem too strong here, and elsewhere Adams suggests that
fabled stories (for instance, narratives alleging the existence
of the Northwest Passage or cherished ideas pertaining to
the Noble Savage) were repeated and reinforced by travel
writers whose perceptions were colored by notions they already held. Two rival theories in particular controlled the
image making about the New World. One was the view,
first espoused by the Comte de Buffon in his *Histoire Naturelle* (1749-1804) and greatly extended by Corneille De
Pauw in *Recherches philosophiques sur les américains* (1768),
that men, animals, and plants in the Americas were degen-
erate forms of Old World species. The counterview was advanced by such writers as Dom Pernetty, J.-B. Bossu, Brissot
de Warville, and Thomas Jefferson, who reported on the
longevity and robustiousness of Indians and American colonists.

A striking example of a deep-rooted tradition spreading
to American soil is the so-called Adario motif, an attachment
to the myth of New World vitality and superiority. Adario
was the name given a Noble Savage, variously designated between 1703 and 1806 as a Huron and a Shawnee, who criticized the institutions of the white man in philosophic vein
directly reflecting the bias of his pretended interviewer.
Christianity, land tenure, and barter in guns and liquor received the barbs of the sage aborigine. Adams reports this

device in the Upanishads, Lucian, and Pausanias and throughout the literature of the eighteenth century. An example of
the device appears in my *American Folklore* in a quoted
passage from the *Boston Evening Post* for August 2, 1736,
in which Lord Lovelace, newly arrived in America, questions
a Christian Indian on his religious beliefs and is given a
pidgin English abstract of Genesis. The First Man's squaw
entices him to eat the forbidden apples. "Den presently
both on 'em turn Rogue, quite Rogue, and ebber since all
his Children Rogue too. Now ebbery body Rogue, now I
Rogue, and you Rogue, too, and ebbery body Rogue." Adams'
study makes clear the long popularity and utility of the
Adario theme for critics of an imperial culture.

*The Western Movement.* Several attractive exhibits fall within
the humorous literature, an ethnographic literature really,
of the Old Southwest. These ante-bellum journalistic sketches
belong to the topic of the American frontier, since they re-
volve around character types and folklife scenes of the backwoods; indeed this corpus is often referred to as frontier humor. Long forgotten, the precursors of Mark Twain have now
come resplendently into their own, and none more rightfully
than George Washington Harris, author of *Sut Lovingood,
Yarns of a Nat'ral Born Durn'd Fool* (New York, 1867).
    Something of a Sut revival has developed in the 1960s.
An annual miscellany, *The Sut Lovingood Papers,* issued from
1962 to 1965 and edited by Ben Harris McClary, maintained
a high level of original and invigorating scholarship. An amus-
ing essay by Brom Weber, who had issued a transliterated
edition of the Sut yarns reviewed in the *New Yorker* by Edmund Wilson, plays with Wilson's revulsion at Harris' ex-
cessive humor of physical discomfiture. Ray Browne in a suggestive article points out that Harris was a literary craftsman
even though he places oral yarns in Sut's mouth in folk style.
Carol Boykin reports Sut's speech to be an accurate rendition
of South Midland dialect as spoken in the east Tennessee
hills, and not a contrived eye dialect. Besides this journal,
separate volumes have dealt with Sut. A splendidly appre-
ciative critical biography, *George Washington Harris* (New
York, 1966), was published by Milton Rickels, and M.

Thomas Inge celebrated the centennial of the first and only Sut book with two new editions, *Sut Lovingood's Yarns* (New Haven, Conn., 1966) and *High Times and Hard Times* (Nashville, Tenn., 1967), reprinting previously uncollected newspaper pieces as well as the 1867 yarns. Along with the renaissance of Harris, other Southwestern humorists have gained attention in two anthologies of John Q. Anderson, *Tales of Frontier Texas 1830–1860* (Dallas, 1966) and *With the Bark On* (Nashville, Tenn., 1967), which concentrate on lesser-known writers, and a third by Hennig Cohen and William B. Dillingham, *Humor of the Old Southwest* (Boston, 1964), parallel in scope to Franklin Meine's *Tall Tales of the Southwest* (New York, 1930), the volume of reprinted pieces that initiated the serious study of frontier humor. Despite all this scholarly endeavor we still await the work fully assessing the folklore and folklife elements in Southwestern humor. Hints aplenty are offered; Rickels concludes that the newly discovered Sut pieces show an increase of unusual fantasy, a greater amount of sexual reference and symbolism, and more use of folklore. The scenes of Sut's madcap escapades, and indeed of all the sketches of the frontier humorists, are vignettes of folklife: camp meetings, quarter-horse races, militia drills, quilting bees, barn dances, wedding frolics, coon and possum hunts. Sut is the true American picaresque hero, upsetting the mores, puncturing pompous windbags, shocking the respectable and the genteel. How fitting that he shocked Edmund Wilson!

*Regionalism.* An unusual and imaginative work of scholarship centering on the cattle-raising region of the Far West was conceived by Austin and Alta Fife in their edition of N. Howard "Jack" Thorp's *Songs of the Cowboys* (New York, 1966). Thorp paid a printer in Estancia, New Mexico, to bring out his little booklet of twenty-three songs in 1908, the first publication of its kind. The Fifes have used these songs as a springboard into the culture and myth of the cowhands that burgeoned in the second half of the nineteenth century and have continued in diluted form through the mass media up to the present. Their edition should be considered on two levels. There is first an expert and thorough tracing of the

history of the individual songs—some of which, like "Cow
Boy's Lament," have so proliferated in tradition that they
consume over forty pages of textual variants and comments,
while others, like "Who's Old Cow," filled with technical
branding terms, have not wandered far from Thorp's pen.
On a second plane, the Fifes recognize the documentary
quality of these hallowed twenty-three ballads and lyrics, whatever their folk popularity, since each embodies some elements
and imagery of what they call the "cowboy myth."

A whole code of cowboy behavior and values can be
constructed from the songs. Cowhands despised the blowhard,
the softy, the schemer, the tightwad. They admired the trickster who outtricked them, pretending to be an "Educated
Feller" (the song title) ignorant of horsemanship but actually
a skilled bronco buster. They prided themselves on their
open-handed hospitality: "Did you ever go to any cowboy
whenever hungry or dry/Asking for a dollar and have him
you deny" ("Old Time Cowboy," p. 241). Some songs like
"The Texas Cowboy," echo the themes of "geographical dis-
placement and culture shock" resulting from the advent of
farmers or "sod busters" who erected barbed wire fences in the
Southwest, or of copper mines blasting rock in Montana, or of
the townspeople brought by the lunge of the transcontinental
railroads. Other songs, mildly deistical to firmly fundament-
alist, hum of transcendental solaces and dreams, employing
cowboy imagery: "there's to be a grand roundup"; "the riders
of judgment"; "the trail to that great mystic region"; "So
for safety you'd better get branded/Have your name in his
big Tally Book." On the obverse side of the coin, there is
the lusty sexual symbolism in "The Bucking Bronco" that
pictures the cowboy as a potent lover who woos a maiden by
jumping in the saddle, riding the bronco, swinging the raw-
hide. Yet the ardent cowboy reveres and idealizes the frontier
woman, who combines feminine virtue with the manly skills
of the range; "Pecos River Queen" could shoot and rope and
ride with the best of the cowpunchers, and none dared follow
her across the teetering Comstock Railroad Bridge, the feat
needed to win her hand and recalling suitors' tests in epic
and folktale.

These are the themes and leitmotifs to which the Fifes adroitly call attention. They have the knack of synopsizing in a few pithy sentences the horizons of cowboy life hidden within the songs. Of "Speckles," they say the song is "spiced with genuine images of life on the open ranges: the drifting horse trader, a grasshopper plague, cowboy hospitality, the use of horses as a medium of exchange, encounters between Rangers and Indians . . . images of the deep arroyos and high mesas that are the proper setting for the cowboy culture" (p. 254). There is a danger in using folksongs as social documents, but in turning to Thorp's *Songs of the Cowboys* the Fifes have cleverly seized on a pioneer collection that is itself a historical source fixed in time and place and reflecting a distinct phase of the American past.

*Immigration.* One of the most appealing but least fulfilled themes in the "Theory" is the folklore of the immigrant, promising so many studies in cultural transition between the Old World and the New. Collections themselves are few, although we now have Pawlowska's Polish folksongs and Hoogasian-Villa's Armenian folktales, both from Detroit, but a depth treatment of history, traditions, and social institutions surrounding the oral texts has only just come to hand, in Jerome R. Mintz's *Legends of the Hasidim* (Chicago, 1968), subtitled *An Introduction to Hasidic Culture and Oral Tradition in the New World.* Here at last is the long awaited work that examines in absorbing detail the transplantation of a European folk culture to the United States and that answers questions as to what happens to these people and their lore when plunked down in the midst of American culture. Nowhere could these questions be more dramatically posed than in the case of the Hasidim, who, driven by the Nazi scourge from rural Poland and Hungary, bring to the streets of Brooklyn a highly insulated religious orthodoxy rejecting and fearing the secular world, the gentile, even the non-Hasidic Jew. Unlike the Old Order Amish who came in colonial times to the unsettled Pennsylvania countryside, these later arrivals met American civilization head on in the twentieth century, seeking economic and spiritual survival in

the city jungle. They have steadfastly preserved their dis-
sonant institutions: the courts with their miracle-working
Rebbes, the web of *mitsvehs* or religious principles and observances that govern their lives, the distinct costume marked
prominently by headgear and beards.

And too they have retained their strength-renewing body
of oral narratives that encase the prophecies and blessings and
moral fables of the Rebbes. Mintz ingeniously keys his ethnography of the Hasidic culture in Brooklyn to his collected
tales, which so intimately refract Hasidic thought and customs. In addition he incorporates passages from personal histories into his introductory general history. One observes with
fascination the shifts in the repertory now borne on American
soil. Old World legends and scenes persist in abundance, although the more extreme expressions of supernaturalism,
such as possession by a dybbuk, have disappeared. Indeed in
one account where a Rebbe fails to exorcise the dybbuk, a
Hasid suggests the demon-ridden child see a psychiatrist. Side
by side with the narrations that could just as well have been
told in the courts in eastern Europe are others revealing
American characters and settings. The Hasidim speak frankly
about their anxieties arising from American pressures. "Even
though we live in America here very peacefully," says one
Hasid, "we still feel very uncomfortable in this country. . . .
You have to rush. Time is so short. . . . Not meeting friends,
and not learning with each other—it's hurting our belief,
it's hurting our customs" (p. 61).

Another expresses his fear of sexual promiscuity in America, where an orthodox man sits next to a woman in a bus, but
comforts himself with the fact that he takes out his *New
York Times* to read and falls asleep within three minutes.
These attitudes expressed in life histories are often repeated
in the tales, which are themselves mainly extracts from the
narrator's knowledge. Above all, the Hasid reveres his Rebbe.
One characteristically American episode tells of a successful
business man who told his Rebbe he had to meet a payment
of five thousand dollars by the next day. The Rebbe bids
him not to worry, God will help, and next day a couple
from Chicago come in the store and purchase a fur coat for
five thousand dollars. A friend in Chicago had recommended

the store. Later the Rebbe explained that this was no miracle but simply the fulfillment of a "tradition handed down from the Baal Shem Tov" that God will help when every other resource fails. Another and deeply moving recital relates how a soldier little versed in Jewish ways went to a Rebbe before leaving for the Korean War and was instructed in the *mitsveh* of washing his hands before eating. In Korea he debated whether to look for water before eating his bread, finally decided to do so, and on returning found that all his comrades had been bombed to bits. Such memorats reinforce the Hasidic culture as it fights for its foothold in America. *Legends of the Hasidim* demonstrates how an immigrant culture can be perceptively explored by the historically and ethnologically minded folklorist. If the Hasidim can be penetrated, then surely so can the other flourishing ethnic societies in the United States.

*The Negro.* Nowhere do American history and folklore intersect more closely than in the "peculiar institution." In the post-"Theory" decade one exceptional study based on the writer's own field materials has extended and deepened the narrow collecting approach to southern Negro traditions. In *Deep Down in the Jungle,* Roger Abrahams has achieved several major firsts. His is the first intensive study of northern urban Negro folklore. It is the first full presentation of such unreported genres in the Negro repertory as the versified narrative known as the toast and the obscene jocular cante-fable known in prettier variants. It is the first attempt to bring to bear sophisticated theories of language and society on American Negro texts.

*Deep Down in the Jungle* bristles with ideas and analytic commentary. Abrahams is an admitted eclectic, vitally concerned with the information about cultural behavior that folklore can divulge. He values folk narrative as "a rhetorical expression of the dialectical unity of the culture" (page 8), terms made fruitful for him by Kenneth Burke. He seeks to relate the individual and his oral expression to social mechanisms approved for molding normal personalities, in this following the ego psychology studies of Erik Erikson. Ultimately he wishes to extend the oicotype concept of von

Sydow from a simple comparativist treatment to a full or-
ganic view of folktale types. Applying these and other theoretical systems to the materials he obtained from the Camingerley neighborhood of Philadelphia, Abrahams detects special
qualities, or "tropisms," of contemporary Negro folklore.

In brief, he finds a "life-style" admired by Camingerley
youths that is projected into their folklore. These youths,
raised in a matriarchal home and thrust onto the ghetto
pavements, compensate for their father-loss with exaggerated
masculinity in their cultural postures and verbal skills. The
hard sport, the tough talker, the strutting badman are admired on the streets and in the toasts and tales. Shine, Stackalee, and Signifying Monkey, the culture heroes of Camingerley, never achieve a dramatic resolution in their stories,
nor do the hard sports of Camingerley ever integrate into family life and middle-class society.

From the point of view of the "Theory for American
Folklore," Abrahams has made two signal contributions, quite
apart from the development of his own theoretical formula-
tions. He has proven that the southern Negro repertory has
considerably altered in the urban North, while retaining its
original vitality and cultural power. In addition he has given
explanations for these changes that relate to the new ghetto
milieu of the tradition bearers. Using comparative texts
he clearly shows the cultural revisions that divide European
and American, and southern and northern variants. Uncle
Remus' bamboozling Rabbit has become the audacious foul-
mouthed ghetto hustler of Camingerley.

*Industrialization.* As originally presented, the "Theory" had
no category for occupational or industrial lore. The forces of
industrialization and technological development certainly
constitute one of the main chapters in American history,
and although at first blush the machine seems hostile to tradition, we are beginning to see that lore does breed in the mill
and the factory, in the department store and the supermarket.
In *A Treasury of Railroad Folklore* (New York, 1953), Benjamin Botkin and Alvin Harlow point the way for field inter-
viewers, who had better get busy before the iron horses run
out of steam. The lore of the labor movement, perhaps the

most enticing for the industrial folklorist, is suggested in the folk documents assembled by Joyce Kornbluh in her anthology of Wobbly literature, *Rebel Voices* (Ann Arbor, Mich., 1964). However there is at hand one work that goes all the way and completely makes the case for industrial lore, Mody C. Boatright's *Folklore of the Oil Industry* (Dallas, 1963).

Beckoning titles of this sort are a dime a dozen, but Boatright's is genuine. He tape-interviewed numerous oilmen and scoured ephemeral printed sources. His great achievement is to extricate from these amorphous materials clear and distinct areas where technological processes slip into rumor and mystery, a no-man's-land between science and speculation. This is largely an uncharted terrain, in which motif and ballad indexes give little direction and the familiar folk genres do not appear. Still this is very much folklore country, and Boatright has erected his own signposts. They indicate the traditions proliferating around the oil-finding witch and seer, dreams leading to the discovery of oil, luck and unluck in locating the liquid gold (reminiscent of the many similar legends told of mining prospectors), frauds and hoaxes perpetrated by inventors of elaborate oil-detecting machines. The role of the oil diviner resembles that of the water witch, examined in detail by Evon Vogt and Ray Hyman in *Water Witching U.S.A.* (Chicago, 1959). As Boatright points out, the doodlebug man preceded the geologist in giving faith to wildcat drillers who needed some assurance that their investment would pay off. In another category of lore Boatright deals imaginatively with popular stereotypes formed in the excitement of oil drilling, and associates them with stock folk figures. The Geologist is an ivory-tower scientist, the dismal pedagogue who is far less reliable than a shaman. Said one oilman, quoted in the *New York Times* in 1922, "Not that I don't believe in geologists. I always use one. I'm that big a fool. Pay him $50.00 a day to chip rocks and write reports. But when I get ready to start, I take a Negro and blindfold him, turn him around three times, and let him throw a silver dollar as far as he can. Where the dollar falls, if I can find it, is the spot where I drill."

Then there is the Old Promoter, a newer version of the Trickster, both sly Yankee and flamboyant confidence man;

the Shooter, a frontier daredevil reminiscent of Fink and Crockett, who detonated nitroglycerin to break up tight rock-formations; the Driller, a taciturn nomad-hero, counter-part of the Cowboy and the Mountain Man; and the Land-owner, a country bumpkin elevated to affluence overnight, in the rags-to-riches formula, who sometimes becomes a Coal-Oil Johnny, squandering his sudden riches in extravagant follies.

Boatright does look at tales, notably the Gib Morgan cycle he had already uncovered, and songs, uncongenial to oil work; but these chapters are an appendage to his main inquiry pursuing folk materials from within the structure of the industry rather than through the categories of folk-lore. One conjectures how many other industries could yield comparable profits. From my recent foray into Gary, populated since its founding in 1906 by dozens of nationality groups and now welded into an uneasy community of steel, I can glimpse the human and folk side of America's number-one industry. The Cecil Sharps and Vance Randolphs of the future may turn up in factory towns.

*Mass Culture.* While mass culture appears antithetical to folk cultures, the "Theory" proposed that their interrelationships be considered, and this is precisely the concern of Charles Keil's brilliant book on *Urban Blues.* Sharing some of the same insights with *Deep Down in the Jungle,* particularly of the Negro as the man of words in many roles, *Urban Blues* concentrates on the new Negro elite who have become celebri-ties in the entertainment world. Although no longer anony-mous folk, they have emerged from a folk culture and adapted folk skills and talents to the ravenous demands of the Amer-ican mass-entertainment media. At the core of his volume Keil provides an urban ethnography of successful Chicago blues-men, concentrating on B. B. King and Big Bobby Blue Bland, whom he has observed, interviewed, and photographed. Keil closely analyzes their live musical performances, their busi-ness associations, and their personal tastes. These specific case studies are intended to provide hard data for broad general theses on the success story—albeit a limited success—of the modern city Negro.

The entertainment world offers the Negro his chief avenue of success into the mass culture, and it serves also as a
bridge into other segments of mainline America. Folksinger,
folk storyteller, folk musician, folk dancer, folk preacher, and
folk healer all parlay their talents, with the breaks, to become well-known comics, revivalists, athletes, recording and
concert artists, politicians, and authors. As in the folk South,
so in the urban North one individual plays several parts. On
the folk level, I think of J. D. Suggs, who was a semipro baseball player, member of a minstrel troupe, and son of a preacher as well as a gifted narrator and folksinger during his life
as a prison guard, short-order cook, laborer, soldier, railroad
fireman, and family servant. On the celebrity level, as Keil
shows, the same combination of roles persists, evident in personalities like Cassius Clay, Adam Clayton Powell, Dick
Gregory, Paul Robeson, Eldridge Cleaver, Ralph Ellison, and
James Baldwin. The interplay of cultural roles is indeed Keil's
overriding theme; he speaks of the transition from country
to city blues singing, of the interchange between Negro
church and blues music and between the blues and preaching
as art forms, of the revitalization of American Negro music
by a return to African sources to counteract its enervation
from white absorption. Entertainers and hustlers—a preacher
can be both—are the subculture heroes, and may become national heroes; Malcolm X is the supreme example. Some of
these points are strikingly confirmed in my own field work.
Charles H. King, Jr., present director of the Human Relations Commission of Gary and a former minister, in a recorded interview explained to me the continuity of techniques from revivalist preaching to civil rights oratory, giving
his own career as one example.

*Urban Blues* is in its largest sense a study of how the
machine civilization of America has acted upon America's
most vigorous folk culture. The "folk myth of Soul" is the
Negro's spiritual gift to America, Keil claims, and, though
Soul itself is nonmachine, the mass culture has now made it a
nationally known commodity. Keil supports his generalizations with intimate empirical and often shoddy details of the
recording industry and its manufacture of popular bluesmen.
The urban middlemen-technicians are the agents that re-

shape the folk performer into the commercial entertainer, and we are allowed to see them at work, tailoring their human product to sell more platters and entice more disk jockeys. Yet even technology bows to magic, as with the oil-field doodle-bugs; and the A and R men (artist and repertoire executives) in recording are regarded as shamans with esoteric powers. Keil looks on both sides of the process; what to the white culture is entertainment to the black is ritual catharsis. Negro life in America is one long sacrificial ritual. Negro culture, in the ghetto as in the South, is auditory and tactile, in contrast to the visual and literate culture on the outside.

All these propositions rest upon a highly sophisticated base. Little that is relevant in anthropological, ethnomusicological, psychological, sociological, and folkloristic theory escapes Keil's notes or his jabs. He quotes McLuhan and Lévi-Strauss, Herskovits and Frazier, Robert Bales on small group interaction, Erik Erikson on psychosocial crises in the life cycle, Robert Merton on measurement of propaganda materials, Alan Lomax, McAllester. and Merriam on the relation of music to culture. *Urban Blues* is an arresting synthesis of library and field, black and white, folk and mass, the loftily theoretical and the minutely empirical.

Two ingenious essays by Alan Dundes can further illustrate the relevance of folk attitudes to the mass civilization. In a contribution to his own anthology of selections on cultural anthropology, *Every Man His Way* (Englewood Cliffs, N. J., 1968), he discusses the symbolic and magical status of the number three with numerous and varied examples that seem to penetrate every nook and cranny of American life. As the Märchen must have triply repeated episodes, so the American mind must think and react in categories of threes: "Strike three, you're out!" Since reading his essay I have come across the following passage in William Manchester's *The Death of a President,* describing the moment President Kennedy was shot, the most fateful moment in the history of our time.

> Merriman Smith had seized the radiophone while they were still on Elm Street. His Dallas UPI bureau heard him bark: "Three shots were fired at President Kennedy's motorcade in downtown Dallas."

Smith was not as astute a reporter as he seemed. Despite extensive experience with weapons he had thought the sounds in the plaza were three shots from an automatic weapon. . . . Before eyewitnesses could collect themselves [the UPI bulletin] was being beamed around the world. To those who tend to believe everything they hear and read, the figure of three seemed to have the sanction of authority, and many who had been in the plaza and had thought they heard only two reports later corrected their memories.[11]

The other paper by Dundes, presented at a Wenner-Gren Conference in Austria on the subject of world-view, considers the futuristic orientation of American life as reflected in folklore. As to this orientation and its responsibility for so many anxieties and compulsions of American citizens, few can doubt who are familiar with the ladder of school, college, and professional degrees, job-seeking, promotion, and retirement. Dundes shows how American popular sayings and rituals reinforce this outlook.

The works singled out for mention here are all theoretical and speculative in nature. None are simply collections, though most make use of original field materials. In examining their sources they employ a variety of concepts and techniques, drawn from literature, anthropology, psychology, sociology, and history, but their final synthesis is a predominantly humanistic folklore method, concerned less with the fantasy of predicting human behavior and more with the reality of interpreting the human spirit in its manifold cultural settings. Their authors may not claim the "Theory," if indeed they know about it, but the "Theory" will claim them as true American folklorists who perceive the intimate bonds between the culture of the folk and the history of the American experience.

11. (New York, 1967), p. 191.

# 4

# Folklore in Relation
# to American Studies

There is before me a new course proposal prepared for an
American Studies program in a large Midwestern university.
The syllabus recommends proven interdisciplinary authors:
Boorstin, Hofstadter, Howard Mumford Jones, Matthiessen,
Perry Miller, Nye, Persons, Henry Nash Smith. In this con-
spectus folklore plays little part. Again here is Robert Walker's survey *American Studies in the United States* (1958) analyzing ninety-one college and university programs in American Civilization. One examines curriculum after curriculum
with extensive lists of fields or departments, but with no mention of folklore. One such list specifies "education, psychology,
language, music, speech, art, zoology, geology, philosophy,
sociology, economics, government, history, and English" (p.
61, University of New Hampshire). Or consider the contents

Reprinted from *Frontiers of American Culture,* ed. Ray B. Browne, Richard H. Crowder, Virgil L. Lokke and William T. Stafford, by permission
of Purdue University Studies, © 1968 by Purdue Research Foundation.

of the *American Quarterly*. The articles and review essays cover a broad spectrum of the arts, literary and cultural history, regionalism, business history and technology, religion and philosophy, and seemingly every facet of American experience; but again folklore is rarely in evidence.

These examples raise the question whether the folklore approach may have any utility for even so eclectic a scholar as the American Studies savant. This question led me to ponder how in my own case an American Civilization program inveigled me ever deeper into folklore, and through folklore to see American culture from new angles. This program was initiated at Harvard University in 1938 under an interdepartmental committee chaired by Kenneth Murdock and it offered the first doctorate in American Studies in the United States. The new degree, titled "History of American Civilization," generated electricity among a memorable group of the faculty and some remarkable graduate students. The coming of Howard Mumford Jones to Harvard in 1936 coincided with the rise to fame on the existing faculty of Francis Otto Matthiessen and Perry Miller, and these American literature experts gave leadership to the loosely organized program. Bernard DeVoto had resigned from Harvard by 1938 but he had participated in the original deliberations and as a confirmed resident of Cambridge and close friend of the Americanists continued to make his presence felt. Ralph Barton Perry in philosophy and Benjamin Wright in government contributed actively to the committee. The American historians played a more passive role, having already discovered America, but the degree candidates had access to Arthur Schlesinger, Frederick Merk, Paul Buck, and Samuel Eliot Morison. First to attain the new degree was Henry Nash Smith, already an assistant professor, on leave from Southern Methodist University. The second was Daniel Aaron; the third Frederick B. Tolles; the fourth Edmund S. Morgan; and the fifth myself, an anomalous refugee from the tennis and squash courts. Like Morgan and Conrad Wright, I entered the doctoral program as a continuation of the Harvard College major in American history and literature.

The talk and the writing in those days was all of the American experience, now suddenly revealed as an indepen-

dent, mature, intricate, and noble civilization. Notable books
flowed from the inspired and inspiring faculty: Miller's *The
New England Mind, the Seventeenth Century,* Matthiessen's
*American Renaissance,* Jones's *Ideas in America,* Perry's *Puritanism and Democracy,* DeVoto's *The Year of Decision: 1846.*
Henry Nash Smith wrote as his doctoral dissertation the work
that would emerge as *Virgin Land.*

All this ferment and stimulation would seem to provide
an excellent test ground for the interdisciplinary approach of
American Studies. Yet it does not appear that the degree reci-
pients abandoned the conventional disciplines. For the most
part they entered history or English departments and func-
tioned as intellectual or religious or colonial or literary historians. I remember Ralph Barton Perry saying that if the
faculty on the committee had to take each other's exams they
would all flunk.

The degree requirements at the time called for the
mastery of six areas, five in American fields and one in a non-
American field. For my outside area I chose folklore, being
the first and the last candidate to do so. In the 1930s and 40s
no courses in folklore were offered at Harvard, with one brief
exception, a course called "Legend and Tradition with Especial Reference to Celtic Material" given by Kenneth H.
Jackson, the Celticist on the faculty. One day I passed Henry
Nash Smith in the catacombs of Widener Library, and he
stopped me to say he had recently met Jackson and learned of
his interest in folklore. Smith knew that my own interest in
the subject had arisen from an undergraduate paper on
frontier humor that led to my publishing in 1939 a selection
from the Crockett almanacs, *Davy Crockett, American Comic
Legend.* The upshot was that I signed up with Professor Jackson for a special reading course in folklore and attended
his lectures. Jackson had come from Cambridge University
and would shortly return to the chair of Celtic language and
literature at the University of Edinburgh. He introduced
me to the mysteries of Stith Thompson's *Motif-Index* and the
historic-geographic method of comparative folklore study.
Since there was no category for folklore offerings in the Harvard curriculum, Jackson had to smuggle this course in as a
Celtic-related subject.

The Crockett almanacs and the humorous literature of the old Southwest to which they belong offer a good case in point of the interrelation between American Studies and folklore. This forgotten subliterature that flourished in the three decades before the Civil War became visible once again through a sequence of notable scholarly anthologies and studies beginning in 1930 with Franklin J. Meine's *Tall Tales of the Southwest*. All the American literature members of the Committee on Higher Degrees in American Civilization relished and praised this newly resurrected body of writings which so happily supported their bright premises. Here indeed was a purely homegrown American prose, catching the idiom and accents of the backcountry and depicting a novel gallery of backwoods characters. Bernard DeVoto had demonstrated in *Mark Twain's America* (1932) how Clemens had learned his craft from this school of journalistic humor relying heavily on the techniques of oral yarnspinners. In place of, or at least alongside with, the tired beadroll of hallowed American authors in the genteel tradition emulating European models and mannerisms, Americanists could now speak of Augustus Baldwin Longstreet, William Tappan Thompson, Johnson Jones Hooper, and George Washington Harris, casual writers whose pieces appeared in newspapers and cheap paperbacks and hardbacks long out of print. Perry Miller lent me his own copy of Harris's *Sut Lovingood,* in the only known edition of 1867, during an undergraduate tutorial. I took it home with me to New York and promptly left it on the train. Panic-stricken I rushed to the Harvard Coop and ordered a new copy, not knowing what else to do. Astonishingly a copy did appear in response to this order, from the Fitzgerald Publishing Company, whose name was pasted in a label over that of the original publishers Dick and Fitzgerald. It seems that the successor company, which now specialized in drama scripts, had kept the original plates and run off a few copies every year in fresh bindings. Apparently Sut's yarns had retained a continuous if slender audience ever since their publication.

The humor of the Old Southwest was clearly an expression of the popular culture. It entered sportsmen's weeklies such as the now celebrated New York *Spirit of the Times,* the daily papers that in the thirties and forties served up a

regular fare of entertaining stories, comic almanacs larded
with woodcuts, knockabout one-act farces, lithographs and
posters and drawings. Book publishers like Carey and Hart
and their successors T. B. Peterson and Company, both of Philadelphia, developed a paperback series called the Library of
Humorous American Works, whose individual volumes included a number of yarns and sketches first printed in the
*Spirit* and other papers. The illustrations of Felix O. C. Darley superbly portrayed the scapegraces and slatterns of the
stories and captured the lowbrow spirit of the series. One reason indeed that this humorous literature disappeared from
sight when its vogue had passed was its lack of recognition or
even awareness by highbrow literary critics. The *Spirit's* correspondents and the playwrights and actors of Yankee plays
mingled freely with the character types they were depicting.
The teller, the subject, and the writer might even merge into
the same person, as in the case of Davy Crockett.

All critics have noted the dependence of frontier humor
on oral storytelling, and this is the point at which the folklorist can render his service. Traditional folktales, repertorial
sketches based on fact, and fictional narratives based in varying degrees on oral tradition lie side by side in the *Spirit*.
Only a trained folklorist employing the system of type and
motif-analysis can make these distinctions. In his generally
excellent study of *William T. Porter and the "Spirit of the
Times,"* Norris W. Yates does mistake a tale well-known
in international tradition, "The Origin of the Twist in Pig's
Tails," for a composed story. We should like to ascertain to
what extent the Southern humorists drew upon floating anecdotes. Reading the new edition of *Sut Lovingood's Yarns*
edited by M. Thomas Inge, which brings together some uncollected pieces, I came across this observation by Sut in an
1868 sketch titled "Sut Lovingood, a Chapter from His Autobiography." Sut is watching a glorious fight between his mom
and old Mrs. Simmons. He says, "So I clomb a dogwood wif
a chip in my mouth, an sot astradil in the fork, to watch the
fust fight I ever seed, whar I had no choise ove sides, so I
meant to holler for bof ove 'em."

Now this seems a likely enough comment to come from
"a nat'ral born durn'd fool." But one of Rowland Robinson's

Vermont raconteurs, Uncle Lisha, tells of the farmer's wife who found her husband in the sheep-pen clasped by a great bear. "Go it, ol' man, go it, bear," she cheered, "it's the fust fight ever I see 'at I didn't keer which licked." The story is told as a Kentucky happening in an 1865 jokebook, as a Wisconsin incident in a 1944 folk booklet, and is credited to Lincoln.[1]

The folklorist can identify such small nuggets of tradition within larger compositions, and he can also locate narratives that are folktales in their entirety. Such narratives are strewn throughout the files of antebellum newspapers, with some papers of course being much richer than others in humor. Only one attempt has been made to extrapolate folktales from their journalistic beds, the article by Arthur K. Moore on "Specimens of the Folktales from Some Antebellum Newspapers of Louisiana."[2] Moore categorized the narratives according to their international types, as set forth in the Aarne-Thompson *Types of the Folktale*. Similarly the folklorist Ralph Steele Boggs identified the tale types placed by the North Carolina humorist Harden E. Taliaferro in the mouths of his raconteurs in *Fisher's River Scenes and Characters*.[3]

Literary historians recognize the presence of traditional anecdotes in the humor of the old Southwest, but they make much too exclusive a definition of this humor. In fact the folklorist is in a position to revise the whole picture. Tall-tale humor and ringtailed roarers are not confined to the old Southwest. In the same period one can uncover other regional screamers, such as Zeb Short, the "Varmounter" who came out of the Green Mountains in a thunderstorm and slung a panther over the mountain by the tail when he was eight years old. A backwoodsman was not a shaving to Zeb, who once grappled a bear on the ground, pulled out its tongue by the roots, and pushed its head into the mud as if it were a child.

1. R. M. Dorson, *Jonathan Draws the Long Bow* (Cambridge, Mass.: 1946) , p. 227.

2. *Louisiana Historical Quarterly* 32 (1949) : 723–58.

3. R. S. Boggs, "North Carolina Folktales Current in the 1820's." *Journal of American Folklore* 47 (1934) : 269–88.

According to the unknown storyteller, Zeb could tie a bear in
a double bow knot around Davy Crockett and heave both
where they would never see daylight again.[4] Or there is the
"true Alleghenian boulder" who came clear from the forks of
the Allegheny in York State alongside the Seneca nation, and
who called himself the "raal prickly grit of America," although
he turned out to be a Yankee trickster.[5] In newspapers and
periodicals throughout New England, the Middle Atlantic,
and the Midwest,- as well as in the Southwest, there percolated
a popular humor close to folk sources. Yet the conventional
literary and cultural histories speak only of literary down-East
humorists represented by Haliburton's Sam Slick, Seba Smith's
Jack Downing, Lowell's Hosea Biglow, and now the earliest
of them all, Josh Strickland, the creation of George W. Arnold
and the discovery of Allen Walker Read.[6] Like the Southwestern humorists, these Yankee writers drew upon folk types
and folk talk, although less obviously. In both regions, a large
body of anonymous tales and anecdotes belonging properly to
folk literature lies scattered through the organs of popular
print. Feeling that the old Southwest had received undue emphasis, I turned to New England printed sources in my own
doctoral dissertation to prove that the tall tale and comic anecdote did flourish down-East as well as on the frontier.

Individual studies already demonstrate that a flood of
humorous folk narratives covered the nation in the antebellum years. The mood of the young republic—gregarious,
mobile, sociable, buoyant—well suited the funmaking of tall
yarn, capital joke, and sly sell. A folklorist can and should
make visible this oral humor frozen in newsprint and analyze
not simply the tall tale but also the trickster story, the local
character anecdote, the jest, the numskull tale, and related
forms of comic fiction. Now that Ernest W. Baughman's
*Type and Motif-Index. of the Folktales of England and North*

4. *Pearl and Literary Gazette* 3 (December 21, 1833) : 79; quoted in Dorson, *Jonathan Draws the Long Bow,* p. 117.
5. New York *Spirit of the Times* 15 (July 19, 1845) : 244; reprinted in
R. M. Dorson, "Yorker Yarns of Yore," *New York Folklore Quarterly* 3
(Spring, 1947) , "A Mouthful of Pickled Dog," 12–17.
6. Allen Walker Read, "The World of Joe Strickland," *Journal of American Folklore* 76 (1963) : 277–308.

*America*[7] has finally been published after a long delay at the printer's, this task would be greatly facilitated. Such an anthology would show the vast store of traditional oral humor on which the literary humorists levied.

The folklorist belongs in the field as much as in the library, and the book that taught me most about American civilization was based on folk traditions collected in the field. Its title is *Bloodstoppers and Bearwalkers,* and I wrote it. One day after years of reading works on American history and literature and society in the library and listening to lectures in the classroom. I found myself outside the university in the midst of real, living Americans brimful of Americana. The experience was heady and exhilarating and provided a totally new kind of education.

When I left Harvard in 1944 for a teaching post at Michigan State College, as it was then called, my initiation into the mysteries of folklore had aroused my desire to taste the field, and the Upper Peninsula of Michigan seemed made to order. Here a variety of ethnic and occupational groups coexisted under the same regional roof, and my purpose was to penetrate equally these separate traditions, rather than to identify with one alone, as collectors were wont to do. For five months I traveled around the friendly towns of the Peninsula talking to lumberjacks, copper and iron miners, Great Lakes sailors, Finnish farmers, Cousin Jacks, French Canadians, and Ojibwa Indians. The Peninsula offered very much of an oral, even a garrulous culture; this was a free and open society, still close to its frontier spirit, devoid of bookstores but abounding in taverns. Now the great advantage of the folklore method for establishing personal relations became at once apparent, for with no previous contacts or acquaintances, I was able to make conversation with hundreds of strangers and to enter quickly into their minds and memories.

What does the ivory-tower intellectual talk about when he finds himself face to face with the folk? Symbolism in Faulkner will not get very far, and the future of the Green

7. (Bloomington, Ind., and The Hague, 1966).

Bay Packers will not last very long. But folklore topics bring the man in the street and the cloistered student of American civilization into an immediate community of interest. Before setting out on the field trip, the lore hunter should prepare himself by reading up on the available history and traditions of the region and blocking out a mental questionnaire that he can draw upon in his conversations. Once in the field, he can speedily adjust, enlarge, and revise the set of leading questions.

The personal and emotional rewards of these five months in the field cannot readily be conveyed, but some concrete findings may be noted. All the information procured bore out the initial assumption that the Peninsula possessed a pluralistic culture, divisible into a number of coequal subcultures. Members of each ethnic and occupational group shared legends, sayings, anecdotes, beliefs, and customs, but the lore of one group never merged with that of another. The white man knew nothing of the Indian's private traditions, nor the lumberjack of the sailor's. One individual could participate in more than one lore, say if he were a Finnish lumberjack, but the traditions themselves remained separate. In addition to these group lores, the region itself had bred an all-enveloping lore that branded each Peninsularite, who could recite dialect jokes with expert mimicry and knew intimately the stereotypes of the uncanny Indian, the Indian-like Finn, the comical Cornishman and *Canadien*, and the whisky-drinking lumberjack. Yet the official culture of the Peninsula, such as it was, comprehended nothing of the fabulous folk wealth within its borders and boasted, through Chamber of Commerce releases designed to attract tourists, that the Peninsula had spawned America's two foremost legendary heroes, Paul Bunyan and Hiawatha. This substitution of fakelore for folklore by promoters is itself a typically American phenomenon.

By contrast, the writer who had faithfully and skillfully drawn upon the regional characters and folkways in short stories failed to attain recognition. John Voelker, prosecuting attorney for Marquette County, adroitly captured the Peninsula folk flavor in *Troubleshooter* and *Danny and the Boys*, books that won him little acclaim. John, who wrote under the pen name Robert Traver, showed me a letter from a publisher suggesting he combine the short stories in *Danny and the Boys* into a novel with a connected plot, perhaps based on a treasure hunt. "But that's not the way I know these people," Voelker sighed. He took me to visit one of his favorite raconteurs, a Cousin Jack named Dave Spencer, who recited rhymes and sang a ballad of "Steve O'Donnell's Wake" that Voelker placed in his fiction and I in my folklore. Eventually Voelker capitulated and wrote for the New York publishers a courtroom novel, *Anatomy of a Murder,* that became the nation's number one best-seller for over a year. But it is far inferior to his short stories.

The history of *Bloodstoppers and Bearwalkers* was curious. Four trade publishers dallied with it for some time before deciding it was not another *Stars Fell on Alabama.* Their readers could not categorize the book. One said that as an American he could not consider the tales of immigrants part of American folklore. Finally I turned the manuscript over to our new university press at Michigan State, which took nine months to reject it, on the adverse report of a female dietitian, somehow on the press committee, whose gorge rose in revulsion at the earthy contents. Harvard then took it in three months, sending me the report of their reader, who I believe was Howard Mumford Jones, saying it was the first manuscript he had ever read for the Harvard Press that he had to force himself to put down. So after six years the book found a home, but it never attracted much attention and, as I say, primarily served to educate me in the folklore approach to American studies.

One obstacle that faces the American Studies folklorist in getting his message across is the professional resistance to local as opposed to national history. Fieldwork must take place in a necessarily limited area, and the folklore collections that cover the whole nation or large regions must inevitably rely on second-hand printed sources. The bona fide field report, say Emelyn Gardner's *Folklore from the Schoharie Hills, New York,* will consequently be lumped by the academic scholar with antiquarian and genealogical studies on the local-history shelf. Theodore Blegen attempted to alter this emphasis with his persuasive plea for *Grass Roots History,*

but professional advancement will not be achieved through
the Association for State and Local History. When I was
presenting my case to the Mississippi Valley Historical Association, now the Organization of American Historians, one of
the panelists, Merrill D. Peterson, author of *The Jefferson
Image in the American Mind,* commented on my paper,
"Who cares about a few obscure Indians?" Like myself, Peterson was a product of the Harvard American Civilization doctoral program. and his identification of American civilization
with the hallowed figures of American history is certainly
a majority opinion. One answer is "Jefferson. He cared and
wrote about obscure Indians, as part of his interest in the
American scene."

In the Upper Peninsula, and on subsequent field trips,
I encountered articulate Americans from the folk stratum
whose life histories deserved public recording. The American
Studies folklorist is well equipped to undertake the task
of writing folk biographies. One example of such a document is John Lomax's narrative of Huddy Ledbetter, better
known as Leadbelly, the Louisiana Negro convict who sang
ballads and plucked a twelve-string guitar before concert
audiences after the Lomaxes discovered him. Similarly I
have recorded the autobiography of James Douglas Suggs,
the remarkable Negro folk narrator I met in Calvin, Michigan. In *Lay My Burden Down* Benjamin Botkin has assembled
a number of poignant slave memories and personal reminiscences. But by and large this kind of folk source is not available for the student of American civilization. In England,
however, the publishing house of Routledge and Kegan Paul,
long sympathetic to folklore and folk-life books, has sought
for and printed several manuscripts of this sort. Routledge's
editor, Colin Franklin, has recently described this venture in
an engrossing article on "Publishing Folklore."[8] Franklin's
most remarkable discovery to date is W. H. Barrett, now a
bedridden invalid, who lived most of his life in the Cam-
bridgeshire Fen country. Routledge has published in the
last four years his *Tales from the Fens, More Tales from the
Fens,* and *A Fenman's Story,* all pungent chronicles of Barrett's experiences and memories as a member of the powerless,

8. *Folklore* 78 (1966) : 184–204.

propertyless class in rural Britain fighting for breath with
his wits and nerve. His tales are not folktales but elaborate
personal narratives, often punctuated with traditional motifs.
This kind of oral history lacks a convenient label, but it
exists and thrives in the folk community, and I encountered
such narrators in the Upper Peninsula. For want of a ready
pigeonhole I grouped them in a final chapter called "Saga-
men." There Charlie Goodman recounts his hunting and
lovemaking exploits, Swan Olson his heroic triumphs over
bullies and thieves, and John Hallen his psychic prophecies
that came true. A volume of these memoirs of uncommon
common men would inform us a good deal more about
American life than another tome on Jefferson.

   A further difficulty the folklorist must overcome before
he is fully accepted in the American Studies brotherhood is
how to translate collection into interpretation. The end product of fieldwork is usually a gathering of tales or songs or
superstitions, often regarded by readers as entertainment.
On my return from the Upper Peninsula I found myself in
great demand as a speaker before all kinds of social and
fraternal groups: Masons, Elks, Kiwanis, Zontas, P.T.A.'s,
an endless wheel. They wished to hear my recitations of Upper Peninsula legends, and in these talks, and on a Sunday
radio broadcast, I began metamorphosing into a performing
storyteller. My own motive was to establish new contacts with
potential informants, a hope that never properly materialized,
while on their part the audiences expected amusement from
hearing Michigan stories. They had of course no interest in
my theories of folklore. My career as a performer ended when
I related some unbowdlerized narratives to a P.T.A. convention. This popularizing aspect of folklore can and has in-
jured serious folklore scholarship, and it is not easily avoided.

   The fact remains that·even the scrupulous, well-anno-
tated collection of field texts cannot greatly·assist the American cultural historian. Texts recorded in the field today
cannot be assigned to the nineteenth or eighteenth centuries,
and texts divorced from the personalities of their carriers and
from their social setting lose much of their historical meaning. A few praiseworthy exceptions to the conventional compilations of texts may be noted. Austin and Alta Fife debated whether to arrange their Mormon folk legends topically

or chronologically and happily chose the latter option, making their *Saints of Sage and Saddle* a folk commentary on the main events in Mormon history from Joseph Smith's vision to the successful establishing of Deseret. Américo Paredes, in *"With His Pistol in His Hand"*, has used the ballad of the outlaw Gregorio Cortez to illumine the mutually hostile attitudes and folk stereotypes of Mexican and Texan along the Southwest border. Vance Randolph in *Ozark Superstitions* has revealed hidden pockets of supernatural convictions in the minds of Ozark hillfolk. Yet one has to dig hard for these few instances of analytical and theoretical employment of American folk materials, and this is why folklore titles seldom appear in American Studies reading lists. Recently the ancient historian Frank Kramer, in *Voices in the Valley,* has attempted to utilize folklore in his interpretation of institutional myths and social symbols shaping the Midwest, but his concepts of myth and symbol are so vague and his insertion of folk tradition so artificial that the book serves as a warning against, rather than a support for, the folklore method. No one falls flatter on his face than an Americanist like Marshall Fishwick or Kenneth Lynn who tries to comment on folklore when he has no competence in the subject.

We have been considering contributions that folklore method can make to American Studies. Let us turn to the question where folk culture fits in relation to American popular culture. The usual view of this relationship communicated to me conceives of folk culture at the bottom of American civilization, with popular, mass, and elite cultures resting above on successive levels, as in the following representation.

| Elite |
|---|
| Mass |
| Popular |
| Folk |

The organs of popular culture point toward the oral and grassroots culture, as in the antebellum newspaper. The organs of mass culture point toward centrally directed signals, as in the modern newspaper with its canned editorials and columnists and wire services. The elite or intellectual culture covers the small cerebral segment of the population at the opposite end of the pole from the folk. This is the picture Americanists seem to have in mind when they speak of folklore.

It is not an accurate picture. The folk culture does not relate more closely to the popular culture than to other spheres of American civilization. In Carl Bode's *The Anatomy of American Popular Culture, 1840–1861,* one will find only the scantiest indications of folk expression, in a passing reference to the folk art of carving and whittling. Yet this is a detailed examination of American taste and temperament in the mid-nineteenth century.

The relationships between folk, popular, mass, and elite cultures in the United States might better be presented this way:

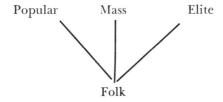

Popular          Mass          Elite

Folk

We may illustrate this model with the case of Davy Crockett. The legends of Crockett developed in the oral humor of the frontier and followed a universal heroic pattern common to folk epics. During Davy's lifetime and in the two decades following his death, the organs of the popular culture played with the oral yarns told by and about Crockett. In the daily press, in the comic almanacs, in the several versions of Paulding's farce about Crockett, *The Lion of the West,* in the graphic humor of woodcuts and cartoons, Davy blossomed as a popular and subliterary hero exhibiting chauvinistic and racist attitudes. The Crockett revival of the 1950s engineered by Walt Disney presented an all-American boy scout type as a mass-culture hero. In an elite view, Vernon Louis Parrington characterized Crockett in his *Main Currents in American Thought* as a frontier wastrel exploited by Whig politicians who constructed a romantic myth about the simple-minded rustic to advance their purposes. All four Crocketts interest the Americanist, but the oral, folk Crockett appears first historically.

Or we may take separate examples of relationships between the folk culture and other cultures. At some points the intellectual culture does intersect with folklore. In the elite realm of religious thought and expression, one can point to Increase Mather's *An Essay for the Recording of Illustrious Providences* (1684) as a synthesis of theology and folklore. The president of Harvard, like other Puritan intellectuals of his time, believed in the providential interpretation of history, and accordingly he and his fellow ministers accumulated oral legends of poltergeists and spectral ships to compose the first book of American folklore. In *The Varieties of Religious Experience* (1902), William James brought together a number of vivid examples in religious history supporting his pragmatic proof of the existence of God. These mystical experiences, visions, and revelations dip into a common store of recurrent folk motifs and folk images.

A case of interaction between mass culture and folk culture is at once apparent in the urban folksong revival. Urban folksingers like Joan Baez have become national celebrities, and the caricaturing of the left-wing beatnik songstress as Joanie Phoanie by cartoonist Al Capp developed into a national incident. The relationship between contemporary left-wing politics and the writing and singing of protest songs is being explored in an Indiana doctoral dissertation by a folklorist with training in American history.

A useful illustration of links between popular culture and folklore is provided in an article in the *Southern Folklore Quarterly* (December 1966) by Marcello Truzzi on "The American Circus as a Source of Folklore." Truzzi points out that circus acts have largely depended upon family tradition for their perpetuation, and he surveys the skills, techniques, personnel, superstitions, terms, legendary anecdotes, and tent-staking chanteys which form categories of circus lore. Circus folktales deal with tricks played by circus people on towns-folk, with origins of circus accessories like pink lemonade, with unusual capacities of circus animals, and with celebrated jugglers, clowns, and aerialists.

Such aspects of American culture permeated by folklore are the fertile research grounds for the American Studies folklorist.

The line of research pursued will necessarily depend on the special training of the inquirer, whether in literature, history, government, sociology, or art history. I remember Russel Nye once saying that when on occasion he teaches a history course he must shift gears from his usual critical analysis of a written work to a chronological consideration of events. The folklorist thinks in still a different groove, com-paratively. Collecting in American folklore has been under-taken by scholars trained in medieval literature and modern languages, or without formal graduate study. Among the new generation of students are some comajors in folklore and American Studies who will master comparative, historical, and critical thinking, and they may produce the sound, perceptive treatments of folklore in American literature or American history that are yet to be written.

# 5

# The Question of
# Folklore in a New Nation

The argument of this paper will be that folklore and folk traditions have formed a large component of emergent nationalism. Frequently the burgeoning interests in a national language and a national folklore reinforce each other. Concern for an estimable national history and national literature also overlap with pride in a distinctive folklore. Circumstances vary from nation to nation, but the promoters of a national self-consciousness, whether in a republic, a monarchy, an empire, or a socialist state, clearly appear to have recognized the value and utility of folklore.

Historians agree that American national feeling began to overshadow state loyalties in the decades following the War of 1812. The 1820s, 30s and 40s were the nurturing decades for the new sense of unity and association, which would be

From *Journal of the Folklore Institute*, 1966; also *Folklore and Society, Essays in Honor of Benj. A. Botkin*, ed. Bruce Jackson (Hatboro, Pa.: Folklore Associates, 1966) , pp. 21–33.

rent by the sectional debates of the 1850s and the outbreak of Civil War in 1861. At the time of the Declaration of Independence, in 1776, the population was divided in roughly equal thirds between rebels against England, Loyalists, and Colonists remaining indifferent. Even the victorious patriots felt their strongest ties to their particular states, joined in a loose confederation. Under the new federal constitution launched in 1789, Americans maintained, as they still maintain, a dual citizenship in state and nation; and in the early years of the republic, a man regarded himself as a Virginian or a New Yorker first, and a citizen of the United States second. This was a wholly natural outlook, for the states preceded the republic, and the colonies, the states: and each colony-state possessed its separate traditions of settlement: Massachusetts with Puritans, Pennsylvania with Quakers, Maryland with Catholics, New York with the Dutch, Virginia with tobacco planters, Georgia with convicts.

The second war with Britain helped Americans harden into a nation. The war itself, while ending a stalemate, solidified the states, strengthened the central government, and added to the meager stock of common traditions. Subsequently, a long stretch of peace and a turning away from Europe to the inward conquest of the continent gave the young nation a chance to fatten and grow. As new western territories were carved out of the national domain and additional states were admitted, a new species of Western American emerged, with national rather than state attachments. A plan for economic self-sufficiency, sponsored by Henry Clay, promoted the flow of internal trade between all sections of the country over newly constructed turnpikes and canals.

In this atmosphere, the notes of philosophic nationalism began to sound. As early as 1823, Charles Jared Ingersoll, a Philadelphia lawyer, could address the American Philosophical Society on the subject, "The Influence of America on the Mind." In his glowing discourse, he discussed the various categories of civilization in which America had already left her special and enlightened imprint: education, the law, medicine, journalism, inventions, and commerce, all prospering in a free society blessed by nature's bounty. The Monroe Doctrine, announced the same year as a cornerstone of Amer-

can foreign policy, drew a distinction between the virtuous
institutions of the New World and the decadent ones of the
Old.

And yet, rhetoric aside, what were these American qualities? Americans spoke the English tongue, read English literature, adopted much English law; their history had barely
begun; the Monroe Doctrine was in reality the tootle from
a cock-boat hiding behind a British man-of-war. In his recent
work, *The Americans, the National Experience,* Daniel J.
Boorstin has ingeniously illustrated some of the trials encountered by Americans seeking to find a national identity.
Local historical societies flourished, but the American Historical Association had to wait until 1884 to be formed. Only
in 1834 did George Bancroft begin the first volume of the
first panoramic American history; before that date, in the
words of Boorstin, "The American who looked back across
his New World past found clusters of documentary collections,
patriotic biographies, and works of state and local filio-piet-
ism." Bancroft's history became itself a symbol of American
achievement.

And who were the heroes of this history? In a delicious
chapter on "The Mythologizing of George Washington,"
Boorstin describes the process in which an all too real and
immediate Washington was transformed and idealized into
a mythical father-figure and founding hero, comparable to
the ancient heroes of long-historied countries shrouded in
legendary mists. This alteration hallowed a figure highly
controversial and even anathematized at the time of his death
in 1799. Still, he was the only candidate suitable for national
apotheosis, in consequence of his roles as victorious comman-
der-in-chief and first president of the requblic. In biography
and portrait, holiday fete and marble statuary, the image-
makers began their task of creating an American Zeus for
a hero-hungry public. The cultural mechanisms they employed
suggest the processes of folk tradition. Though spun out of
whole cloth, the now celebrated tale of young George Washington and the cherry tree, conceived by Washington's most
famous hagiographer, "Parson" Weems, soon passed into the
nation's lore:

"I can't tell a lie, Pa; you know I can't tell a lie. I did
cut it with my hatchet."

"Run to my arms, you dearest boy," cried his father
in transports, "run to my arms; such an act of heroism
in my son, is more worth than a thousand trees, though
blossomed with silver, and their fruits of purest gold."
Packed with such cautionary fables, the *Life of George Washington: With Curious Anecdotes, Equally Honourable to
Himself and Exemplary to His Young Countrymen* sold
enormously from 1808 on into the century. Dreams of pro-
phetic greatness and accounts of heroic invincibility trapped
out the saga. The cult of Washington represented a triumph
for national over regional hero worship; and Professor Boorstin has traced the controversy between the Virginia and
Massachusetts claimants to Revolutionary greatness, Patrick
Henry and James Otis, each of whom, his champions contended, had been the first to defy the British tyrant. Again
the process of mythologizing produced apocrypha; there is
no factual evidence for the peroration dear to schoolboys
which Henry supposedly uttered in the Virginia House of
Burgesses in 1775, "Give me liberty or give me death."

Sometimes the first author of a national legend can be
identified, as with Weems and the cherry tree, or with the
popular writer George Lippard and his sentimental relation
in 1874, in a book on *Washington and His Generals,* of a
dim-eyed old bell-ringer pealing forth the Liberty Bell from
the Philadelphia statehouse to announce the signing of the Declaration of Independence. "The Liberty Bell," writes Professor Boorstin, "was destined to be reproduced endlessly
on coins, postage stamps, and government bonds, finally becoming one of the most cherished emblems of American nationality, American purpose, and the American mission."
Yet the incident was pure Lippard. In other cases, the first
contriver is not known, and the source may well be oral. Ask
any American schoolboy, or grown-up, who uttered the im-
mortal words, "Don't give up the ship," and the chances are
he will say John Paul Jones, the Revolutionary naval hero,
or Oliver Hazard Perry, the War of 1812 victor in a Great
Lakes naval engagement. The actual speaker was the obscure

Captain James Lawrence, commander of the thirty-eight gun
frigate the *Chesapeake,* which sailed out of Boston harbor
in 1813 to fight a duel with the British frigate the *Shannon.*
Apparently Lawrence, mortally wounded, gave this dying
injunction to his officers, but the schoolboy seldom realizes
that they did give up the ship, fifteen minutes after Lawrence
died, and that it was towed into Halifax as a prize. "Millions
for defense but not one cent for tribute," is another cherished
national adage, attributed to Charles Cotesworth Pinckney,
one of the American commissioners in the so-called XYZ affair of 1797–98; he is supposed to have said this when asked
for a bribe by an intermediary of the French Minister Talleyrand. Pinckney denied authorship of the slogan throughout
his life, but on his death the utterance was relentlessly en-
graved on his tombstone.

The quest for a national history impinged on folklore
in such instances, and similarly the quest for a national
literature skirted across folk materials. Beginning in the
1820's, two major authors began writing on American themes
and characters, although still under the domination of English
and continental literary models. James Fenimore Cooper, the
American counterpart to Sir Walter Scott, initiated a cycle
of frontier novels laid in the forests and prairies, centering
on a hero-woodsman alternately called Natty Bumppo, Hawkeye, Deerslayer, and Leatherstocking. As Henry Nash Smith
has shown in *Virgin Land: The West as Symbol and Myth,*
Hawkeye is a fictional drawing of the historical Daniel Boone,
who quickly passed into the national mythology on the level
of popular literature as the intrepid Indian-fighter and wilderness scout. This generic Western hero has remained vivid
in the American imagination down to the present day, when
he is glorified in a hundred variants of a standard television
plot. Also influenced by Scott, whom he visited in 1817, Washington Irving turned out graceful sketches dipping into
German, English, Spanish, and American folklore; his tales,
set in the Hudson Valley at the time of the Dutch settlement
in the seventeenth century, drew upon what appeared to be
native legends of headless horsemen, compacts with the Devil,
ghostly sailors, and hundred-year sleepers. At the close of
this period, in 1855, the poet Longfellow sought in *The Song*

*of Hiawatha* to construct an American epic based on his conception of American Indian myths; his verses, immediately clasped to the collective American bosom, climaxed a number of similar but abortive efforts. The creation of an American literature was not undertaken in solitary parlors by questing artists in search of their muse, but in a public spotlight beamed by patriotic critics and editors, who demanded a literature growing from the native soil and reflecting the national glory. Americans never did forget the sneer of the English critic Sydney Smith (1771–1845), "Who reads an American book?" The campaign for an American literature is elaborately traced by Benjamin T. Spencer in *The Quest for Nationality* (1957).

So too with language, Americans began consciously to draw distinctions between the speech they had imported from England in the seventeenth century and that which they spoke in their republic in the nineteenth. In the first half-century of the new nation, Noah Webster devoted his energies to standardizing the vocabulary, spelling, and usage of the American idiom; in 1828 he published his famous *American Dictionary of the English Language.* The concept of an "Americanism" as a newly minted word arising from the circumstances of American society and geography, or an inherited word converted to new employment, itself entered the language; John Russell Bartlett compiled a *Dictionary of Americanisms* in 1848. Meanwhile in the backwoods and the backcountry—terms that had themselves become American-isms—novel styles of expression were forming among the novel breeds of settlers, and from the 1820s on their "tall" and "cute" talk, comic imagery, bold metaphors, and home-spun rhythms increasingly caught the notice of newspaper editors, travel writers, humorists, and playwrights. This flavor-ful and extravagant speech entered into popular oratory of the period, from the rolling phrases of the 4th of July dec-lamations to sonorous Congressional speechmaking. A special mouthpiece of American wisdom emerged in the "crackerbox philosopher," a homely sage speaking in native wit and proverb, who would recur in many guises, historical and fictional, throughout American history.

The national quests for an American history, an American literature, and an American language proceeded consciously and deliberately. But because the spirit of nationalism was kindled in the United States before 1846, the year when the word and the idea of *folklore* were articulated, patriots could not intentionally search for folk traditions. Such traditions did rub against the newly constructed history, literature, language. But they also occupied their own separate niches in the fermenting national culture. If the name for folklore did not yet exist to clarify the process, still the process of folk-hero creation and folk-legend formation was clearly at work, and was encouraged by the promoters of Americanism. Between 1820 and 1850, five folk heroes sprang from the city pavements and the Western clearings into the public limelight. These hero-buffoons—Davy Crockett, Mike Fink, Sam Patch, Mose the Bowery b'hoy, and Jonathan the Yankee —have been discussed in various research studies in the last thirty years, but I would like to regard them from the vantage point of aspiring nationalism.

As the nation needed a mythological founder-hero and father-figure like Washington, so it craved more intimate, popular demigods to identify with its down-to-earth American traits and sky-soaring American ambitions. Where were such heroes to be found? They began to edge in from the corners of American life in the 1820s, until they literally held the center of the stage. A comic drama of 1821, Alphonso Wetmore's *The Pedlar,* produced in St. Louis, Missouri, brought together a gallery of native character types already visible: the Revolutionary veteran, the old salt, the ringtailed roarer, the Mississippi keelboatman, the Yankee peddler. Curiously, the military and the naval figures never crystallized in the popular imagination, probably because they were too transient; the deeper rooted ones typified American regions and occupations. Mike Fink, though always a shadowy brute, became best known of the breed of lusty riverboatmen who poled keelboats of produce down the Ohio and Mississippi Rivers to New Orleans before the era of the steamboat. Davy Crockett achieved celebrity as a congressman from the western state of Tennessee, which first elected him in 1827, but his legendary role cast him as a representative not of a new state but of

a new species, the frontier braggart. Though Crockett and
Fink were personalized and historical, their folk-hero quality
lay in their portrayal of an entire genus, the hunter and the
boatman of the Western woods and waters. In the case of the
Yankee, the regional type never jelled into a single individual; but throughout myriad newspaper yarns, theatrical
farces, and doggerel verses, the Yankee displayed a consistent
portrait, that of a New England bumpkin fresh from the
farm, often a sly trader, alternately crafty and loutish. In
Wetmore's play, the Yankee was the title character, as he
would be in many other simple comedies. He always bore a
rustic name, like Deuteronomy Dutiful, Solomon Swop, Jedediah Homebred, or Jonathan Ploughboy. Most often he was
called Jonathan.

Two other personalities joined these three, this time
from eastern cities and factories. Sam Patch was fully as eccentric as the others, but less a type; he belonged to the new
class of factory operatives and worked in cotton mills in Pawtucket, Rhode Island, and Paterson, New Jersey. Patch gained
notoriety by jumping from bridges, ships' masts, and plat-
forms erected over waterfalls, and after a fatal plunge in 1829
speedily passed into legend. The final mock-hero, Mose, burst
upon the New York public in 1848 as a shaggy hero in a knockabout skit of New York City low life called *A Glance at New
York,* and soon acquired his own legendary status. Mose, as
portrayed originally by the actor Francis Chanfrau, was actually modeled upon an urban character type conspicuous in
the Bowery area of lower New York, a combination street
loafer, low-class dandy, and cocky volunteer fireman, known
as the "b'hoy," a term indicative of Irish origins.

Regional and local as were these incipient heroes, with
peculiarities of speech, costume, and manner at first familiar
only to their immediate circle, all became nationally renowned.
The public responded with immediate delight to their antics
and heroics, adopting their names and sayings as household
words. Through the media of popular culture which thrived
in the pre–Civil War decades—the sporting weekly, comic. almanac, theatrical entertainment, literary gift-annual, regional
newspaper, woodcut and lithograph—the adventures of the
quintet were widely disseminated to all parts of the country.

In their elevation from regional to national celebrity, they quickly transcended the limits of oral folk homage and entered the popular rather than the folk channel of culture. The distinction between oral-folk and popular-printed channels of legend should not, in the years from 1825 to 1855, be too sharply drawn. Trickster anecdotes and lying tales swirled orally around the Yankee and the frontiersman and found their way into the cheap printed media which, before the day of national and international news services, lay close to and fed upon local talk, gossip, and yarns. To such periodicals as the New York *Spirit of the Times* and the Boston *Yankee Blade,* quite without counterpart in the post–Civil War decades, correspondents sent humorous sketches of backcountry life and character which frequently reproduced storytelling scenes, and within these scenes presented texts of international tales, usually about tricksters and Munchausens. Conversely, in the cases of Mose and Sam Patch, the newspaper notices and stage performances that brought both to general attention propelled their slang sayings and daredevil escapades into the everyday conversation of newsboys and bootblacks and the public at large.

From the perspective of cultural nationalism, these cock-alorum heroes offered both potentialities and problems. On the positive side, they were all thoroughly and indelibly American, spawned on the new continent, and rising into view on the tide of Jacksonian democracy. As the election of Jackson had ushered in an era of the common man, so these were the uncommonest of common men, slattern democrats in all their glory, straight from the canebrakes and street corners, mocking the aristocratic dude and effete intellectual. They were Jacksonian Americans, too, in their formulaic boasting and tall feats of hunting, fighting, jumping, drinking. Against the Injuns and varmints of the backwoods, and the sharpers and cozeners of the metropolis, they won an incessant string of triumphs; eventually, as their legends grew, they bobbed up in far parts of the world. The stage Yankee particularly illustrates this pattern, for he had a prehistory, beginning with the first Yankee servant of 1787 in Royall Tyler's play *The Contrast,* and continuing in a succession of minor roles designed mainly for comic relief. But in 1825 he takes the

central part, as Jonathan Ploughboy in *The Forest Rose,* and
thenceforth, in farce after farce, assumes an heroic stance.
Comedians like "Yankee" Hill and Dan Marble closely studied
the live New England rustic to make their own performances
more realistic. No longer a servant, the Yankee, too, had become an all-conquering hero, sometimes cast as a Revolutionary War soldier or War of 1812 sailor. These commoners,
clad in buckskin breeches and coonskin cap, or pearl-but-
toned peajacket and stovepipe hat, corresponded to the peas-
ants of Europe in whom the romantic poets, from Herder to
Wordsworth, were discovering moral virtues. While refresh-
ingly realistic in one sense, with their slangy talk and barnyard and gutter manners, these American yeomen at the same
time conformed to the romantic tradition, for underneath
their shaggy crusts beat hearts of purest gold. Distressed dam-
sels and befuddled greenhorns could inevitably look to them
for succor.

So in these jokers, American nationalists could find their
demigods. The problem was to convert regional eccentrics into
national properties. More than that, these figures of fun had
to be taken somewhat seriously; they had to be elevated as
well as rendered familiar. In the United States of the Jacksonian era, three flourishing popular media effectively nation-
alized the local scalawags; the humor-filled newspaper, re-
plenished through the mechanism of the exchange; the comic
almanac; and the theatrical farce.

In the case of Crockett, all three worked overtime to make
him a national legend. When the Tennessee congressman-
elect first appeared in the nation's capital in 1827 to take
his seat, he created a sensation, as a real live specimen of the
half-horse half-alligator breed. Decorous Easterners gaped at
this wild Westerner, and the newspapers played him up as
fertile copy, gleefully printing his salty sayings and backwoods stories. The antebellum press doted on humor, and
both dailies and weeklies hunted for original "good ones" to
spread before their readers; more often, they had to rely on
their exchanges with other papers for filler. A good story was
reprinted around the country and stayed alive for years.

The celebrity of Crockett began in this way. By 1833,
when Crockett had broken with the Jacksonian Democrats

over internal improvements, the Whig party thought him suf-
ficiently well-known to promote him as a counterfoil to Jackson. His political career fizzled, but his legendary career soared
when a series of almanacs featured his adventures and escapades in the backwoods. The series commenced in 1835,
the year before his death at the Alamo in Texas, and lasted
till 1856. At first these annual numbers were printed in Nashville, Tennessee, but in the 1840s and 50s printers in New
York, Philadelphia, and Boston issued them, and they must
have circulated very widely. The farmers' almanac had provided a staple reading and consulting fare for Americans all
through the eighteenth century, and Benjamin Franklin developed its humorous and subliterary potentialities with *Poor
Richard's Almanac.* Hence the Crockett almanacs found a
ready and receptive public. As for the third medium, the
popular theater, a Crockett character under the pseudonym
of Nimrod Wildfire cavorted across the stage for two decades
from 1831 on in James K. Paulding's play *The Lion of the
West.*

The theater was perhaps the most successful means of introducing Americans to their newly acquired heroes. Like the
newspaper of the day, it was a grassroots affair, close to its
audience; skits and farces were often hastily constructed and
improvised; character actors specialized as rustics and villains
drawn from life; theatrical entertainment verged on the circus
and carnival. The theater then was an all-American institution; troupes traveled to cities and towns throughout the nation with the plays of Broadway; events of the moment were
easily transmuted by the play hacks and star performers into
the stuff of melodrama. Yankee Jonathan and Mose the fire
laddie were primarily stage creations; Sam Patch reenacted
his jump over Niagara Falls on stage; Crockett talked tall
in *The Lion of the West,* and Mike Fink rough-and-tumbled
in Wetmore's *The Pedlar.* Through these knockabout dramas,
a whole series of publics became acquainted with the hero-
clowns, and could see them in the flesh in regional costume
and hear them speaking in regional dialect. To some extent
the heroes tended to coalesce. The title of *Sam Patch; or the
Daring Yankee* indicated the identification of the jumping
hero with Jonathan; and the role was played by Dan Marble,

one of the most celebrated Yankee impersonators. Another
well-known Yankee comedian, James H. Hackett, took on the
character of Nimrod Wildfire. Such popular actors as George
H. "Yankee" Hill and Francis Chanfrau became so associated
with their projections of the Yankee and Mose that in a sense
they continued the parts in real life; monologues and anecdotes were published of "Yankee" Hill, and lithographs
printed of Chanfrau as Mose.

When these actors played before their home audiences,
the spectators whooped with delight; but on tour in strange
localities, the problem of introducing a local hero to the rest
of the nation became acute. What would citizens of Louisville,
Kentucky, for instance, make of a swaggering bully from the
Bowery? We are in a position to answer this question from a
surviving playbill for October 31, 1856, announcing the ar-
rival of Mose and his "gallus gal" Lizey.

> Mose, the far-famed and world-renowned, presents him-
> self at our Theatre this evening. In all the pieces of this
> class, there is scarcely a single incident that is not cal-
> culated to warn the unwary against the arts of the design-
> ing, and prepare the adventurer for the trials he must
> expect to encounter. All the spirit, fun and knock situa-
> tions, are rendered prominent; but in this, as in every
> other Mose piece, produced by Mr. Chanfrau, the hero
> is always found defending right against wrong; protect-
> ing the weak against the assaults of the strong; and in-
> variably siding with innocence, helplessness, and distress.
> No two characters have been more misunderstood than
> Mose and Lizey. This hero and heroine of humble life
> have been too often considered perfect rowdies and
> profligate outcasts, while the very reverse is the case.
> Mose, it is true, is one of the fire b'hoys, full of fun,
> frolic and fighting, but without one vicious propensity
> in his nature; and Lizey, is a good-hearted, worthy and
> virtuous woman, attached to Mose, with no other prom-
> inent fault than the very excusable one of striving to
> imitate the peculiarities of the man of her heart.

Thus at some pains did the tour promoters seek to allay the
fears and misapprehensions felt in the hinterland by theater-
goers who had clearly already heard much about Mose. From

the tone of the playbill one can appreciate, too, the independent existence that Mose had acquired, apart from his stage
incarnation; he was a personality and a living hero in his own
right. Mose came, was seen, and apparently conquered, for
a playbill of November 6 called his attraction (an adaptation
of the original *A Glance at New York*) "the most successful
drama ever produced in Louisville."

So Mose, like his fellow braggarts before him, met the
people, both in his heroic adventures and on his stage tours.
As the Gold Rush to California took place the same year
Mose made his Broadway debut, one of the subsequent Mose
pieces dealt with *Mose in California,* and the company actually performed in San Francisco. The Yankee peddler became as familiar a figure in the South and West as in his native down-East; fittingly Wetmore's drama *The Pedlar* opened
in St. Louis. In their later, national phases the heroes left the
United States to disport and conquer in foreign lands. A booklet of colored lithographs showed Mose gawking at the sights
in London; "Sam Patch in France" followed on the first Patch
drama laid in Sam's home cities; the stage Yankee fought
in Poland, Algiers, and Cuba; and the almanac Crockett defied
the emperor of Haiti and wrestled an anaconda off the coast
of Brazil. Now fully accredited national representatives, the
swaggering demigods carried the torch of liberty and the in-
signia of democracy overseas.

These bellicose commoners each spoke a regional dialect,
a badge of their common origins and American nurture. On
stage the Yankee actors and impersonators of Mose talked in
a carefully practised idiom; we know that "Yankee" Hill and
Dan Marble studied New England rural speech, and that
Chanfrau modeled the patois and dress of Mose on one Moses
Humphreys, who ran with Lady Washington fire engine no.
40. Yankee comedians frequently appeared between the acts
to deliver a recitation in down-East vernacular. In newspaper
yarns, the Yankee's talk is rendered phonetically in an ob-
vious attempt to catch the sound of his words and the spirit
of his phrasemaking. In the almanacs Crockett regularly
spouts Western tall talk flavored with backwoods imagery,
in the manner frequently reported at firsthand by travelers
and correspondents in the Southwest.

Because these figures often appear in so ludicrous a light, and in media so truly vulgar, one may question whether they represent a genuine folklore impulse. My view is that they were indeed the cherished popular folk heroes of the young American nation, catching perfectly the brash humor and daredevil impudence of the Jacksonian period, yet comparable to the legendary creations in other national cultures. A case can be made, as I have suggested elsewhere, for Crockett as an Heroic Age champion, the blood-brother to Achilles, Siegfried, Grettir the Strong, Cuchulain, Arjun, and Antar, even though in the United States the conditions of Heroic Age society and the bardic reworking of the oral legends were enormously compressed and condensed. American history ran the gamut from the seminomadic, warring society of the Heroic Age, found on the frontier, to modern nationhood in less than two centuries. Both the Heroic Age and the nation-making eras contributed to American folklore. Analogies can be found in other histories for the process whereby nationalism promotes folklore.

A word needs to be said about the tidal wave of interest in American folklore that commenced to surge in the 1920s. There are similarities with the period a century earlier: the nation had emerged from a major war; the spirit of national-ism manifested itself in a renewed call for an American lan-guage, this time trumpeted by H. L. Mencken; Paul Bunyan was uncovered as a one hundred percent, giant, all-American folk hero, and was shortly followed by other giants, none hav-ing any actual folk basis. The nineteenth-century heroes were excavated, dusted off, and trotted out in shiny new colors alongside the Bunyans. With the awareness of *folklore, folk-song,* and *folk hero* as terms now in the language, publishers and performers could vend their wares with labels not avail-able a century before. But the world power of 1925–50 bore little resemblance to the upstart nation of 1825-50; this was the age of mass culture, and it processed products called folk-lore for sale to a mass audience. The question here is of folk-lore in an older nation.

# 6

# Folklore Research Opportunities
# in American Cultural History

The dramatic possibilities for folklore research within the frame of American cultural history are best visualized in the light of European achievements in folklore study. In Europe *folklore* got its name in 1846 and gained its status in the second half of the nineteenth century. Italy, France, and England had their day, when their private scholars attained international distinction, and now Finland, Sweden, Ireland, Germany, and Russia take the lead in folklore activities, their governments all actively supporting the cause.

Finnish nationalism runs parallel to the evolving science of folklore, which developed from the collecting of Kalevala runes and charms by Elias Lönnröt into a nationally sponsored Finnish Literature Society in 1831. In collecting folklore the society also sought to preserve the ancient language and poetry. In 1935, after a century of collecting, a new com-

From *Research Opportunities in American Cultural History,* ed. J. F. McDermott (Lexington, Ky.: University Press of Kentucky, 1961).

petition netted 133,000 items. The folklore archives of the society contain a million and a quarter items, contributed by thousands of citizens from all social classes, and indexed on 275,000 cards.[1] From the Finnish scholars has come the so-called historical-geographical method, practiced by most leading folklorists today, who compare hundreds of texts of a single tale or ballad to trace its original starting point and subsequent wanderings. This method is demonstrated in an international series of renown, the Finnish Folklore Fellows Communications.

The Irish Folklore Commission, organized in 1935, has similarly served the movement of Irish nationalism and the revival of Gaelic speech. Its intensive collecting program and corps of full-time and part-time field workers have accumulated in the Irish archives over a million pages of manuscript, largely in Gaelic. To assist the collectors, an exhaustive *Handbook of Irish Folklore* provides a questionnaire for every conceivable aspect of traditional life in Ireland. Sean O'Sullivan adapted this handbook from the classification system developed by the Swedes from their documents in four vast folklore archives at Stockholm, Uppsala, Lund, and Gothenburg, and the artifacts in their eight hundred provincial and urban folk museums.[2]

In Russia, where the scientific collection of *byliny* from individual narrators began in 1831 with P. V. Kireyevsky, the Soviet Union has fully exploited propaganda potentialities in folklore materials. By party decree in 1936 the academic folklorists openly recanted the bourgeois theory that folklore filtered down to the working people from the upper class, and professed the new gospel, that the farm and factory workers have created the songs of protest and the legends of anti-Tsarist and revolutionary heroes which are the genuine Soviet

1. Jouko Hautala, "The Folklore Collections of the Finnish Literature Society," *Studia Fennica* 5, no. 6 (1947) : 197–202. See also, by the same author, "The Folklore Archives of the Finnish Literature Society," *Studia Fennica* 7, no. 2 (1957) : 3–36.

2. A good discussion of the work of the Irish Folklore Commission by Sean O'Sullivan is in *Four Symposia on Folklore,* ed. Stith Thompson (Bloomington, Ind., 1953), pp. 2–16; Sigurd Erixon talks about the Swedish folk-life museums, *ibid.,* pp. 175–81.

folklore. The party recognizes folklore both as a weapon in
the class conflict and as a force for national unity among the
diverse peoples of the Soviet Union. Collective farm workers
are encouraged to compose songs. For example, a brochure
published by the political division of the Starozhilov machine-
tractor station in 1934 and presented to the Writers' Congress
proudly announced that thirty-six of the thirty-eight collective farms served by their station had produced authors or
collectors of their folk poetry.[3] Quite apart from their propaganda use of folklore, the Russian-Soviet concern with the ar-
tistry and biography of the individual narrator and folk poet
far eclipses comparable studies in other countries.

   In most European states one or more professorships of
folklore or institutes of folklore and folk music exist. Cooperative scholarship has produced such monuments as the *Handwörterbuch des deutschen Aberglaubens,* the ultimate reference on folk beliefs.[4] In August 1959 the vitality of European
interest in folklore received a new proof in the successful first
International Folktale Congress held at Kiel and Copenhagen. Some three hundred folktale scholars attended, including
the largest delegation from the United States yet to attend a
European folklore meeting.

   The folklore situation in the United States presents a
striking contrast to the picture in Europe. Instead of a con-
stant growth of folklore organization, interest has surged and
ebbed. A wave of enthusiasm followed the founding of the
American Folklore Society in 1888, ten years after the birth
of the English society. A dozen branch societies held meetings
in various cities. An especially active group met in Boston
and Cambridge, where Francis James Child issued his famous
edition of the English and Scottish ballads, and even a Harvard Folklore Club thrived from 1894 to 1900. During the
1880s and 1890s a Negro folklore branch met regularly at
Hampton Institute, Virginia, and published summaries of
papers and the texts of Negro folklore in the *Southern Work-*

3. Y. M. Sokolov, *Russian Folklore,* tr. Catherine R. Smith (New York,
1950) , p. 26.
4. In ten volumes, edited by E. Hoffman-Krayer and Hans Bachtold-
Staubli (Berlin and Leipzig, 1927–42) .

*man.* A rival organization, the Chicago Folk-Lore Society, came into existence in 1891 under the leadership of Lieutenant Fletcher S. Bassett, U. S. N., and established its own branches in various states. George Washington Cable, for instance, was appointed head of the Louisiana branch of the Chicago Folk-Lore Society! Bassett edited one issue of a journal, *The Folk-Lorist,* and arranged an impressive international folklore congress in 1893 in conjunction with the Chicago World's Fair.[5]

Yet these promising beginnings all faded out. By the turn of the century the Chicago Folk-Lore Society and the local branches of the American Folklore Society had dissolved. After the death of its first editor, William Wells Newell, in 1900, the *Journal of American Folklore* fell for the next forty years into the hands of professional anthropologists, to whom folklore was necessarily a secondary interest.

During the 1920s and 1930s a new trend developed, as folksong collectors followed the exciting vistas opened up by John Lomax and Cecil Sharp. Volumes of Child ballads and cowboy, lumberjack, and Negro folksongs rolled from the press. Reed Smith in South Carolina, H. M. Belden in Missouri, Arthur Kyle Davis in Virginia, and Phillips Barry in New England made solid contributions to the young literature of folksong in America.[6]

The 1940s and 1950s witnessed a spurt of interest in the folktale, and from the southern Appalachians and the Ozarks the collections of Richard Chase, Vance Randolph, Leonard Roberts, and Marie Campbell have demonstrated that the elusive Märchen still abounded in parts of Anglo-Saxon United States.[7] With the vigorous pursuit of the two main forms of

5. See "North American Folklore Societies" and "North American Folklore Societies: A Suplement," compiled by Wayland D. Hand, *Journal of American Folklore* 56 (1943) : 161–91, and 58 (1946) : 477–94.

6. Reed Smith, *South Carolina Ballads* (Cambridge, Mass., 1928) ; Henry M. Belden, *Ballads and Songs Collected by the Missouri Folk-Lore Society* (Columbia, Mo., 1940) ; Arthur K. Davis, *Traditional Ballads of Virginia* (Cambridge, Mass., 1929) ; Phillips Barry, ed., *Bulletin of the Folk-Song Society of the Northeast,* 1930–37.

7. Richard Chase, *The Jack Tales* (Boston, 1943) ; Vance Randolph, *Who Blowed Up the Church House? and Other Ozark Folktales* (New York. 1952) ; Leonard W. Roberts, *South from Hell-fer-Sartin* (Lexington, Ky., 1955) ; Marie Campbell, *Tales from the Cloud-Walking Country* (Bloomington, Ind., 1958) .

oral folklore, the ballad and the tale, a renewed enthusiasm
for the whole field of folklore became apparent. Upon the
initiation of the Southeastern Folklore Society in 1934 and its
offspring, the *Southern Folklore Quarterly* in 1937, a host of
state and regional folklore societies and publications came
into being or revived, until at this writing about thirty such
societies exist. The printed quarterlies, *Western Folklore*,
*Midwest Folklore,* and *New York Folklore Quarterly,* are followed by various bulletins, newsletters, and leaflets, issued
through photo-offset, mimeographing or similar process. The
membership in these societies customarily consists of a few
academic folklorists surrounded by amateur genealogists, folksingers, and hobbyists of various kinds. Meanwhile a generation of professional folklorists has emerged to take over the
reins of the American Folklore Society. Since they have entered folklore from a variety of disciplines, chiefly English
literature, modern languages, and musicology, their primary
allegiance of course goes to their own professional organizations, and so the American Folklore Society is plagued by inconsistent attendance and lukewarm support. The Society
now meets in alternate years with the Modern Language Association and the American Anthropological Association.

This rapid survey indicates the haphazard and rather
unprofessional character of American folklore studies as compared with the European. The vast institutional archives in
Europe, the team field trips, the salaried collectors, the cooperative encyclopedias, and the rival schools of interpretation so common abroad are yet to appear in the United
States. An Archive of American Folksong does exist in the
Library of Congress, but its recorded treasures are due chiefly
to the collecting efforts of its first curators, Robert Gordon
and the Lomaxes, and with its diminished budget and the
loss of its director, the archive is severely crippled. During
the WPA days a folklore collecting program of a sort did
develop under the Federal Writers Project, and its amateurish
results at least suggested the accomplishments that might be
attained with trained collectors. Actually the universities of
Indiana and Pennsylvania and U. C. L. A. have provided the
chief institutional support for folklore curriculums, library
collections, archives, and publications. The foundations are

noticeably cool to folklore. "What is the real purpose in col-. lecting all this folklore?" an official of one of the major foundations has asked.

For better or worse, the genius of American folklore study has so far expressed itself in the wayward, individual collector. The illustrious names are those of solitary figures, unacademic and nonprofessional, who drift into some special groove of interest and collect assiduously along that line, with little heed to other traditions, other collectors, or considerations of bibliography, scholarship, and theory. We think of John Lomax recording from cowboys and penitentiary Negroes; Vance Randolph scouring the Ozarks, and only the Ozarks, for all kinds of lore; Phillips Barry combing New England for folksong, and only for folksongs; George Korson, a Pennsylvania newspaperman, wondering if coal miners sang ballads; J. Frank Dobie, glamorizing the lore of the Southwest in volume after volume while scoffing at the "science of folklore." The most intensive single collection of American superstitions, *Folk-Lore from Adams County, Illinois,* was privately published in 1935 by an individual then completely unknown to the folklore fraternity, Harry M. Hyatt. The most extensive collection of all kinds of folklore from a single state was gathered in North Carolina by a professor at Duke University, Frank C. Brown, who was so much the hobbyist that he could never classify, annotate, and steer his finds into print, and a group of specialists had to perform these tasks after his death.

In library studies as well as in field collections, the same individualistic tendency appears, even in works of an essentially cooperative nature. The one attempt at a comprehensive *Bibliography of American Folklore and Folk Song* (1951) was undertaken by a concert singer and music historian, Charles Haywood, who describes ruefully his painful attempts to transfer the contents of shoebox files directly into cold type; one box in fact was lost in a closet and never did turn up until after the book was published. As it stands, this gigantic work is indispensable, but it must also be used with extreme caution because of the numerous errors in citation and the loose definition of *folklore.* This kind of task required a division of labor among specialists, or at least an advisory board. Yet when a group of experts was assembled for the *Standard Dictionary of Folklore, Mythology and Legend* (2 vols., 1949-50), the work proved to be uneven in coverage and content, and fell far short of expectations. The editor, Maria Leach, is a writer of children's folklore books.

Not only does folklore in America lack the hard core of professional scholars taken for granted in other disciplines, but the firmness of its data is softened by the widespread popular interest in folklore. Broad avenues of publication are wide open for so-called folklore materials. Compilers of treasuries, writers of juveniles, vendors of magazine and newspaper articles, cabaret folksingers, recreational camp directors, organizers of folk festivals, all these extend a warm welcome to whatever savors of folklore. The confusion between reworked and genuine folk materials is found even among scholars, as well as in the general public, who are not particularly exercised about such matters.

By contrast with the lavish attention given half-baked folklore books aimed at the mass public, sometimes painstaking works of considerable merit are ignored. Two of the oustanding field collections done in the United States, both by highly competent folklore scholars, have remained unpublished dissertations for over a decade. The collection of tales and legends from the New Jersey piney country made by Herbert Halpert is a superb example both of fieldwork and annotation.[8] Also the collection of the tales told by and about Oregon Smith, and the analysis of his reputation and narrative techniques, undertaken by William H. Jansen, is a unique and valuable study.[9] But publishers, the university presses as well as the commercial firms, dislike variant texts, and in fact tend to disapprove of exact texts which reproduce the words of the narrator with all their repetitiveness and meanderings. (Stith Thompson tells how one well-known university press to whom he submitted his manuscript of *Tales of the North American Indians* asked him to rewrite the tales. Eventually

---

8. "Folktales and Legends from the New Jersey Pines; a Collection and a Study" (Indiana University, 1947).

9. "Abraham 'Oregon' Smith: Pioneer, Folk Hero, and Tale-Teller" (Indiana University, 1949).

Harvard University Press published the book in its original form.) Hence scholarly folklore studies cannot easily find their way into print, and when they do, too often attract relatively few readers. The most skillful American collection of the full range of a folklore within a limited area—and proper fieldwork can only cover a limited area—is *Folklore from the Schoharie Hills, New York* by Emelyn E. Gardner, a book that has received little acclaim.

A long step forward in American folklore studies can be made if folklore in the United States is seen in its proper relation to major periods and themes in American history which gave a special character to folklore in the United States, themes such as colonization, the westward movement, immigration, the Indian and the Negro, and even modern mass culture. A would-be American folklorist should divide his training equally between comparative folklore and the history of American civilization, as a preparation for his researches.[10]

The American folklorist who is exploring research opportunities must seek for raw materials in two directions: printed (or manuscript) sources and field collections. Both avenues offer many inviting leads.

Because printed sources can provide him with texts for the seventeenth, eighteenth, and nineteenth centuries, before field collecting was consciously undertaken, certain printed media are valuable and necessary to the worker in American folklore. Yet the folklorist usually feels ill at ease among newspaper files, while the literary historians who have stumbled on buried folk matter are frequently at a loss to recognize and identify their finds. The files of American newspapers from the mid-1820s up to the mid-1850s are extremely rich in humorous and legendary tradition. Both ordinary newspapers and the popular literary-sporting-family weeklies using a newspaper format tapped oral tradition. The New York *Spirit of the Times* has been repeatedly mined and continues to yield new humorous tales and sketches of merit. At the American Antiquarian Society the author stumbled onto a

10. Richard M. Dorson, "A Theory for American Folklore," in *Journal of American Folklore* 72 (1959) : 197–215.

good run of the *Spirit's* closest rival, the *Yankee Blade*—no
complete file surviving—and excavated over a hundred Yankee yarns. The same library also possessed issues of similar
still-rarer, short-lived comic weeklies, such as *Union Jack,
Saturday Rambler,* and *Yankee Privateer.*[11] Antebellum papers
filled with humorous lore are reported by Philip Jordan and
George Kummer for Ohio, by Eugene Current-Garcia for
Georgia, by Eston E. Ericson for North Carolina, and by
Thomas D. Clark for Kentucky.[12] For the Far Western papers,
the spadework of Duncan Emrich in Nevada, Randall V.
Mills in Oregon, and Levette J. Davidson in Colorado has
dug into profitable veins.[13]

The *Index to the Burlington Free Press in the Billings
Library of the University of Vermont* (Montpelier, Vt., 1940),
compiled under the Federal Writers Project, lists well over a
thousand entries under the headings "Stories," "Humor," and
"Sketches." These stories traveled the rounds of the press,
via the exchange, and for the decade 1848–58 alone the *Free
Press* listed more than three hundred exchange credits. Working from such a list, a roster of papers juicy in humor could
be compiled, and those papers examined for folktales. Eventually, by analyzing the contents of key papers in each state
and territory, the folktales current in the heyday of frontier
humor would be very fully uncovered, for in those humor-
hungry times it is safe to assume that a folk anecdote of any
currency found its way into newsprint.

11. Comic tales from these four papers are reprinted in the author's
*Jonathan Draws the Long Bow* (Cambridge, 1946).
12. Philip D. Jordan, "Humor of the Backwoods, 1820–1840," *Mississippi
Valley Historical Review* 25 (1938): 25–38; George Kummer, "Specimens
of Ante-Bellum Buckeye Humor," *Ohio Historical Quarterly* 64 (1955):
424–37; Eugene Current-Garcia, "Newspaper Humor in the Old South,
1835–1855," *Alabama Review* 2 (1949): 102–21; Eston E. Ericson, "Folklore and Folkway in the Tarboro (N. C.) *Free Press* (1824–1850),"
*Southern Folklore Quarterly* 5 (1941): 104–25; Thomas D. Clark, *The
Rampaging Frontier* (Indianapolis and New York, 1939).
13. Duncan Emrich, ed., *Comstock Bonanza* (New York, 1950); Randall
V. Mills, "Frontier Humor in Oregon and Its Characteristics," *Oregon
Historical Quarterly* 43 (1942): 229–56; Levette J. Davidson, "Colorado
Folklore," *Colorado Magazine* 18 (1941): 7–8, and with Forrester Blake,
eds., *Rocky Mountain Tales* (Norman, Okla., 1947).

The technique for this research depends on familiarity with the type and motif indexes of folk literature. Those reports we now have on the antebellum newspapers and family weeklies usually fall short of the folklorist's demands in two main respects: they fail to reprint complete texts and they fail to identify tales by type and motif numbers and known variants, and so to separate traditional from literary or factual narratives. One shining exception testifies to the rewards obtainable from the proper application of professional folklore methods, when Arthur K. Moore excerpted folktale texts from antebellum Louisiana newspapers.[14] (See p. 25.) In this batch of thirty-one reprinted texts, we find not only early nineteenth-century recordings of well-known and still popular tall tales and sells, but also specimens of once familiar lying tales now vanished along with the circumstances that gave them point, such as the stories about violent "shakes" from fever and ague.

In combing these files, the folklorist can catch besides tall tales many other types of folk tradition: legends, beliefs, hoaxes, proverbs, conundrums, riddles, folk speech, rhymes, anecdotes, jokes. C. Grant Loomis has unearthed numerous items of humorous wordplay from these papers.[15] Other kinds of printed sources can also be searched for such traditions. Novels and short stories constiute a source for proverbial sayings of a bygone day, as Archer Taylor and B. J. Whiting have recently demonstrated in *A Dictionary of American Proverbs and Proverbial Phrases, 1820–1880*. Their sources included the humorists of the Old Southwest, and Mark Twain, Cooper, Emerson, Irving, Lincoln, Lowell, Melville, and other, lesser authors. Under Archer Taylor's stimulus, a graduate student at Indiana University, Jan Brunvand, has just published *A Dictionary of Proverbs and Proverbial Phrases from Indiana Books Published before 1880*, based on the check list of Indiana novels by R. E. Banta. Reading

14. "Specimens of the Folktales from Some Antebellum Newspapers of Louisiana," *Louisiana Historical Quarterly* 32 (1949): 723–58.

15. E.g., "Jonathanisms: American Epigrammatic Hyperbole," *Western Folklore,* 6 (1947): 211–27.

through nearly one hundred of these often unreadable romances, Brunvand located some 1500 traditional sayings, comparisons, and miscellaneous phrases in a model study that
can be emulated for other states. Wayland D. Hand, the
compiler of the forthcoming dictionary of American popular
beliefs and superstitions, has pleaded for listings of folk beliefs from early printed sources, in order to provide historical
dates for the tens of thousands of superstitions which he is
cataloguing and annotating from contemporary oral tradition.
The long files of *The Old Farmer's Almanac* and *Nathan
Daboll's Almanac,* to name two of the various almanac series
available, would yield many examples of weather lore, folk
medicine, signs, omens, taboos. Kittredge opened the door
to this wealth of late colonial folk beliefs in *The Old Farmer
and His Almanac;* now the folklorist seeks an orderly listing
of all texts in chronological sequence. Texts of ballads, folk
lyrics, and folk hymns as well can be recovered from periodicals, travel writings, and songsters, as Ralph Leslie Rusk
and Harry Stevens have indicated.[16]

The copious bibliography of nineteenth-century songsters offers for the ballad specialist a hunting ground similar
to that provided for the folktale specialist in the *Spirit of
the Times* and other periodicals. Traditional and composed
songs are printed promiscuously in these songbooks which,
like folksingers, make no distinction between individual and
folk pieces. Some traditional ballads originated with printed
broadsides, and the several thousand entries given by Worthington Ford in his *Broadsides, Ballads, etc. Printed in Massachusetts, 1639–1800,* document the abundance of printed
ballad texts in colonial days.[17] The American jestbooks described by Harry B. Weiss will also furnish valuable texts for
the research folklorist when he begins, as inevitably he must,

16. Ralph L. Rusk, *The Literature of the Middle Western Frontier,* 2
vols. (New York, 1926), 1: 303–19; Harry R. Stevens, "Folk Music on the
Midwestern Frontier 1788–1825," *Ohio Archaeological and Historical
Society Publications* 57 (1948): 126–46.

17. See the discussion of broadside printing in America in Malcolm G.
Laws, *American Balladry from British Broadsides* (Philadelphia, 1957),
pp. 44–49. The need for a classified index to traditional pieces in broadsides and songsters is expressed by D. K. Wilgus, *Anglo-American Folksong Scholarship Since 1898* (New Brunswick, N. J., 1959), p. 258.

to trace the antecedents of American jocular tales.[18] Vance Randolph has now under way an annotated collection of Ozark jokes.

One type of printed source which should prove highly rewarding in folklore materials is travel literature. A systematic examination of the titles listed in Wagner and Camp's bibliography of travel books for the Far West, or Thomas D. Clark's for the South, or Vail's for the old frontier, should yield volumes of social folklore—not merely texts, although they will appear, but also the settings in which folk custom and belief flourished.[19] Travelers are especially concerned with manners and customs, they listen to reports and stories of all kinds, and they devote full time to observation of local and regional culture. The traveler is a kind of amateur ethnographer. John Josselyn, the Englishman who reported on two seventeenth-century voyages to New England, may well deserve the title of America's first folklorist, so extensively did he note the legends of enchanted islands, mermen, sea serpents, quill-throwing porcupines, and the marvelous properties of tobacco. In documenting the spread of Yankee humor through the West, Walter Blair relied principally on the accounts set down by travelers who kept hearing tales about the cunning of Yankee peddlers.[20] While the celebrated travel books of Frederick Law Olmsted deal primarily with the economics and sociology of the antebellum plantation, they incidentally describe the folk religion of the slaves, whose shouting, singing, dancing, and exhorting bred traditional forms of song, music, dance, and sermon. The *American Diaries* listed and described by William Matthews offer another type of writing, akin in some ways to travel literature.[21]

18. *A Brief History of American Jest Books* (New York: New York Public Library, 1943), pp. 3–19.

19. See R. W. G. Vail, *The Voice of the Old Frontier* (Philadelphia, 1949); Henry R. Wagner and Charles L. Camp, *The Plains and the Rockies: A Bibliography of Original Narratives of Travel and Adventure 1800–1865* (Columbus, Ohio, 1953); Thomas D. Clark, *Travels in the Old South*, 3 vols. (Norman, Okla., 1956–59).

20. Walter Blair, *Native American Humor (1800–1900)* (New York, 1937), p. 27, n. 1.

21. *American Diaries, An Annotated Bibliography of American Diaries Written Prior to the Year 1861*, compiled by William Matthews (Berkeley, 1945).

A close examination will repay the student of folk custom and folk speech. Indian captivities represent a bridge for the passage of Indian supernatural beliefs and myths, in garbled form, into white culture.[22]

A library folklorist may not only scan separately the newspaper, periodical, chapbook, broadside, jestbook, almanac, diary, or travel book, but he can investigate all these sources concurrently on a regional basis. In *Jonathan Draws the Long Bow*, the author relied on such printed materials for a picture of New England legends and humorous folktales in the first three centuries of American history. The town history proved to be a particularly rich repository of local legends. In his *Tall Tales of Arkansaw*, James R. Masterson surveyed the printed folk humor of one state from a miscellany of writings, coming up with a meaty spread that serves as an excellent complement to the field collections of Vance Randolph from the Ozarks. One social historian, Thomas D. Clark, had the sagacity to observe, "There is no richer source for the study of human activities on the frontier than its thousands of humorous stories."[23] From the *Spirit of the Times,* the reminiscences of preachers and travelers, Kentucky newspapers, and even published statutes he constructed *The Rampaging Frontier,* which illustrates folkways in the backwoods society of the trans-Allegheny West.

When Clark describes the traditional games on the frontier, such as throwing shoulder stones and long bullets, or gander-pulling and dog-fighting, he provides fresh materials and valuable datings for the comparative folklorist, who must depend on the printed accounts of eyewitnesses in the backwoods for information about now vanished pastimes and recreations. The student of games will find special rewards in the accounts of frontier sports and pleasures, from shooting matches to corn huskings, assembled by R. Carlyle Buley from Indiana, Illinois, and Michigan newspapers, travel

22. See "The Indians' Captives Relate Their Adventures," in Vail, *The Voice of the Old Frontier,* pp. 28–61; and Howard H. Peckham, *Captured by Indians: True Tales of Pioneer Survivors* (New Brunswick, N. J., 1954).

23. Thomas D. Clark, *The Rampaging Frontier* (Indianapolis and New York, 1939), p. xii.

books, and pioneer recollections.[24] Arthur Palmer Hudson
prepared his anthology *Humor of the Old Deep South* from
the printed resources of Alabama, Louisiana, and Mississippi.
No anthologies have yet appeared which take for their objective the recovery of the full range of identifiable folklore—
songs, tales, proverbs, beliefs, customs, speech—from the printed resources of a state or region. Some attempts have been
made, however, to trace the legend of the regional character
symbolizing the folkways of the state. Masterson has suggested the legendary outlines of the Arkansawyer, Leach of
the Texan, and Moore of the Kentuckian:[25] what of the Missouri puke, the down-Easter from Maine, the Georgia cracker,
the Ohio Buckeye, the Illinois Sucker, the Indiana Hoosier?

Printed sources capture oral traditions only by accident
and must always rank below field collections. Today the folklorist deliberately seeks out these traditions with notebook
and tape recorder; yet collectors in the United States have
barely tapped the immense resources of oral folklore. A few
regions are relatively well collected—the Spanish Southwest,
for instance—while others, like New England, have been virtually ignored. Here I shall suggest three lines of fieldwork
which would attempt to explore systematically the oral wealth
of the American heritage.

In order to achieve representative samplings of folk tradition which will permit cross-regional comparisons, a series of
planned and coordinated field trips is necessary in place of
the casual and haphazard collecting that is now the practice.
One approach to the task of selecting regions for intensive
collecting can be made by following the guidelines already
available in the relic areas of folk speech mapped by fieldworkers on the Linguistic Atlas of America. This Atlas, directed by Hans Kurath, with the assistance of the late Marcus
L. Hansen, was designed to plot the historical movements of
American population, but has unfortunately suspended oper-

24. R. Carlyle Buley, *The Old Northwest, Pioneer Period 1815–1840*
(Indianapolis, 1950), 1: 315–36.
25. James R. Masterson, *Tall Tales of Arkansaw* (Boston, 1943); Joseph
Leach, *The Typical Texan* (Dallas, 1952); Arthur K. Moore, *The
Frontier Mind* (Lexington, Ky., 1957).

ations after mapping speech areas of eastern United States. After discussions with Kurath, who suggested that the eastern seaboard had been unduly neglected by folklore collectors fleeing to the mountains during summer vacation, this author, in July, 1956, essayed a pilot field trip to Jonesport, high on the coast of Maine, to determine whether such a relic area would prove rich in other types of folklore besides folk speech. Seventeen days in the field yielded over three hundred tales and songs from twenty-two of these Yankee lobstermen, who had clearly preserved a vigorous folk tradition of maritime lore, local anecdote and rhyme, and supernatural legend.[26] For comparative purposes, similar trips should explore relic areas all along the coast: Essex County and Cape Ann in Massachusetts; the Narragansett Bay area of Rhode Island; Long Island Sound; the Delamarva peninsula lying between Chesapeake and Delaware Bays; Albemarle Sound in North Carolina; and the coastal strip from Cape Fear to the mouth of the Peedee River in South Carolina. The results of comparable quests in these zones would inform us whether or not these relic areas are indeed reservoirs of folk tradition and whether the nature of these traditions alters markedly with the regions. Inland relic areas can also be tested, although beyond the Appalachians these have not yet been fully mapped.

Collecting possibilities on an ethnic basis are so overwhelming that one scarcely knows where to begin. The great collections of nationality folklore in the United States all belong to the future. Only one book-length study exists, *South Italian Folkways in Europe and America,* by Phyllis Williams, published in 1938 by a sociologist wishing to prepare a handbook for social workers dealing with Italian immigrants. Her case studies are chiefly drawn from New Haven. Just to illustrate the potentialities in this type of tradition: in one day's recording with a Greek-American family in northern Michigan the writer obtained some twelve thousand words of ex-

26. A sample of the collection is given in "Collecting Folklore in Jonesport, Maine," *Proceedings of the American Philosophical Society* 101 (1957) : 270–89.

cellent texts on a variety of legendary themes, involving
saints, demons, heroes, and possessors of the evil eye.[27]
One can only wildly surmise what is collectable from a
Greek-American population of 180,000 families, and how the
acculturation process may differ among Greeks who stayed in
the Boston area, opened restaurants in the Midwest, or formed
a sponge-fishing community in Tarpon Springs, Florida. Dorothy Lee has already shown the possibilities of differentiating
Greek immigrant lore according to geographical areas of
emigration.[28] What holds for the Greeks will apply of course
to the whole spectrum of nationality traditions. We have
been tantalized with articles on Czech songs in Nebraska,
Portuguese folklore in New Bedford, Basque tales in Oregon,
Armenian stories from Detroit, Chinese customs in San Francisco[29]—but in place of a ten-page article we would like to see
a ten-volume collection.

One ethnic group has indeed seen·the wish come true.
The Lithuanian collections made by Jonas Balys in the United
States demonstrate the rewards attainable by the skilled col-
lector with the knowledge of the Old Country language and
culture. Most of the publications covered in the eighteen
Library of Congress cards of his writings on this subject are
in Lithuanian, but translated texts or notes are available in
his articles on "Fifty Lithuanian Riddles" and "Lithuanian
Ghost Stories from Pittsburgh," his Folkways recording of
"Lithuanian Folk Songs in the United States," and his volume

27. "Tales of a Greek-American Family on Tape," *Fabula* 1 (1957):
114–43.

28. Dorothy Demetracopoulou Lee, "Folklore of the Greeks in America,"
*Folk-Lore* 47 (1936): 294–310.

29. See the references in my notes to ch. 4, "Immigrant Folklore," in
*American Folklore* (Chicago, 1959), pp. 295–96, and such other refer-
ences as Jon Lee, "Some Chinese Customs and Beliefs in California,"
*California Folklore Quarterly* 1 (1942): 337–57; C. Merton Babcock,
"Czech Songs in Nebraska," *Western Folklore* 8 (1949): 320–27; Susie
Hoogasian and Emelyn E. Gardner, "Armenian Folktales from Detroit,"
*Journal of American Folklore* 57 (1944): 161–80; Stanley L. Robe,
"Basque Tales from Eastern Oregon," *Western Folklore* 12 (1953): 153–
57; Leah R. Yoffie, "Yiddish Proverbs, Sayings, etc., in St. Louis, Mo.,"
*Journal of American Folklore* 33 (1920): 134–65.

*Lithuanian Folksongs in America,* which contains 472 song
texts and 250 melodies.[30]

More than mere collecting is involved in the gathering of
immigrant folk traditions, for all kinds of acculturation studies are possible in the vast laboratory of the United States
population. We can compare the early mid-nineteenth century Irish immigrants with the latest Puerto Rican influx;
we can contrast Italians in the city with Italians in the countryside, Sicilians with north Italians, Red Finns with anti-Red
Finns, Issei with Nisei Japanese, the Jews of Brooklyn with
the Jews of Los Angeles, the Scandinavian with the Slav, the
European with the Asiatic. From such rural-urban, cross-
regional, cross-generational, and cross-ethnic studies we can
learn much about the social life of immigrant groups and
their compromises with American civilization. Also we can
obtain texts and customs of European folklore now obsoles-
cent in the Old Country. In developing a collecting program
among nationality pockets, the international institutes and
ethnic organizations in all large northern cities would prove
immediately helpful.

A third large area for collecting folklore in the United
States comes under the head of occupational lore. Men working together in a common trade or under one factory roof develop the cohesiveness, and the esoteric traditions, of an in-
group. In the early days of folksong collecting, the song repertoires of cowboys and lumberjacks were revealed as surprisingly
extensive hoards, but other aspects of their lore were slighted.
It remained for a newspaperman, George Korson, to penetrate the grim and forbidding company towns of Pennsylvania
coal miners, and dredge up hidden veins of balladry, legend,
union lore, and craft traditions.[31] No comparable collections

30. Balys describes his techniques for making contacts among Lithuanian
immigrants—through ethnic newspapers, priests, ethnic clubs—in *Four
Symposia on Folklore,* pp. 74–78. "Fifty Lithuanian Riddles" was published in the *Journal of American Folklore* 63 (1950): 325–27, and
"Lithuanian Ghost Stories from Pittsburgh" in *Midwest Folklore* 2
(1952): 47–52. *Lithuanian Folksongs in America* is published by Lithuanian Encyclopedia Publishers, Boston, 1959.

31. George Korson, *Minstrels of the Mine Patch, Songs and Ballads of
the Anthracite Industry,* and *Coal Dust on the Fiddle, Songs and Stories
of the Bituminous Industry* (Philadelphia, 1938 and 1943); *Black Rock,*

of occupational lore have yet been published, but a rich cache of material in the Indiana University Folklore Archives bears witness to the mass of folk tradition to be found in army barracks. Eighty-five folders hold texts of jinxes and hoaxes, bawdy ballads and song parodies, war tales descended from earlier wars, goldbricking yarns, atrocity legends, folktales of lucky escapes and unlucky fatalities, devoutly believed superstitions, glossaries of special terms, cycles about swashbuckling officers and offbeat GIs.

We can postulate similar categories of tradition for other modern American occupational groups—railroaders, truck and taxicab drivers, the crews of passenger liners and freighters; factory workers and labor union members; professionals in show business and sports; journalists; workers in specialized trades, like printing, whose customs Thorstein Veblen referred to in the *Theory of the Leisure Class;* and office workers of the white-collar world. Salesmen are the Yankee peddlers of today, glib of tongue, carriers of tales as well as of goods. In the public relations culture of twentieth-century America, everybody must be a storyteller, from the college president to the political campaigner. Nor are the older outdoor occupations once so productive of lore now all vanished; there are still quarry workers, shrimp and lobster fishermen, migratory fruit pickers, Erie canallers.

We have spoken about research opportunities in the library and in the field, but another large area, the folk museum, invites attention. Here the contrast with European accomplishments is most glaring for systematic presentation of the material objects in folk culture dates back only about a decade and a half in the United States. Yet in this time some notable publications, richly and handsomely illustrated, have depicted existing collections of folk art. They include Jean Lipman's *American Folk Art in Wood, Metal and Stone* (1948), Erwin O. Christensen's *The Index of American De-*

---

*Mining Folklore of the Pennsylvania Dutch* (Baltimore, 1960)); and "Songs and Ballads of the Anthracite Miners," Recorded Album 16, issued from the Collections of the Archive of American Folk Song. Library of Congress.

*sign* (1950), and *The Abby Aldrich Rockefeller Folk Art Collection* (1957). Although the definition of folk art is even more tenuous than that of folklore, it applies broadly to objects painted, hewn, carved, chiseled, woven, spun, and decorated by nonprofessional craftsmen and artists in a traditional manner. In the seventeenth, eighteenth, and nineteenth centuries, before the advent of mass-produced factory goods, traditional crafts and folk arts flourished in the city as well as on the farm.

The first problem of the American folklorist concerned with this subject is to locate and rescue examples of folk art for preservation and exhibit in the folklore museum. While the collector of songs and tales enters the living room seeking to record members of the family, the collector of pottery and quilts searches the attic, the basement, and the barn. In the future a single folklorist may engage in both these quests simultaneously.

Collecting for the folk museum promises indeed to rival the collecting of oral traditions. Only one American folklorist has so far ventured deeply into the folk museum sphere—Louis C. Jones, director of the New York State Historical Association. The Association's properties at Cooperstown include the Farmers' Museum, which displays farm and village buildings of frontier times, and the American Folk Art collection housed in the Fenimore House.[32] One example related by Dr. Jones may suggest the abundance of physical items obtainable by the enterprising searcher. In 1950 the authority on American primitive paintings, Nina Fletcher Little, asked Jones if there were houses in central New York with wall paintings or stencilings. He knew offhand of only one, in Ithaca, and its stenciled scenes had long been covered with wall paper. But upon initiating a hunt, he discovered within ten miles of Cooperstown itself a tavern covered from floor to ceiling with free-painted landscapes, and eventually he located half a dozen buildings within a twenty-mile radius of Cooperstown with

32. Louis C. Jones, "The Cooperstown Complex," *Antiques* 75 (February, 1959): 168–69. The William J. Gunn collection of over 600 American primitive paintings, acquired by Fenimore House, is described in Agnes Halsey Jones and Louis C. Jones, "New-Found Folk Art of the Young Republic," *New York History* 41 (April, 1960): 117–231.

extensive stencilings on their walls. The tavern was transported bodily to the Farmers' Museum, and the other wall paintings were acquired for the Folk Art collection.[33]

In a culture rich in home crafts, like that of the Pennsylvania Dutch, the folk arts extend to the kitchen utensils, the household furniture, the daily costume, the carriages, the tombstones, the barns. Here the question arises as to how far folk art in the United States encompasses folk architecture. The Pennsylvania German barns, decorated with traditional designs, clearly reflect the distinctive culture of their builders.[34] In most regions the data is still meager, but Austin Fife has acquired an impressive collection of colored slides of wooden fences, gateposts, and hay derricks in the Rocky Mountain states, and can illustrate their patterns of regional design.[35] José E. Espinosa published in 1960 an extensive monograph on the *santos,* or family images of patron saints, an indigenous expression of religious folk art in the Spanish southwest.[36]

As these artifacts of regional folk cultures are gathered in folk museums, the American folklorist will need to ponder their relationship to the oral forms he has studied in the past. Dov Noy, the director of the Ethnological Museum in Haifa, Israel, has actually traced magic amulets and rings to their possessors from allusions in folktales.[37]

Giant tasks face the collector of folk materials on several fronts, and their fulfillment can produce scholarly monuments, worthy of a place alongside the ballads of Child, the customs of Frazer, the motifs of Thompson, the riddles of Taylor. But the accumulation of texts and objects is not an end in itself. The documents and artifacts will offer data for

33. Personal letter from Louis C. Jones, dated 16 October 1959.

34. Charles H. Dorbusch, *Pennsylvania German Barns,* with introduction and descriptive text by John K. Heyl, Pennsylvania German Folklore Society Yearbook, vol. 21 (Allentown, Pa., 1958).

35. See Austin E. Fife and James M. Fife, "Hay Derricks of the Great Basin and Upper Snake River Valley," *Western Folklore* 6 (1948) : 228–39.

36. *Saints in the Valleys: Christian Sacred Images in the History, Life and Folk Art of Spanish New Mexico* (Albuquerque, 1960).

37. Dov Noy, "Archiving and Presenting Folk Literature in an Ethnological Museum," *Journal of American Folklore* 75 (1962) : 23–28.

broader and deeper syntheses within American cultural history. The historian of American life has steadily expanded his concerns to include literature, the fine arts, science, religion, and indeed all the manifold aspects of a civilization. He has made gestures toward folklore, and we can see the rewards in such seminal works as Theodore Blegen's *Grass Roots History* (1947), calling for historical treatment of the folk, and the studies of American cultural myths by Dixon Wecter in *The Hero in America* (1941), Henry Nash Smith in *Virgin Land* (1950), and Arthur K. Moore in *The Frontier Mind* (1957).

Yet in no area of American culture is the historian so misinformed as in folklore. The standard bibliographies in *The Literary History of the United States* and *A Guide to the Study of the United States of America* cannot fully be trusted.[38] Because the pursuit of folklore in this country is riddled with so many amateurs, from writers of children's books to urbanized folk singers, the scholar in other fields frequently takes the wrong turn when he enters the maze of folk tradition.

For the future we can look toward an increasingly profitable synthesis between American history and folklore. Scholars in the two fields are gradually moving toward common ground, where all kinds of inviting research topics suggest themselves: the feed-in and feed-back between folk and popular culture; the folk stereotypes of politicians and the rituals of political behavior; the role of Old Country tradition in the life of the immigrant; the history of occultism in America; the development of regional identities and regional myths; the transition from supernaturalism to science in early American thought. As folklore study in America approaches maturity, its prospects for fresh and original explorations in the years immediately ahead appear exciting and adventurous.

38. For example, such works as Stanley D. Newton, *Paul Bunyan of the Great Lakes;* Frank Shay, *Here's Audacity! American Legendary Heroes;* and Walter Blair, *Tall Tale America,* lack any validity as specimens of folk tradition (*Literary History of the United States,* ed. Robert Spiller et al., vol. 3, Bibliography [New York, 1948], pp. 200, 203, 205). The unscholarly "treasuries" of American folklore by B. A. Botkin are recommended in D. H. Mugridge and Blanche P. McCrum, *A Guide to the Study of the United States of America* (Washington, D. C., 1960), pp. 785–98.

# 7

# Oral Tradition
# and Written History
# The Case for
# the United States

Scientific historical method, reverencing the documentary source, gives short shrift to oral tradition. Such standard manuals for the United States as Homer C. Hockett's *Introduction to Research in American History*[1] and J. Franklin Jameson's *The American Historian's Raw Material*[2] warn the graduate student and serious scholar to avoid legend and tradition and folklore, all dirty words in the current lexicon of historiogra-

From *Journal of the Folklore Institute,* 1964.

1. (New York, 1931), p. 90. In his expanded and rewritten edition, *The Critical Method in Historical Research and Writing* (New York, 1955), Hockett introduces a section on "Myths, Legends, and Traditions" (pp. 51–54). He sees no value in them. Yet in a discussion of "New Trends," he recognizes a recent rapprochement between Local History and Folklore (pp. 238–40).

2. (Ann Arbor, Michigan, 1923), p. 29. Jameson's address, delivered at the dedication of the William L. Clements Library of the University of Michigan, stressed library resources of printed books and manuscripts for the history of man: "All his story lies within the period since the invention of printing. . . . "

phy. In *The Historian and Historical Evidence* (1926), Allen
Johnson explains his omission of oral tradition from "The
Sources of Information" on the grounds that tales take on
exaggeration and embellishment from their tellers, even from
such careful narrators as the Icelandic saga reciters.[3] H. B.
George in his treatise on *Historical Evidence* (1909) dis-
parages traditions of the people as unreliable; in the work of
Livy, for example, they veer continually from fact to legend.
George gives in illustration a local English tradition of a track
named Rounday Down marking the site of a battle fought
near Devizes during the Great Rebellion, and won by the
Royalists. A "rustic" informed a stranger that Julius Caesar
had defeated the French here, they had "runned" away, and
the place had ever since been called "Rundaway" Down.[4]

A few historians do give cautious heed to tradition. Edward
A. Freeman in a lengthy discussion of "The Mythical and
Romantic Elements in Early English History" (1866) accepts
a kernel of truth in mythical stories.

> A real action of a real person is distorted, exaggerated,
> incrusted with all kinds of fictitious details, details some-
> times transferred to a wrong person, or to a wrong time
> or place; but we see that a real action of a real person
> did form the groundwork, after all.

He gives the legend of Charlemagne as a case in point. "We
are too often apt . . . to forget that tradition is really a means
of information essentially of the same kind as history."[5]
Thomas Henry Buckle in his *History of Civilization in England* praises the general accuracy of ballads and oral tradition,
before the advent of writing diminished their value and increased the spread of falsehood by mingling and confusing
local traditions.[6] Discussing "Historical Tradition and Ori-

3. (New York, 1926), p. 5. A recent debunking of "legend" and "folklore," in contrast to "the facts," is Larry Gara, *The Liberty Line: the
Legend of the Underground Railroad* (Lexington, Ky., 1961), although
Gara says (p. 17) the history of the legend might well be worth its own
study.

4. (Oxford, 1909), p. 73.

5. Freeman, *Historical Essays*, 2d ed. (London, 1872), pp. 27, 31–32.

6. 2d ed. (London, 1858), 1: 211–15.

ental Research," J. H. Breasted provided examples of Oriental
records confirming Greek oral traditions.[7]

In her study of *Historical Material,* chapter 5, "The Record of Myth, Legend, and Tradition," Lucy Maynard Salmon
summarizes the position of recent historians, especially on
ancient history, as sympathetic to tradition and legend. The
basic truth behind, say, the legends of the Minotaur and of
the siege of Troy can be reached by patient winnowing of in-
crustations. Accepted history may be shown to be legend, but
also legend can be restored to historical standing, as in the
cases of Jonathan Carver and John Smith. Salmon emphasizes
the point, however, that the initial core of truth is less of value
to the historian than the "unconscious record" offered by the
legend of the times and civilization in which it circulated.[8]

In an address to the American Historical Association in
1935 on "The Predicament of History," Eugen Rosenstock-
Hussy contended for a "careful study of the relations between
scientific history and group memory. . . . History is corrected
and purified tradition. . . . The important facts, experienced,
remembered, and created into traditions and instincts, must
once more become the foundation of historical research."[9]
Samuel Eliot Morison in his presidential address of 1950 to
the association quoted Rosenstock-Hussy with approval, commenting "A historian owes respect to tradition and to folk
memory. . . ."[10]

A vast literature deals with the usability and validity of
oral traditional history. Not merely historians, but archaeologists, geologists, ethnologists, classicists, Biblical scholars, mythologists, and psychologists have heatedly debated the question.[11] In Polynesia and Africa, tradition forms the main
source for the historian. It is, however, the folklorist who has

7. *Nature* 114 (1924) : 757.

8. (New York, 1933) , pp. 46–58.

9. *Journal of Philosophy* 34 (1935) : 93–100. Quotations from pp. 93, 95.
100.

10. "Faith of a Historian," *American Historical Review,* 56 (1951) : 270.

11. The writer analyzed this literature in a research report for the Department of Justice, United States Government, for use by the Indian
Land Claims Commission, "The Historical Validity of Oral Tradition,"
submitted 11 November 1961 under contract No. J-40973.

chiefly concerned himself with the properties of oral tradition, whether historical or fictional, and with the techniques for pinning down their mercurial nature.

A number of fairly specific uses, or areas of usefulness, of oral tradition to the historian may be enumerated. The examples to support these points will be drawn chiefly from American history, as the history best known to me, and also the field of historical research most adamant in rejecting folk and other oral traditions.

## As a Source for Popular Attitudes, Prejudices, Stereotypes

In seeking to assess and convey reactions of the people to a given historical issue, American historians dig into newspaper files and sample editorial opinion. But newspapers may not accurately mirror popular sentiments, as the pollsters and columnists who picked Dewey over Truman in the presidential election of 1948 ruefully concede. The rewards of personal interviews in depth to sample regional political biases have been demonstrated by the astute political analyst, Samuel Lubell, in our own day. For earlier periods we can at present merely surmise what the oral cycles buried in diverse printed sources, or perhaps still current, might reveal—for instance, about Abraham Lincoln.

Stories rife in the southern mountains about Lincoln's paternity are offered in a book of reminiscence and anecdote, *Random Thoughts and Musings of a Mountaineer,* by Judge Felix E. Alley (Salisbury, N. C., 1941). Judge Alley was born in 1873 on a farm in the foothills of Whiteside Mountain in southern South Carolina. Alley's father fought in the Confederate Army, but one brother served with the Union forces. The judge had an ear for mountain yarns and devoted one chapter to folk anecdotes of "Uncle" Boney Ridley, an eccentric character, and other specimens of mountain wit. In the three chapters he gives to supporting the thesis that "Abraham Lincoln was a native of the Carolina Mountains," the judge takes mountain traditions very seriously, and incorporates them into the testimony of affidavits, letters, and publications he adduces to prove that Lincoln was the illegitimate son of John C. Calhoun and Nancy Hanks, who once resided in Anderson County, South Carolina. Alley even prints facing photographs of Lincoln and of Calhoun with Lincoln's hair and beard style (after page 386) to show their resemblance. The Calhoun tradition is only one, though the most amply documented, of nine dealing with Lincoln's parentage.

Alley declares (page 383) that this tradition circulated widely in northern Virginia, Mississippi, and Georgia, and that he heard it from several sources. One source was a prominent lawyer in Surry County, Virginia, R. A. Freeman, who in turn heard it from a Professor J. M. Harris, a former professor of Furman University who had fought in the Civil War and interested himself in its history and traditions. In his version of the tradition, Freeman refers to still another story declaring that Lincoln and Jefferson Davis were half-brothers (page 384). In this, as in the other eight traditions, we can readily see the process of word-of-mouth transmission from one carrier to another. For instance, the account that ascribed one Abraham Enloe of Swain County as the father of Lincoln was spread throughout the mountain counties during a long lifetime by a peddler named Phillis Wells (pages 386–87), who bought ginseng, feathers, and furs and sold tinware, and claimed to have heard from Enloe, a married man, how he had gotten Nancy Hanks in trouble and sent her to another county to bear their son Abraham. Wells was ninety when he told his tale to a Lincoln biographer, and he had been repeating it orally since his youth.

The appeals of this vigorous oral tradition lie, one, in regional pride, by giving Lincoln a birth among the southern mountaineers, and two, in national loyalty healing the sectional rancor that had divided the mountain people, through the blood union of a great Northern and a great Southern leader. In addition, the folk mind perceived a logic in the story of Lincoln's illegitimacy, for it explained his persistent melancholy (page 382).

In *Legends that Libel Lincoln* (1946), Montgomery S. Lewis endeavored to correct the record about Lincoln's allegedly sordid boyhood and shiftless father. He refers to a work of 1921, *The Boyhood of Abraham Lincoln* by J. Rogers Gore, as being largely responsible for this distorted picture.

"It is astonishing that this book should be considered as more than pleasant fiction based upon folklore," Lewis writes (page 26), "but it has served as a source book for numerous writers." Gore depended largely upon the reminiscences given him in 1896 by a man of ninety, Austin Gollaher, who related incidents of Lincoln's birth and childhood in considerable detail. Gollaher had his father and mother present and assisting with the birth of Abraham in the Lincoln cabin on February 12, 1809—although tax records show that his family did not move into Hardin County until 1812. However, Gollaher represents a type of pioneer family stock who through long years of yarning and recollecting helped fix the stereotype of Lincoln's squalid beginnings and attach it to the American myth of rags-to-riches success—a myth studied most recently (1963) by John W. Tebbel.[12]

Historians like Lewis customarily reject oral tradition as muddying the record and creating legends. But the popular prejudices and stereotypes nourished by oral tradition have affected the course of history.

## Strengthening the Concepts of Myth, Symbol, and Image

The concept of myth, currently so attractive to literary critics, cultural anthropologists, Jungian psychologists, and political philosophers, has begun to intrigue historians. National myths as analyzed by historians differ of course from the tribal myths recorded by anthropologists. The historian cannot "collect" or record the secular myth of a nation-state, for it exists in no one place or document, but permeates the culture; he must piece it together from a thousand scattered sources, and render it explicit. The national myth tells no connected story, although it contains biographies of culture heroes and their triumphs. But national myths resemble the tribal ones in unifying their possessors and providing them with common values, symbols, sanctions, and demigods. Immigrants who enter the United States must painfully learn the myths of

12. *From Rags to Riches: Horatio Alger Jr. and the American Dream* (New York, 1963).

Democracy, Free Enterprise, and the Pursuit of Happiness, and become acquainted with their symbolic rituals in Fourth of July orations, the World Series, and the unveiling of next year's auto models.

American historians, especially those with an American Studies orientation, are now nibbling at mythic interpretations. Henry Nash Smith's *Virgin Land, the West as Symbol and Myth,* led the way in 1950 with an examination of the West as an idea and an imaginative construct in the minds of eighteenth- and nineteenth-century Americans, an idea which motivated easterners to emigrate west, but which did not always correspond with historical reality. Even the great Frederick Jackson Turner had succumbed to the myth of the West as the garden of Eden, in shaping his thesis of the influence of the frontier on American history. Smith made extensive use of unconventional sources, such as dime novels, but he did not dip beneath subliterature into the wells of oral tradition. Among the studies that have followed Smith's, the opening chapter in Richard Hofstadter's *The Age of Reform* (1956) on "The Agrarian Myth and Commercial Realities" gives a succinct statement of the force of myth in American history. The agrarian myth of the yeoman farmer as the most virtuous and productive American citizen originally possessed a substantial basis in economic fact, but through the nineteenth century, though the myth persisted, the realities moved steadily away from agriculture to industry, from the country to the city, from the West to the East. In *The Image, or What Happened to the American Dream* (1962), Daniel J. Boorstin brilliantly assessed the role of image-making in modern American life, and the substitution of fabricated products for the genuine.

Oral tradition and popular folklore would certainly add to the sources available for the historian concerned with myth, symbol, and image. The central myth of American history, Manifest Destiny, is reflected in the hyperbole of the frontier boast and the backwoods composition of American folk heroes. Intellectuals and business men never attain apotheosis in folk tradition and popular culture. In the Crockett almanacs the educated Easterner is a ridiculous dude; in the movies the professor is a figure of fun. The business man, the banker,

the robber baron, the Wall Street tycoon become interrelated
symbols of predatory greed and exploitation. Jesse James, who
robs the banks and gives to friendless widows, becomes the
folk hero. As Wall Street is identified with the East, so the
folk heroes—Boone and Crockett, Johnny Appleseed, Kit Carson and Buffalo Bill, Jesse James and Billy the Kid—are associated with the West and its qualities of virility, fertility,
and individual daring. Manifest Destiny, as it rose to full cry
in the 1840s, linked the future greatness of American democracy with the occupation and settlement of the transcontinental lands stretching to the Pacific. The war with Mexico,
the dispute with England over the Oregon territory, the an-
nexation of Texas, all culminated during Polk's administra-
tion from the surging spirit of Manifest Destiny. Frederick
Merk has most recently retold and reanalyzed this story in his
painstaking study *Manifest Destiny and Mission in American
History* (1963).

Folklore sources can amplify the story. In such a figure as
Abraham "Oregon" Smith, the teller of tall tales who himself became a folk character in Indiana and Illinois, we see
attitudes toward the fabled West at the grass-roots level. Smith
won his sobriquet from the wild tales he told his fellow townsmen after returning from a trip to the Oregon country in
the 1850s. He spoke of oranges as large as watermelons, of
pleasant rain that never dampened those on whom it fell, and
of milk flowing from buffalo cows that churned itself into
butter in the mountain streams. Such folktales form a counterpart to the glowing wonders of Oregon and California
painted in the emigrant guidebooks and the political speeches
of Western-minded Congressmen like Senator Thomas Hart
Benton of Missouri.

Folklore can also illuminate the reaction to Manifest
Destiny on the part of those peoples who stood in its way.
Mexicans failed to share the faith of United States citizens
that they were destined to straddle the continent, and in the
excellent analytical studies of the Mexican *corrido* by Merle
Simmons and Américo Paredes the hostility to and defiance
of the Yankee colossus are plainly revealed. In tracing nine-
teenth- and twentieth-century attitudes of Mexico toward the
United States, as seen through *corridos,* Simmons shows how

the decline of Manifest Destiny coincided with an upsurge of
friendly feeling toward their northern neighbor by the
*pueblo.*[13] Paredes has collected *corridos* of Mexican border
heroes like Gregorio Cortez and Jacinto Treviño, counterparts
to Billy the Kid and Sam Bass, who mock Texas Rangers and
sheriffs.[14] In an article cleverly analyzing Mexican folk attitudes toward the railroad as expressed in *corridos,* John T.
Smith, a student of Paredes, presents the railroad as a symbol
of exploitation and greed, "a monster of the very worst kind"
that "runs after money / and eats the cobs as well as the
corn." The monster is of course identified with the gringos,
and the wrecks and loss of life caused by the monster are
laid at the feet of the Yankee.[15] When Mexico declared war
on Germany in 1917, as a result of diplomatic pressure from
the United States, many of the *pueblo* danced in the streets,
thinking it was the gringo they were about to fight. The ethno-
centrism of folk history is not so far removed from that found
in professional history. The battle of Lundy's Lane, in the
War of 1812, lightly tossed off as a stalemate in United States
histories, is regarded by Canadians as a national triumph
against the invading bully from the south.

An historical study has just appeared (1964) which for
the first time deliberately employs the concept of myth and
the materials of folklore to illuminate American history. Frank
R. Kramer explains the method of his book, *Voices in the
Valley,* in its subtitle, *Myth Making and Folk Belief in the
Shaping of the Middle West.* Kramer concentrates on the
Lower Middle West as a cohesive community shaped by a
sequence of historical events: the entrance of French Jesuit
missionaries into the Huron tribal villages; the emigration of
New England Yankees, Pennsylvania Germans, and southern
Appalachian Scotch-Irish into the Ohio Valley; the emergence

13. Simmons, *The Mexican Corrido as a Source for Interpretive Study of
Modern Mexico (1870–1950)* (Bloomington, Ind., 1957) .
14. Paredes, *"With His Pistol in His Hand": A Border Ballad and Its
Hero* (Austin, Tex., 1958) ; and "Corrido de Jacinto Treviño," in R. M.
Dorson, *Buying the Wind* (Chicago, 1964) , pp. 483–85.
15. John T. Smith, "Rails Below the Rio Grande," *And Horns on the
Toads,* ed. M. C. Boatright, W. H. Hudson, and A. Maxwell, Publication
of the Texas Folklore Society, vol. 29 (Dallas, Tex., 1959) , pp. 122–135.

of agrarian settlements, symbolized by the homestead and
the grange; the transition to heavy industry and a new influx
of immigrants—Czechs, Bohemians, Poles—symbolized now by
the factory and the labor union. For each of these groups
Kramer delineates a communal myth that gives their world
meaning, a myth supported by symbols, rituals, codes, and
ceremonies, and by what he calls folk philosophy and folk
logic. To support his thesis he draws upon collections of folktales, folksongs, and folk beliefs, and intersperses these materials with conventional historical sources. He fails to fuse his
sources into a coherent narrative, but the failure is due not
to their incompatibility but to the author's over-impression-
istic method of presentation.

## Disentangling Fact from Fancy

A knowledge of the folklore properties of oral tradition can
enable the historian—especially the local historian—to separate fiction from fact. The history of town, county, and region
abounds in legendary traditions, which often parade as real
occurrences.

An example is afforded in the reminiscences of a northern
Michigan lumberjack, Ira Farrell, published in 1961 under
the title *Haywire: Growing Up in the Upper Peninsula 1905–
1925*. For the historian of this colorful region, Farrell's string
of earthy anecdotes constitutes a prime source; here is a rare
document, unpolished experiences and incidents set down in
print by a member of a folk group. The little book is as
formless as life itself. From my own fieldwork in the Upper
Peninsula, I can testify to the accuracy and authenticity of
its lumber camp and saloon scenes, odd character types, and
rowdy humor. But among the numerous anecdotes are some
already familiar. There is the story of the tough camp boss
who, when the choreboy asks him what time to wake up the
lumberjacks, roars, "Any goddamn time you find them
asleep." Farrell repeats this twice (pp. 68, 102–3) and I
heard it more than once in the Upper Peninsula and printed
it in *Bloodstoppers and Bearwalkers*.[16] Farrell sets down as

16. (Cambridge, Mass., 1952) , p. 198.

fact other folktales. One is the conversation of a minister with a woman living deep in the woods, who comically misinterprets his religious metaphors; this is Type 1833E, *God Died for You*, known in Europe and the United States. Another is the episode of the hunter who claims sole credit for shooting a deer but, when the deer turns out to be a horse, shares the credit with his companion. Baughman assigns this anecdote Motif X584.2*, and it appears among Aesop's *Fables*.[17] The presence of such traveled fictions in the pages of Farrell's little book by no means invalidates its claim to record faithfully life in the Upper Peninsula. Farrell can indeed enlist Herodotus as a predecessor in generosity to floating traditions. The storytelling culture of northern Michigan inevitably attracted folktales congenial to its temperament, and these stories of a boastful hunter and an ignorant backwoods woman fit perfectly into the frontier conditions of this region.

Local tradition tends to transmute legend into fact. An example of this process was brought directly to my notice during a field trip to the coast of Maine. In the village of Kennebec I tape-recorded a place-name tradition of Yoho Cove, two miles down the bay, from Curt Morse and his daughter Eve, who stated that the name derived from an episode known to everyone in the area. A wild man, who uttered only the word Yoho, abducted a white woman some time in the early days of settlement and lived with her for a couple of years until she was rescued by a boating party; in anger the Yoho tore their baby in two, and flung a half after the boat. The people of the township believe this happened, and a local historian might include it in his annals. But the Yoho has performed the same way in Persia, Canada, and Kentucky. Leonard Roberts recorded four variants of the Yoho legend in Pine Mountain, Kentucky.[18]

17. Ernest W. Baughman, *A Type and Motif-Index of the Folktales of England and North America* (Bloomington, Ind., and The Hague, 1966) ; Dorson, *Negro Tales from Pine Bluff, Arkansas, and Calvin, Michigan* (Bloomington, Indiana, 1958) , pp. 90–91.

18. R. M. Dorson, "The Legend of Yoho Cove," *Western Folklore* 18 (1959) : 329–31, elaborating on Archer Taylor and Leonard Roberts, "A Long-Sought Parallel Comes to Light," *Western Folklore* 16 (1957) : 48–51.

The Creeks, Micmacs, Wyandots, and Lenapees all speak
of a treaty they concluded with the white man, who offered a
good price for as much land as could be covered by a cow-
hide.[19] The white man then cut up the hide into strips and
spread the strips over a very large area. This same act of de-
ception was attributed to Dido in Virgil's *Aeneid,* and has
been reported from Turkey, Iceland, France, Estonia, Greece,
Egypt, and Siberia. This trick is indexed as Type 2400, *The
Ground is Measured with a Horse's Skin,* and Motif K185.1,
"Deceptive land purchase: ox-hide measure." Yet if the event
is historically false, it is psychologically true, and its incorpora-
tion into tribal histories is a fact for the American historian
to note.

## Verification of Incidents

The foregoing examples seem to support the theory so vehe-
mently contended for by Lord Raglan and Robert Lowie that
after a sufficient lapse of time, say a century and a half, all
oral tradition becomes pure fiction. There exist, however,
numerous cases, from Great Britain to Africa, and from Polynesia to Iceland, to illustrate the veracity of tradition. A recent
finding is presented in the *Journal of American Folklore* in
1959 in the article "Folk Traditions as Historical Fact: A
Paiute Example." Two archaeologists, David M. Pendergast
and Clement W. Meighan, working on American Indian sites
at Paragonah, Utah, recorded observations in 1956 and 1957
from four Southern Paiute informants about a Puebloid people who lived in this area from 800 to 1150 A.D., when the site
was abandoned. The Paiute statements concerning the people
they called "Mukwitch" generally supported archaeological information about the southern migration, deer hunting, short
physique, underground homes, and use of metates in food
grinding by the occupants of the site. The authors stated,
"Although no single informant knows all of the information

19. Marius Barbeau, *Huron and Wyandot Mythology,* Publications of
the Geological Survey of Canada, Anthropological Series, 11, no. 80
(1915) : 271; Mabel Burkholder, *Before the White Man Came: Indian
Legends and Stories* (Toronto, 1923), pp. 20, 23; Jay J. Woodman,
*Indian Legends* (Boston, 1924), p. 9.

about the *Mukwitch,* the collective knowledge of the group
seems to include an abbreviated but accurate history of events
and peoples some 800 years in the past."

Lord Ragland attacked the article, pointing to contra-
dictory statements by the Paiute, a reference to trains and
roads which would date one tradition in the nineteenth century, nontraditional observations on probability elicited from
the informants, and the incapacity of primitives to distinguish mythic from real persons.

In reply Meighan pointed to the high degree of consensus
among the informants and to their exclusion of mythical characters like Coyote from the *Mukwitch* accounts ("There are
no stories about the Mukwitch"). He cited four other North
American oral traditions validated by ethnogaphers, covering
a time span of from two hundred to eight hundred years. Why,
he asked, do the illiterate Paiutes know more about these
archaeological sites than the neighboring white farmers?

> The answer, we feel, is simply that it is their land, they
> have been there for thirty generations or more, their an-
> cestors saw these communities when they were living
> villages, and the old people talked about it to the young.[20]

Historical facts may lie embedded in narratives filled with
distorted and folkloristic elements. In the "Kiowa-Apache
Tales" collected by J. Gilbert McAllister, Old Man Hastchian
and Solomon Katchin tell historical stories about "How an
Apache Band was Exterminated" and "The Battle with Kit
Carson" (1864-65). The first contains a fabulous account of
a contest in magic (Motif D1719.1), in which an Indian medicine man named Tijjena triumphs over a white medicine
man. It also includes an historical inaccuracy, which McAllister points out, namely that an American officer rides a
horse, although the events take place supposedly before the
introduction of the horse. But the use of the cannon, which
McAllister at first thought an error, he later found verified by

20. Clement W. Meighan, "More on Folk Traditions," *Journal of American Folklore* 73 (1960): 60. The previous article in the same journal by
Meighan and David M. Pendergast, "Folk Traditions as Historical Fact:
A Paiute Example" appeared in 73 (1959): 128–33, and Lord Raglan's
comment, "Folk Traditions as Historical Facts," in 73 (1960): 58–59.

the testimony of army officers reported in James Mooney's
*Calendar History of the Kiowa.*[21]

## Providing Data on Minority Groups

Sociologist David Riesman in his provocative analysis of
American society, *The Lonely Crowd,* has distinguished three
main segments of the population: the other-directed, which
constitutes the main stream of contemporary American life,
dominated by the mass media and symbolized by the organization man; the inner-directed, of which the Puritans, motivated
by conscience and the will of God, are a prime example; and
the tradition-directed, those pockets and enclaves of immigrants and minority groups preserving an older, even archaic
culture. For the first two segments, the historical record is
amply documented: these have been the public and articulate
sectors of American civilization. But for the impoverished
immigrant, the submerged Negro, the ejected Indian, the
record is pitifully meager. The historian accustomed to rely
on published sources can find little from these illiterate or
semiliterate peoples. Dependent on the spoken rather than
the written word, and strongly bound by ethnic solidarity,
these groups perpetuate oral traditions of sufferings and
triumphs.

To them, oral history possesses a personal and intimate
quality. John Joseph Mathews in his tribal biography, *The
Osages,* tells of coming to recognize the importance of oral
"father-to-son" history when he returned to his home among
them after a ten-year interval.

> The history was a part of them, of the informants and
> the tribe, and they could not be detached from their
> narratives as were literate Europeans detached from their
> written narratives.[22]

Indian, Negro, and immigrant historical traditions venerate
heroes little known to students of textbook history. Here are

21. J. Gilbert McAllister, "Kiowa-Apache Tales," in *The Sky Is My Tipi,*
ed. M. C. Boatright, Publication of the Texas Folklore Society, vol. 22
(Dallas, Tex., 1949) , pp. 110–20, 133–39.
22. (Norman, Okla., 1961) , p. xii.

a few examples from my own field experience. A 93-year-old Potawatomi woman related to me in Escanaba, Michigan, in 1946 an account of a great battle down toward New York, in which the French were defeating the Americans, who turned to the Indians for help. Chief Eight Feathers (Ne-shaw-so-ge-nebbi) blanketed the French with a fog from a special stone, and killed them with his tomahawk. The stone and tomahawk were given him by a big bird up in the mountains, a bird in the form of a man who could make lightning. Chief Eight Feathers told the American general an eagle had given him his power, and in gratitude to their saviors the Americans put the eagle on the silver dollar, half dollar, and quarter, and the Indian on the penny.[23]

In contrast to their own heroes, the Indians see white Americans as villains. An Ojibwa, Mike Sogwin, told me a tradition he had heard from his great-grandparents of how United States government officials kidnapped his people on a Great Lakes vessel, dumped them in the hold, and gave them smallpox-infected blankets. When they died off on their Kansas reservation, the agents never reported their deaths, but continued to collect the Congressional allotments per head.[24] A Sioux, Herbert Welsh, informed me of the incident leading up to Custer's last stand; on the rifle range, Custer drunkenly shot a squaw and her baby watching a train pull into Fort Lincoln.[25]

Any folklorist or historian who speaks with Southern-born Negroes can rapidly accumulate a litany of horror and atrocity tales of slavery times. Atrocities are countered by heroic escapes, and these are remembered with close detail, even to conversations and meals along the escape route. The tendency of tradition to take on legendary hues can be seen in the saga narrated to me by Georgia-born E. L. Smith about his slave grandfather, Romey Howard, who "told us he could outrun bloodhounds, till they were too tired to jump over the fence." Romey frightened off the ghost-fearing poor white

23. R. M. Dorson, *Bloodstoppers and Bearwalkers* (Cambridge, Mass., 1952) , pp. 39–40.
24. Ibid., 38.
25. Ibid., 38–39.

patterolls by stretching out on the cemetery slabs, and when
caught, slid from their grasp and ran back to his Old Miss.[26]
Though a slave, it is Romey who possesses the mana, and the
whites who are superstitious and physically and mentally inferior.

In a day-long recording session in Iron Mountain, Michigan, the Corombos family narrated in full detail the family
saga of their emigration from Bambakou, near Sparta in
Greece. They described the struggle to get established in Boston, the drifting of the Greeks into the candy business and
eventually into restaurant ownerships in the Midwest, a completely new pattern from Old Country, where the husband
never entered the kitchen. Yet Old Country ideas and practices
retained a vital hold, manifested in a large body of saints'
legends and occult beliefs, for example, in the evil eye. These
traditions have reinforced the connections between the United
States and Old Country, leading Greek-Americans to return
on occasion and lay an offering at the icon of the local saint,
in fulfillment of a vow for his miraculous healing of the be-
liever. The cherishing of family traditions about an ancestral
hero, Janaikis, who outwitted the Turks, and the patron saint
of Bambakou, Saint Haralampos, who blanketed the attacking Germans in World War II with a fog—much as did Chief
Eight Feathers in the Potawatomi tradition—keep fresh a
spirit of Greek cultural patriotism in the midst of American
life.[27]

Oral traditions may well exasperate the historian of a
literate, or at least print-glutted society, with their quick-
silver quality and chronological slipperiness. But they can be
trapped, and they offer the chief available records for the beliefs and concerns and memories of large groups of obscured
Americans. The historian can find history alive in the field as
well as entombed in the library.

26. Dorson, *Negro Folktales in Michigan* (Cambridge, Mass., 1956), pp.
85–86.
27. Dorson, "Tales of a Greek-American Family on Tape," *Fabula* 1,
nos. 1–2 (Berlin, 1957): 114–43.

# 8

# Local History and Folklore

Nowadays the academic fashion calls for much communion among the various fields of learning and subject matter. The political scientist should double in sociology, the classicist should know linguistics, the European historian should acquire an Asiatic language. Among these belated courtships the least likely, and yet one with unsuspected elements of romance, would bring together history and folklore. Historians who have been "retooling" in the social sciences no doubt find themselves more distrustful than ever of the imprecise and unstatistical vagaries of folklore. The printed document and archival manuscript are the source and the law and stand ever opposed to the unverified tradition. Mindful of the credulity of Herodotus, the modern historian reveres the written and rejects the spoken word. Hearsay, rumor, gossip, folklore are close cousins, and no relations of recorded facts. Folklore indeed is nonfact.

Reprinted from *Detroit Historical Society Bulletin,* vol. 18, no. 1 (1961), with permission of the Detroit Historical Society.

It will be my argument that this schism is falsely imposed by the worshipers of facts, and that one branch of history—local history—is naturally and inescapably linked with the study of folklore. One of the great attractions indeed of research in local history is the opportunity to record folk traditions and employ them for the enrichment of the historical narrative.

A more tolerant attitude toward oral historical sources, evident for instance in the Oral History project of Columbia University, is now developing. In his stimulating address to last year's Local History Conference, Madison Kuhn pointed out this and other examples of the increasing reliance by historians on the verbal testimony of eyewitnesses and participants in the events described.[1] Samuel Eliot Morison has declared that such oral reports may give a sharpness and immediacy to the historical account not otherwise obtainable from conventional documentary records. Still oral history of the Nevins-Morison kind, derived from interviews with sailors and businessmen recounting events in their own lives, is far removed from the matter of folklore. Slips of memory and biases of recollections are not folklore in the sense intended by the professional folklorist.

That sense can be briefly stated as orally transmitted *tradition*. In the first half of the nineteenth century, antiquaries in England and philologists in Europe began to pay serious attention to the orally inherited tales, beliefs, songs, sayings, and customs preserved by the peasantry. A century of systematic study has yielded certain clear principles or properties of oral tradition. This oral traditional folklore shows ever recurring themes and motifs; legends held to be true by many peoples are now known to be wandering traditions which become attached to different persons and regions. Fabulous, supernatural, and magical conceits thrive in the floating mass of oral tradition, no matter how solidly grounded in chronicle and genealogy. A man in his own lifetime may reconstruct his early years with some hope of partially accurate reconstruction, but his son's conception of those adventures may

1. Kuhn, "Writing Institutional History," *Detroit Historical Society Bulletin* 16, no. 9 (October, 1960) : 9.

be heavily clouded, and his grandson's can be largely fictional. One school of folklorists, led by Lord Raglan in England, contends that after one hundred and fifty years all oral history has become folklore, structured and molded according to the properties of word-of-mouth tradition.

How then can folklore be counted a handmaiden of history, rather than its most insidious foe? One answer lies in the conception of a fact. A fact, in orthodox historiography, is the objective statement of the *res gesta* (an ideal which itself partakes of the nature of fantasy). The historian reads the sources on both sides and all vantage points of the battle, or the political campaign, to reconstruct the story of what really happened. There is, however, another class of facts, in a way more solid because they are not hypostatized, and these are the traditional beliefs of a group of people as to what happened. This shared belief is a fact which can be established by a folklorist or a local historian. Cotton Mather took careful pains to establish the fact that many persons in New Haven in 1648 believed they had seen a spectral ship sail across the sky after a thunderstorm, with a man standing on top the poop stretching a sword toward the sea. (See p. 31.) From the town suddenly arose a great smoke, which covered the ship, and in that smoke she "vanished away." So wrote the governor of Massachusetts, John Winthrop, in his diary. and fifty years later Cotton Mather was able to secure much fuller details for his *Magnalia Christi Americana*. The minister of New Haven, James Pierpont, in his "relation of that apparition of a ship in the air" which numerous credible observers had beheld, also furnished Mather an explanation of the prodigy, as interpreted by the first minister and founder of New Haven, the Reverend John Davenport. The Lord had willed this sight to answer the prayers of His sorely disturbed people, who had heard no word from the precious ship laden with their goods and bearing their kinfolk from their town in 1646. For His own good reasons, the Lord has decreed, and in His mercy now permitted, His people to comprehend this disaster.

No modern historian would accept the spectral ship of New Haven as a factual occurrence. Cotton Mather boldly recorded the apparition in his early history of America "for a thing as undoubted as 'tis wonderful." Undoubtedly many citizens of New Haven in the spring of 1648 believed they had seen a vessel in the sky. Mather did not accept this fact uncritically; he checked on it carefully and secured the most trustworthy documentary evidence. Nor was this an idle or trivial fact, but one of central interest in the providential history of the Lord's plantations in America, for here was a well-attested public prodigy illustrating God's special concern and means of communication with the saints of New England. While Mather was following the rules of evaluating historical evidence, he was also using the techniques of the folklorist; in effect, he recorded an oral folk tradition. Reports of spectral ships were rife among Englishmen and colonists of the seventeenth century, and the vitality of this folk belief has won it a place in Stith Thompson's *Motif-Index of Folk-Literature,* as E 535.3, "Ghost ship."

This union between the historical and the legendary narrative is firmest at the level of local history. (Mather's *Magnalia* is really local history, whose actors all knew each other intimately.) The local historian is concentrating on a well-defined and bounded community, with its own strong sense of identity and continuity, of roots and past—a much stronger sense than the nation as a whole possesses of its history. Within the township and county borders the family names and local landmarks perpetuate a history that is visible and immediate and borne in the mind, rather than buried in history books. Local history is in a very large sense traditional history. If we look to the so-called nonliterate or underdeveloped areas of the world, we find that the tribal—and the new national—histories are wholly traditional, and often formally preserved through the trained memories of court chroniclers who must retain awesome lists of genealogies in their heads. In the literate civilizations, where the facts are endlessly stored in print, and the populations are crammed in vast cities, the personal sense of history has all but vanished—save in the local community. And community annals receive short shrift from the professional guild.

In his sheaf of essays felicitously titled *Grass Roots History,* Theodore C. Blegen made a persuasive and largely unheeded plea for a redirection in the writing of American history. The perspective of academically trained historians had been almost exclusively focused on the national scene and the federal government. Of the settlement and growth of grass-roots America we had heard very little. Washington, D. C. is at the center, and Small Town far out on the circumference. Where is the story of the individual immigrants and homesteaders, merchants and laborers and farmwives who peopled the empty land? Dean Blegen's volume suggests the conceptual framework and the methods of research for the successful writing of American local history. In such sources as the "America" letters written home to the Old Country by the immigrant settlers, or the emigrant ballads composed on the new soil and printed in the foreign-language press, he illustrated the kinds of novel and rewarding source materials available to the grass-roots historian. Although the essays do not quite cross the border from local history to local folklore, they skirt all around the area of popular, traditional, and folk sources and artifacts.

There are of course town and country histories aplenty on the library shelves. As a graduate student writing a dissertation on New England legends, I combed every such history published in New England, whose every hamlet possesses at least one. These proud old tomes all told one rigid, undeviating story. They began with a reference to Indians and the wilderness topography; hailed the first settlers; noted the first churches, the first schools, the first stores; devoted a chapter to the Revolution and the local patriots; swung into full stride with the establishment of the newspaper, the militia, the fire department, and the waterworks; rhapsodized about the fraternal lodges and civic organizations; recounted the prominent citizens of the community, and enumerated famous personages (chiefly Washington and Lafayette) who had passed through; listed the roster of the Civil War dead; and rounded off the saga with descriptions of the newest edifices on Main Street. Somewhere toward the end there was apt to be a chapter on village witches, appearances of the Devil, reports of Captain Kidd and his treasure, and sketches of local characters and eccentrics; and for these nuggets I blew the dust off hundreds of township chronicles.

While some rewards were forthcoming, these stepchildren of Clio had missed their opportunities in local folk tradition as much as in straight history. Yet they point the way, and for all their homely, antiquarian, genealogical flavor—or because of it—their pages, and the illustrations of the town fathers, convey a sense of sturdy humanity. Here is history of common people, of a folk. To Dean Blegen's recipe for professional and imaginative writing of grass-roots history, I would add one extra ingredient, the folk history of the community.

By folk history I mean the episodes of the past which the community remembers collectively. Folk history will be composed of a number of local traditions. These traditions may or may not be written in the formal histories, but their retention is chiefly by word of mouth, and so they will diverge from the printed accounts, if such exist. Much or most of history on record would never of course survive without the crutch of print; the details of Pendleton's Civil Service Reform Act of 1883 scarcely set our pulses to tingling. But folk history survives purely on its own merits, because some element of shock, surprise, heroics, humor, or terror has captured the folk mind. From the viewpoint of the scientific historian, the folk memory is highly unselective; it may dwell on events of major consequence or of utter triviality. Surely the highfalutin speech of ore trimmer Pat Sheridan at the turn of the century is not memorable to the historian of America, but it has proved so to the folk of Escanaba, and from them I learned it in 1946.

## Pat Sheridan's Speech at Escanaba

More than half a century has passed since an Irishman from County Clare delivered a solemn speech to the ore trimmers union in Escanaba on the question of striking for a pay raise. The speech has lived through the years in word of mouth repetitions, and become an esteemed Escanaba tradition. Its texts of course vary considerably.

In the 1880s and 90s the Escanaba ore docks held a key position in the economy of the lakes. Iron ore from the newly found Menominee and Gogebic ranges poured by rail to the outlet port of Escanaba, to be shipped down the Lower Lakes to Buffalo and thence overland to Pittsburgh. Before the invention of a mechanical buffer to divert the ore evenly into the hold of the ore boats—its inventor, a boss trimmer named Mike O'Brien, was run out of town in 1897—ore had to be "trimmed" by hand with long rakes. With the light boats then in use, this operation called for considerable skill in leveling the ore as it poured from the chute on the docks into the hold, or the boats would easily capsize. Consequently the profession of ore trimmer, which was largely monopolized by the Irish, came to be held in high regard, and considerable esprit de corps developed among the different crews.

The crews numbered ten or a dozen, with fifteen men to a crew. Each crew had its boss, who would holler at the saloon where they awaited calls in between jobs, naming the boat and the dock. A call might come any hour of the day or night. The men marched out in their blue denim overalls, stained deep red from the ore, seized their picks and shovels from under the wooden sidewalks, and swung briskly down Ludington Street to the docks. On offdays the Irish trimmers organized a fife and drum band and played "The Wearing of the Green," "The Irish Washerwoman," and "The Harp That Once," with great enthusiasm, up in McCauley's saloon.

Each trimmer received two cents a ton for trimming. Since the bosses were paid on a contract basis, so much per ton, the trimmers gained slight reward for their skill and speed. The union met at the trimmers' hall on North Jenny Street to discuss striking for three cents a ton. Following the banquet different members were called on to express their views. Only the rhetoric of Pat Sheridan survives. (Some say he addressed the City Council.)

Pat was the top boy of the ore trimmers. He was a serious widower given to reading, and very dignified in his ways. He drove a white horse that had developed a saddleback from getting in and out of the barn door, because the manure which Pat never shoveled away had steadily risen toward the rafters. He was a tall, well-built man who walked the streets with his shoulders held back and his arms swinging sideways, so that his neighbors thought him pompous. He never washed himself from the time he started trimming in April

until he finished the last day in November. He cut his curly
hair only once a year, to clean it of ore dust.

Harold Lindsay of the Cloverton Paper Company gives
his speech in this form.

> I wish I had the humor of a Bobby Burns, the sterling
> oratory of a Robert Emmet, and the stately dignity of
> Alderman John Powers. I would climb the highest pin-
> nacle of the Swedish Lutheran church before I'd ever
> move a damn ton of ore for less than tin cents.

Sam Kitchen, who remembers how the entire ore trimmers
union would come to his father's garden for flowers for their
lapels, gives a fuller rendering.

> Ladies and gentlemen (no ladies present) : I come to
> you not as Robert Emmet; I come to you not as John
> C. Calhoun, but as plain Philip Sheridan of whom you
> all may know. But I want to say this, that I would climb
> the highest pinnacle of the Lutheran Church, and see
> the prancing cohorts go marching by, but I'd come down
> again, before divil of a ton of ore would I thrim for less
> than two cents.

But Tom J. Daley, one of Escanaba's oldest citizens, offers still
another account, illuminated by his own pungent asides—
which, incidentally, explain the reasons for the survival of
the speech.

> Gintlemen, and brothers of the trimmers' union here as-
> sembled: I come not before ye as Daniel O'Connell,
> Robert Emmet, or John B. Cahill (whoever the hell he
> was) , but as plain Patrick (not plain Pat but Patrick)
> Sheridan, as yez all may know. I would climb to the
> highest pinnacle of the Luterian Church (it was a frame
> church with the highest steeple in town) , and watch
> the prancing cohorts go passing nigh. (He was flowery!)
> And I would come down again. (It was nice of him to
> come down.) But damned if I'd shovel a pound of ore
> for less than three cents a ton. (That was from the sub-
> lime to the ridiculous.)

Mrs. George Harvey, who often saw Sheridan before he died in
1911, claims that his peroration ended this way.

> If I was to stand on the pinnacle of the Swedish Luterian
> Church, I wouldn't shovel a shovelful of ore in the lower

hatch or the upper hatch of any Northwestern dock for
less than four cents a ton.

From Charles Follo, an adept raconteur of Finnish dialect
stories, comes this tableau:

Well, the ore-trimmers were on strike, and on the first
day of the strike they all gathered downtown on one of
the main corners on the main street, and they stood
around for a while and someone thought that the occasion called for a speech, but none of them had ever made
a speech before. But the most likely person that they
thought might give a speech was Pat Sheridan. Well, so
they got a-hold of a box somewhere, and they got Pat
to get up on the box, and Pat wasn't quite sure what he
should say. So he started out in the oratorical manner
that he'd heard others use, and he said:

"I have not the iloquence of a William Jinnings
Bryan or an Honorable John Power." But he says, "I
would climb to the tallest pennicle of yonder Lutherian
Church and watch the cohorts go marching by." And
then he was stuck. He didn't know what to say then, and
he paused for a moment, then finally he says:

"And thin I'd come down again, but I'll be darned
if I'll go down in the hold of a boat and trim ore for
thirteen cents a ton."

Strangely enough, the story always stops at that point, leaving
the issue of the strike in uneasy suspense. For plain Patrick
Sheridan's oratory so captivated his listeners that his words
rather than his message came to lodge in their hearts.

The account of Pat Sheridan's speech is a prime example
of a local historical tradition. The variant texts illustrate the
course of oral transmission, the growth of legend is already
visible around the central actor, and the exegesis of their texts
by Tom Daley and Charles Follo explain the folk appeal of
this rhetorical flight. Half a century is a worthy span to test
the survival power of legend. And as historical tradition, the
speech is set intimately in the economic and social facts of
Escanaba's ore-shipping heyday on the Lakes. The background historical details were indeed supplied to me by the
raconteurs.

While this particular tradition was, to my lasting regret, cut from the final draft of my *Bloodstoppers and Bearwalkers,* several other Upper Peninsula legends from oral sources are included in that book. The "stealing" of the courthouse by Crystal Falls from Iron River, well known in both towns, casts light on the zealous rivalry of aspiring population centers for the booty of county seats and railroad stops. In "The Lynching of the McDonald Boys," frontier lawlessness in the days of the white pine lumber boom is grimly displayed. Since these are traditions collected from oral folk history, they reveal folklore elements. In the grisly recital of the abduction of the McDonald boys from the Menominee jail, their brutal lynching by some of the leading citizens, and the subsequent retribution visited upon the lynchers, who escaped trial but who all died mysteriously "with their boots on," I sensed a well-structured narrative pattern. Yet no close analogue turned up, probably because so little folk history is collected. Then one day in July 1959, while sharing the platform at an American Folktale seminar of the New York State Historical Association in Cooperstown, New York, with Dean Hector Lee of Chico State College in California, I heard him relate very much the same sequence of events as having occurred in Gouger's Neck in northern California, where a town lynching took place in 1901, and folk justice followed in the ensuing years. This structuring process characterizes oral tradition, but does not necessarily invalidate the truth of history.

Some local traditions, completely credited by the local resident, the folklorist can prove never occurred. One of the most widely reported local traditions in the United States is the Graveyard Wager. Some boaster or daredevil makes a bet that he will spend the night sleeping on a grave. In the morning he is found dead. During the night he had thrust a knife with which he was whittling in the dark through his raincoat lapel, thus pinning himself to earth, and frightening himself to death when he attempted to arise. This incident is told with variations in many towns in the United States and in Europe with names of local persons and places given—but never as an eyewitness account.

The Big City too generates local traditions, which pass for gospel truth. A colleague at Michigan State University

first told me of the Death Car, a Buick being offered for sale
at $50 by a downtown dealer. The owner had been accident-
ally shot in the north woods by a deer hunter, and the body
had not been recovered for days, hence the stench of death,
which could not be eradicated. This being World War II,
cars were at a premium, and the dealer was deluged with calls.
So were dealers in Detroit, Pontiac, Flint, and even cities in
Florida and California. But no dealers had such a car—or
rather, only one. In *Negro Folktales in Michigan* I described
how I stumbled upon the only case of eyewitnesses to, and
riders in, the death car, in tiny Mecosta, Michigan, from where
the legend must have taken flight. Right here in Detroit a
notorious tradition has grown around a Haunted Street,
where passing cars hear the thud and a dragging body and
sometimes the wails of a little girl who was run over and
dragged along with the automobile for some distance.

So large and unexplored a subject as folk history can here
only be briefly outlined. A threefold division for local traditions may be suggested, according to whether they primarily
concern persons, places, or events. Local personal traditions
center around strong men, big eaters, hermits, shrewd traders,
wily politicians, eccentrics, mad geniuses, necromancers,
saviors. The Mormon legends of the Three Nephites typify
the savior legends still to be found in the United States.

Place traditions are connected with landmarks and buildings: caves, cliffs, streams, trees, haunted houses, roads, bridges.
John Brown's Cave, where the abolitionist was supposed to
hide runaway slaves on the underground railroad, or Devil's
Rock, which bears an imprint of a cloven hoof, are examples
of place legends. Place names frequently give rise to, or preserve, legendary traditions through folk etymologies.

Local traditional events cover conflagrations, floods, murders, robberies, battles from the French and Indian to the
Civil Wars, the coming of the railroad, and whatever turns of
fate have influenced the destiny of towns and cities. These
three compartments are not of course watertight: such a tradition as the Mountain Meadows Massacre of 1857, infamous
in Mormon and Western history, embraces all three. The
battle itself is an event involving the whole community and
giving rise to legends and a ballad; the meadow is the specific

landmark, where the devil has subsequently been sighted; and John D. Lee is the despised figure in the ballad onto whom blame for the Mormon assault has been shifted.

In its emphases and omissions, folk history differs substantially from the history of documented record. But the writer of local history should give attention to both. The community is a living library, whose memories and traditions the local historian can comb with the interview techniques of the folklore collector. Nor is the verdict at all clear, despite the strictures of Raglan, as to whether or not the transmitted word bears false witness. As to what proportions of fact, distortion, and fiction are present in a given tradition, only the folklore-minded historian (or historically-minded folklorist) can ascertain. Folklore can help to humanize local history, and local history can provide a frame and context for folk tradition.

# 9

Defining the
American Folk Legend

*Legend* is as vague, slippery, and elusive a word as its sister terms *folklore* and *myth*. Unlike the ballad, the proverb, or folk art, the legend has received little scrutiny from American folklorists, although everybody at large talks about legends. To my taste, this is the most attractive and intriguing species of United States folk tradition, for it most closely involves history, particularly local history, and most specifically reflects American experience.

We begin by contrasting European and Asiatic with American legends. In Europe today a high-powered committee is considering an international legend classification. There already exists the system proposed by Reidar Christiansen in *The Migratory Legends,* based on Norwegian examples. For Asia, *Folk Legends of Japan,* edited by myself, presents translations of typical texts grouped according to dominant themes. A glance at these volumes shows a world unfamiliar

Read to the Utah Folklore Society at Logan, Utah, 26 July 1968.

to a Yankee. Visitations of the plague in the guise of an old
man, antics of trolls, sympathetic bleeding of stone buddhas,
the malevolence of kappas and tengus—such phenomena have
no place in the American scene. One vast difference between
the New and Old Worlds lies in the inheritance in long settled countries of a demonic mythology and an ancient faith.
Legends in the United States have at the longest a mere four
centuries, and in much of the Far West less than two centuries,
to find anchorage, whether imported from abroad or arising
from local circumstances. As for the Indians, their relationship to American legendry will require a special footnote.

If remembrances of pagan monsters and medieval magicians must be eliminated from the New World context, where
then do we look for American legendary traditions? We can
find an abundance in the fast-moving drama of American
colonization, settlement, and national growth. But at this
point we must grapple with the concept of legend.

Folklorists will agree that legend as one outcropping of
folk narrative must enter at some point into word-of-mouth
circulation. They recognize that legends, while frequently hard
to believe, are nevertheless believed. Another general proposi-
tion holds that the legend is relatively unstructured and loose
in comparison with the symmetrical Märchen. Finally there
is the recognition that the legend is known to a group of
people. This group awareness is indeed one of its key properties. In a particular community, one or two people may be
active storytellers or ballad singers, but almost all will know
and be able to say something about the local legends. They
may not deliberately repeat the legend narratives, but more
likely they will allude to them conversationally and proverb-
ially.

The distinction between legend and fictional folktale is
clear enough, but two further distinctions seem needed to
separate the legend from other kinds of oral narratives told
for true. One relative is the marvelous personal experience,
now pretty generally called by von Sydow's term *memorat*. If
others retell the adventure, the memorat may in time acquire
legendary status. A second relative is the *family saga,* aptly
designated by Mody Boatright. As a memorat is bound to the
individual, so the family saga is bound to the family circle,

who alone are concerned with the past haps and mishaps shaping their present situation. Rarely will the family tradition attract enough attention to become a regional legend, as did occur with the celebrated male witch who haunted the Bell family in Tennessee and Mississippi.

With this preamble, we may turn to some representative volumes of American legendry. Three recent books with *legend* in their titles are *The Western Hero in History and Legend* by Kent Ladd Steckmesser (Norman, Okla, 1965, 2nd printing 1967); *New England Legends and Folklore*, edited by Harry Hansen (New York, 1967); and *Profile of Old New England: Yankee Legends, Tales, and Folklore* by Lewis A. Taft (New York, 1965). These exhibits exemplify the casual current usage of the term *legend*.

In his study Steckmesser recapitulates the biographies of Kit Carson, Billy the Kid, Wild Bill Hickok, and George Armstrong Custer, and separates factual from fictional elements. The words *legend* and *legendary*, which occur in profusion throughout the work, indicate any embroidery, whether in the direction of a badman, a Robin Hood, or a trailblazer, through any medium, whether oral tale, dime novel, colorful biography, movie script, television series, or Wild West show. His concept of legend emerges as the manipulation, selection, and distortion of historical data, mainly by writers addressing a national audience, to arrive at or reinforce a stereotype. "Any criticism of this idealized figure, any challenge to the legend," he writes, "provoked an emotional response" (page 245).

The title of *New England Legends and Folklore* reveals its composition: *Based on Writings by Samuel Adams Drake and Others, and Illustrated with Photographs by Samuel Chamberlain.* This is a nostalgic picture book, a publisher's production, issued by Hastings House, who specialize in the photographic albums of Mr. Chamberlain. They provide a text to accompany the scenes of historic homes and churches and scenic harbors and shorelines by dusting off Drake's bedside companion of 1884, called *A Book of New England Legends and Folklore*, and having the professional book reviewer Harry Hansen trim it for modern browsers. Drake leaned heavily on the nineteenth-century New England poets and

romancers, Hawthorne, Longfellow, Whittier, and the colonial chroniclers, Cotton Mather, William Bradford, John
Winthrop, for traditions of witches and specters, pirates and
gentlemen. Although Hansen claims that Drake collected tales
along the post roads of the New England seaboard, Drake's
compilation smacks chiefly of library clippings and local-
color jottings. The so-called legends are inserted into snatches
of early history and sketchings of the landscape. No sources
are offered in the new edition, except as casually mentioned
in the text.

The *Profile of Old New England* covers some of the same
ground as *New England Legends and Folklore,* but abjures
pictures and historical filler to concentrate on forty retold
narratives. In his preface Taft states: "Here is a selection of
legends and anecdotes of Old New England which have lived
with great vitality through the years. . . . A few decades ago,
several legend and folklore collectors took the most popular
of these yarns, abridged and condensed them without regard
to their entertaining values until they became only skeletal
remnants of what had been interesting and lively tales."
Clearly Mr. Taft has in mind as one culprit my *Jonathan
Draws the Long Bow* (1946), in which I endeavored to trace
the earliest printed sources of New England legends. Mr.
Taft retells many of the old chestnuts: "Tom Walker and
the Devil" (taken straight from Irving). the peripatetic Peter
Rugg (taken straight from William Austin), the wreck of
the *Palatine,* the Windham frog fright, the Micah Rood apple, all reprinted and rewritten dozens of times before. The
author does not acknowledge debts, but he does append a
three-page bibliography, lacking in any title of field-collected
prose traditions—a pardonable omission, for no such volume
exists. What we are dealing with in all these books is a literary, not a folk process.

In order to distinguish legends perpetuated through town
histories, tourist brochures, local-color literature, Sunday sup-
plements, and similar printed channels from spoken legends,
I will employ the terms *literary legend* and *folk legend.*
Where the two kinds of sources reinforce each other, I will
use the term *popular legend.*

The first systematic displayer of American legends was Charles M. Skinner, a correspondent for the *Brooklyn Eagle.* In *Myths and Legends of Our Own Land* (2 vols., 1897), *Myths and Legends beyond Our Borders* (1899), *American Myths and Legends* (2 vols., 1903), and *Myths and Legends of Our New Possessions and Protectorate* (1902), Skinner employed a sure-fire formula. He narrated with flair and verve a string of brief macabre episodes scattered at convenient locations across the continent. Skinner gave no sources, but from my own digging for *Jonathan Draws the Long Bow* I recognize a number that he must have used for New England. Drake and Taft are simply quarrying the same vein. As Skinner moves inland, and American history becomes shorter, his sources dwindle, and he turns to romanticized versions of Indian tales to fill his geographical quota. Skinner's retellings are literary legends, although some may once have lived orally. His formula has been emulated all through the present century, up to the *Life Treasury of American Folklore,* whose corps of rewriters have managed to squeeze the juice out of their mass-cultured traditions.

The formula requires that the legend be told as if it were a straightforward, consecutive, smooth-flowing narration. And this of course is the style of writing that appeals to readers. But it is false to the nature of oral folk legend. No one individual knows the whole legend, for by definition it is a communal possession. The legend may be a cycle of anecdotes about a strong or clever or comical hero, and even if one raconteur knows a baker's dozen, there will be new variants and new incidents to be gleaned from other tellers. Every man, woman, and child I encountered in Jonesport and Beal's Island on the Maine coast responded to the name of Barney Beal, the muscular lobsterman whose feats of strength had been talked about for more than half a century. Most people repeated that he could drum on the floor with his hands when sitting in a chair, and that he had once killed a horse with a blow of his fist. But now and again a novel exploit or unusual twist would be heard, until a sizable list of titanic deeds had accumulated. A money-minded writer could easily weave these together into a fluent Paul Bunyanesque chronicle, filling in

the interstices between episodes with local color and local history of the Maine coastal islands and fishing industry. But his
product would fail to represent the fragmentary and sporadic
character of folk legend.

Or take an illustration from an avant-garde sector of
American civilization, the hippie-drug culture of the San Francisco Bay area, which has generated a subculture antihero
known as Owsley. A student collector, Arvalea Nelson, has
written:

> The character sketched in the following texts is . . . aptly
> described as a living legend. Augustus Owsley Stanley
> III, born January 22, 1935, in Arlington, Virginia, is a
> charter immortal of the Lysergic Acid Diethamide (LSD)
> Hall of Fame. The first great mass producer of LSD, his
> peers of the hippie community have dubbed him "The
> Henry Ford of Acid." Tales of great strength and valor
> are less fascinating to today's drug-oriented youth of the
> psychedelic milieu than the eccentric career of an under-
> ground hero who has to date produced more than ten
> million consciousness-expanding tablets of LSD.

What is the legend of Owsley? Like that of Barney Beal,
it must be constructed from the anecdotal observations of
participants in the subculture, in this case hippie panhan-
dlers, dancers, folksingers, street-corner gurus, artists' models,
unemployed poets. The themes of the anecdotes turn on the
potency of Owsley's blue and purple tablets, the vast sums he
has acquired through their manufacture and sale, his skill in
eluding narks (narcotic agents) and fuzz (the police), his
daredeviltry and recklessness. The scenes of his escapades
cover the hippie hangouts from California to New York. The
only way that one can sell acid, according to Berkeley students, is to say that it is Owsley's. However, they also say
that much of the acid bearing Owsley's name is not made by
Owsley. One rumor alleged that he gave $20,000 to the "Grate-
ful Dead," whom he considered the first psychedelic rock
band, to go out and buy "equipment" to further the psychedelic experience.

On one occasion Owsley, elegantly dressed in a purple
velvet suit, visited a group of Free Speech Movement activists
in jail and astonished them by pulling a Bible from his pocket

and reading aloud from it with a grave mien. After a bit he
revealed that the Good Book had been dipped in acid so
that the inmates could "groove" on the pages. He passed it
around, each tore out a page from his favorite section, one
from Jeremiah, most from Job, and sucked on the pages until
all were "wiped out." One rumor had it that Owsley enjoyed
an agreement with the cops to hold onto his market in order
to keep the Mafia out. A counter rumor asserted that he was
in with the Mafia and that the syndicate kept the cops paid
off. Like J. Golden Kimball, the profane Mormon elder
known throughout Utah in waggish anecdotes, Owsley contributed to his own legend. Some say he started rumors about
himself. As one informant put it, "He grooves on being a
legend."

Here are two hero-legend cycles from the opposite poles
of American life. One comes from the nineteenth-century
setting of outdoor occupations, pioneer values, the admiration
for brute strength. The other comes from the twentieth-
century urban milieu of the antiestablishment, peopled by
youthful grass smokers, hippies, drug addicts, homosexuals,
black militants, student activists. But the folk processes in
both cases are the same. Of course the Owsley proto-legend
needs the weathering of time to determine its staying power.

When we turn to the actual resources of field-collected
American folk legends, we see how rarely the tradition of oral
reality ever gets set down in print, and also how constricted
is the quest for legends. The four valuable folktale volumes
of Vance Randolph contain a variety of narratives, some
recognizable Märchen, some floating jokes, some migratory and
local legends, but all processed by the master collector-author
in the same way, to emerge as fluent, idiomatic yarns, ascribed
to named individuals who sound alike. Information on group
knowledge of the legends is lacking. Two publications that
particularly command our interest are *Legends of Texas,* edited
by J. Frank Dobie (Hatboro, Pa.: Publications of the Texas
Folklore Society, 1924, reprinted 1964), and volume one of
Fred W. Allsopp's *Folklore of Romantic Arkansas* (New York:
Grolier Society, 1931). The contents in the Texas book are
divided according to "Legends of Buried Treasure and Lost
Mines," "Legends of the Supernatural," "Legends of Lovers,"

"Pirates and Pirate Treasure in Legend," "Legendary Origins
of Texas Flowers, Names, and Streams," and "Miscellaneous,"
a sheaf of eight leftovers that includes two of the best known
Southwestern traditions, the stories of Sam Bass and of the
White Steed of the Prairies. The chapter headings of the Arkansas collection are "Prehistoric Days," "Indian Cosmography
and Religion," "Romantic Legends of the Streams of Arkansas," "Arkansas Place Names," "Legends of Places," "Romantic Love Legends," "Indian Legends," "Legends of Lost
Mines and Hidden Treasures," and "Notorious Outlaws."
These rubrics give a fair idea of the categories generally used
to classify American *Sagen*. The prominence of underground
treasure, Indian lovers, and humorous place-names unites the
collections. In my *Jonathan Draws the Long Bow* I used the
four captions "Indian tragedies," "Haunts," "Buried treasure," and "Place-names" in the chapter on local legends.
Community traditions of historical events rarely appear in
field reports.

Looking at the Dobie and Allsopp texts, we find them
for the most part loosely rewritten, with the exact words of
tellers seldom given. For instance, in "The Woman of the
Western Star: A Legend of the Rangers," the writer names
Judge Hugh C. Duffy as her source, and after an introductory
paragraph states:

> I tell the tale now as it was told to me, when the moon
> was full and shone on a merry group of friends seated
> on the ground, in the neighborhood of Polly's Peak.
> The narrator began with these words: "It was on just
> such a night as this." Then followed the legend in the
> time-honored style sacred to legendary lore, impossible
> for me to imitate.[1]

What this style is, and why it should be so difficult to reproduce by a writer addicted to literary phrases, we are not
told. In some instances, multiple versions are given or synop-
sized with named informants, but commonly there are vague
generalities declaring that "old cowpunchers" say they have
seen the ghost of a murdered nester astride a "blindfolded
horse" on Stampede Mesa, that "herd bosses" fear these

1. *Legends of Texas* (Hatboro, Pa.: Folklore Associates, 1964) , p. 116.

phantom steers, and that "it is said" that since the nester was murdered, every herd stopping on that mesa has stampeded.[2] Perhaps the haunting of Stampede Mesa is indeed talked about among cattlemen, but we cannot be sure until we see the sequence of verbatim texts with identified speakers, and are given additional data about the frequency of repetition and degree of credence in the spectral narrative. Still it is not merely the defective method of collecting that is at fault. In addition there is the constricted view of the legend as a landmark tradition connected to a mine, a stream, or a rock. While *Legends of Texas* can be supplemented in the Publications of the Texas Folklore Society with *In the Shadow of History* (1939), which contains historical legends of the Alamo and the death of Jim Bowie, and anecdotes about Stephen F. Austin and Sam Houston, they are chiefly from print.

Three examples of community traditions I collected in Michigan's Upper Peninsula illustrate themes of American history folk-legends, although I now see they were improperly presented. "The Lynching of the MacDonald Boys" is an event of 1881 known to every citizen of Menominee by oral hand-me-down. Only this past summer Jim Borski sent me from Menominee a photostat of a photograph, described to me by hearsay, of the two MacDonalds strung up to a jack pine tree. In local folk belief and saying, every member of the lynch mob died with his boots on, a statement that has become proverbial. Catholics assign the curse to a priest; Protestants to God. In my reconstructed composite account I listed nine retributive deaths, but no one teller knew more than two or three. If I were printing it today, I would set down the fragment of each speaker separately, along with a ballad text recovered by Ivan Walton from Beaver Island. A striking parallel has been unearthed by Hector Lee from northern California in the town of Lookout, where a lynch mob in 1901 met similar enigmatic deaths. Recently Dean Lee told me that he had pieced his television script together from five informants, and that everyone he met in Lookout knew of the event but were reluctant to discuss it. Here again the legend of the folk, resurrected by the folklorist, was larger than the

2. Ibid., p. 114.

knowledge of any individual. One teller used the phrase
"Hell overtook 'em, everyone of 'em," but it does not seem
to have become a local proverb. At any rate we are clearly
dealing here with a repeated folk pattern.

A second example, titled "How Crystal Falls Stole the
Courthouse from Iron River," is known in a general way to
every resident of Crystal Falls and Iron River, the towns in
Iron County competing in 1885 for the county seat. Unlike
the lynching tale, no supernatural elements enter into the
multiple accounts of how, through cunning, fraud, duplicity,
and chicanery of one sort or another, the men of Crystal Falls
stole the blueprints, county papers, or cash from an Iron
River warehouse. The handsome lemon-colored building subsequently erected atop a dizzy hill overlooking the main street
of Crystal Falls continues to reinforce the memory of the
theft and the election that followed, also marked by charges
and countercharges of deceit. This is a mirthful legend, larded
with jocular touches that bring wry grimaces in Iron River
and smug chuckles in Crystal Falls. Unlike the Menominee
event, where an act of frontier lawlessness resulted in a divine
judgment, the lawless behavior in Iron County is regarded as
American high jinks. Again, if I were printing this story today, I would set down dozens of individual observations and
commentaries side by side, along with the contemporary newspaper version. The theme of intrastate rivalry for a capitol,
a university, a county seat, a railroad station is nationwide.

A third community legend, "Pat Sheridan's Speech at
Escanaba," which a publisher's reader cut from *Bloodstoppers
and Bearwalkers,* actually best illustrates the pristine form of
this kind of narrative, for it did juxtapose variant texts. (See
pp. 150–53.) Townspeople kept repeating this speech whose
comical pomposity tickled their fancy. Each individual rendition is funny to the teller and his listeners knowing the in-
terior references, but the full humor comes from comparing
the five texts and seeing how the allusions and metaphors
become wildly garbled. Yet the outside reader for Viking Press
(who rejected the book anyway) singled out this tale for his
severest criticism, an indication of how the nonfolklorist objects to reading variants and demands a smooth, continuous
story line.

How many of these community folk legends exist or once throve on the American land we cannot even surmise, but I am sure they are numerous. An excellent early example is the Windham Frog Fright, concerning a supposed invasion of Indians in 1754 in the then frontier town of Windham, Connecticut. The panicked townspeople mistook the cries of thirsty frogs for an invitation to their leading citizens to treat or negotiate. The report of this misadventure spread far beyond the town and even the county, and enjoyed a continuous life in prose retellings, mock epics, humorous ballads, and pictorial representations through the nineteenth and twentieth centuries. The county historian of Windham could say in 1874, "Few incidents occurring in America have been so widely circulated."[3] At the heart of the Windhamites' discomfiture is a recurrent folklore motif, often found in anecdotes of simpleton Irishmen, of the mistaking of frogs' croakings for human utterance. There is no doubt that this legend first throve by word of mouth, for we are told so, but the many extant accounts are all literary, not verbal texts.

Another process to be considered in the analysis of American legendry is the history of the career of certain legends from an oral-folk-local circuit to a print–mass-media–national circuit. Such histories may prove highly complex, if we could ever unravel them, since print, movies, and television can sow or resow new oral growth. A case in point is the reviving of a late nineteenth-century tradition about the only American ever to be convicted of cannibalism, Alfred E. Packer, who disappeared into a cave during a blizzard while prospecting for gold in Uncompahgre County, Colorado, with five companions. Packer reemerged some months later, without his comrades. A Democratic judge in Lake City, Colorado, pronounced sentence upon him. "There were only seven Democrats in Hinsdale county and you, Alfred Packer, you maneating so-and-so, you ate five of them. I sentence you to be hanged by the neck until you are dead, dead, dead." The occasion for resurrecting this macabre matter was the renaming of the Roaring Fork Cafeteria at the University of Colo-

3. Dorson, *Jonathan Draws the Long Bow* (Cambridge, Mass.: Harvard University Press, 1946) , p. 17.

rado as the Alfred E. Packer Cafeteria, thereby signifying student distaste for the fare. Chet Huntley recited this development gleefully on his television newscast, and next day the newspapers carried the story.[4] Huntley pointed out with a grin the factual error that as the prospectors had recently come from Utah they could not have resided long enough in Colorado to vote. Here the grisly tale has entered two quite distinct cycles of circulation and will now be constantly memorialized for college students in Boulder through a storied place-name.

In referring to a legend, then, we should indicate what point it has reached in its own history and genealogy. The John Henry legend has exhibited very different meanings and attracted quite different audiences at intervals over the past half century, as I have tried to show in an article tracing "The Career of 'John Henry' "[5] John Henry has gone through stages of being a ballad legend, a literary legend, a juvenile legend, a hit-song legend, but never what he is generally alleged to be, a legendary folk-hero of American Negroes. The endless discrepancies and mutations that enter into American legend-making are on view in Bruce Buckley's dissertation on Frankie and Johnny, whose names, deeds, and residences shift with kaleidoscopic variety in popular tradition.[6]

There is a synchronic as well as a diachronic aspect to the American legend. What is its habitat, who are its bedfellows, how does it look in its setting? These questions cannot be answered by text collectors but by ethnographers, and as yet the folklorist has stuck mainly to his texts. Some noteworthy exceptions are Vance Randolph's *The Ozarks* and Emelyn E. Gardner's *Folklore from the Schoharie Hills, New York*. But far and away the most panoramic and delectable spread of local legendary traditions is *The Jonny-Cake Letters* of "Shepherd Tom" Hazard (1880), written originally as a series of letters to the *Providence* (Rhode Island) *Journal*. Hazard was no conscious folklorist but a patrician land-

---

4. *San Francisco Chronicle,* April 25, 1968.

5. *Western Folklore* 24 (1965) : 155–63.

6. "Frankie and Her Men: A Study of the Interrelationships of Popular and Folk Traditions" (Indiana University diss., 1962) .

owner, sheepraiser, and writer on social issues who possessed
a sure instinct for every variety of oral narrative that took root
in his beloved Narragansett country: place-name etymologies,
anecdotes of curmudgeonly characters, culinary tall tales,
strong-man exploits, salty sayings, haunted sites, practical
jokes. These are the genuine American *Sagen,* set in conversational vignettes of daily life and manners in rural Rhode
Island. *The Jonny-Cake Letters* belong to literature as much
as to folklore, but they can serve as an ideal, if not a model,
for the ethnographer of folk legends.

Still another way of viewing American legends is in terms
of simple and complex formations. The most frequently collected specimens are the simpler texts of one or two motifs dealing with haunted houses, buried treasure, tricksters, heroes,
healers, and place-names. They fall into two main divisions:
place legends associated with a specific geographical landmark
or building, and personal anecdotes connected with colorful
and renowned individuals. But the community or local-history or event legends, whatever we may call them, contain a
larger cast of characters and a more complicated, or perhaps
more blurred, scenario. In his valuable pioneering fieldbook,
*Tales and Songs of Southern Illinois,* Charles Neely included
a number of history legends from the turbulent annals of
"Egypt," but they seemed so shapeless that I reprinted none
in *Buying the Wind.* It is surprising how few event legends
appear in the regional collections of such sterling fieldworkers
as Emelyn Gardner and Leonard Roberts. But their few examples possess uncommon interest. In *South from Hell-fer-
Sartin,* Roberts gives a text about Everlasting Water at High
Knob, Kentucky, describing an event of 1870. A Baptist
preacher fell out with his brother-in-law over a well and had
to ride five miles to a water-mill to cart back water in an open
churn on the back of his jenny. He swore to his old lady
that he would pray to God on the dry bank for everlasting
water. The story proceeds in graphic fashion until the preacher
does indeed get his everlasting water. Essentially this is a
miracle legend, centered on Motif D1766.1, "Magic fountain
produced by prayer." The teller concludes, "And that happened at High Knob, Kentucky. That's a true fact now. And

I can find you twenty different old men and women that will swear to the facts of that."[7] We would welcome their renderings of this fresh and unusual tradition.

In his introduction to "The Legend of Stampede Mesa" in *Legends of Texas,* J. Frank Dobie remarked that it contained the most "native originality" of any in the book. This relation too involves a complex event, in refreshing contrast to the hackneyed repetitions of lovers' leaps and lost mines.

Murder is one of the complex events in community life most apt to generate local traditions. Ballads inspired by murders have been gathered together by Olive Woolley Burt in *American Murder Ballads and Their Stories* (New York, 1958), but folk legends of murders have not been assembled or much investigated. Steward Holbrook appended to his *Murder Out Yonder, An Informal Study of Certain Classic Crimes in Back-Country America* a source chapter titled "Folklore of American Murder." Here he offered tantalizing morsels of the legendary lore swirling about these crimes in the localities where they had been committed decades before. In referring to the magnetic prophet Joshua Creffield, who attracted women in droves to his Oregon campsite and was shot by the irate brother of one, who was in turn murdered by his own sister, Holbrook merely hints at the prophet's storied powers. "The folklore concerning Creffield and his band deals mostly with the prophet's unquestioned great virility, and is wholly unprintable."[8] (That was before the obscenity issue of the *Journal of American Folklore*!) Holbrook's final chapter could well have been a book in itself, and one to be treasured by the folklorist.

Yet another perspective on American legendry may be obtained by identifying the most representative themes of a given historical period. In the seventeenth century, the age of providences, spectral ships were often seen and speculated upon, such as the one sighted over New Haven harbor in 1648. In the eighteenth century, the throes of the American Revolution created folk heroes like swashbuckling Ethan

7. Leonard Roberts, *South from Hell-for-Sartin* (Lexington, Ky.: University of Kentucky Press, 1955), p. 173.
8. Stewart Holbrook, *Murder Out Yonder* (New York: Macmillan, 1941), pp. 221–22.

Allen, goggled at in awe and astonishment by his English captors. In the nineteenth century, murdered peddlers, the traveling salesmen of a preindustrial day, left tell-tale clues behind them in the form of ineradicable blood stains. In the twentieth century, the ubiquitous automobile has become an appurtenance to the legends of the Death Car, the Vanishing Hitchhiker, and the Stolen Grandmother.

Turning from the collecting to the study of American folk legends, we find the pickings even leaner. Legends have not, like ballads and proverbs and folktales, been subjected to close analysis. Very rare is the kind of behind-the-story investigation presented by Edward D. Ives in "The Man Who Plucked the Gorbey: A Maine Woods Legend."[9] Ives reports how he pursued a belief of Maine woodsmen, that if one harmed a gorbey (the Canada jay), the hurt would be revisited on the man. An extensive newspaper campaign yielded him over one hundred texts, which he grouped into six geographical areas in the Maine-Maritimes region, and ultimately traced to a Scotch or north England source. Here a folklorist has treated a folk legend with the same respect accorded a Märchen. Ives obtained a quantity of texts, analyzed them by the geographical-historical method, observed their variations and stability, noted their use in literature, related them to an occupational belief, and reconstructed the path of their entry into the United States. In the core plot, the hardhearted woodsman who plucks the feathers off the gorbey and throws it out the bunkhouse window to freeze in the wintry night, wakes up the next morning denuded of every hair on his body. One can see how the humanitarian and retributive aspects of this credited tale would readily fit into the American ethos.

The one folklorist who has assiduously studied the history of some American local legends is Louise Pound, in various papers in *Western Folklore,* reprinted in her book *Nebraska Folklore* (Lincoln, Neb., 1959). Her particular subject has been the synthetic Indian-white place legends—and I use the word synthetic in its double senses—of Nebraska, which have their counterparts throughout the country. In her

9. *Journal of American Folklore* 74 (1961) : 1–8.

studies of "Nebraska Legends of Lovers' Leaps," "Legend of the Lincoln Salt Basin," and "The Nebraska Legend of Weeping Water," Pound engaged in ingenious detective work to ascertain the degree of authentic Indian content in these presumptive traditions. Her conclusions are straightforward and convincing. These narratives are primarily literary, although oral versions influenced by literary texts are extant; they date from the nineteenth century and appear to originate with white authors pursuing the romantic conventions linked to the Noble Savage; they represent white man's concepts of courtship and marriage and not those of the Pawnee.

Pound identifies the legend-initiating romancers. One was John Treat Irving, Jr. (1812–1906), nephew of Washington Irving, who traveled west in 1833. Another was Professor Orsamus Charles Dake, first professor of English literature at the University of Nebraska, guilty of a volume of sentimental poetry in 1871. In the place-name stories of Lovers' Leaps she perceives a literary form extending back to the Greek poetess Sappho and including the Elizabethan dramatist John Lyly and Addison in the *Spectator*. Pound does not close the door to the possibility of some Pawnee elements entering into the white man's compositions, but she demonstrates its unlikelihood. Irving's legend of the Lincoln salt basin, for instance, is strongly reminiscent of the biblical account of Lot's wife turned to salt. Her documented findings prove what some folklorists have suspected, but she produces the evidence. Pseudo-Indian legends are still proper game for the student of folk processes, since there is feedback into popular and even oral channels, and since the student of folklore should in any event consider purported folklore.

# 10

Print and
American Folktales

To the carefully wrought discipline of folklore study, created
by a century's painstaking scholarship, United States civilization poses a frontal challenge. For, in the field of American
folk narrative alone, enigmas and surprises occur: the absence
of universally common tale types; the presence of somewhat
pseudo superheroes; the leavening of oral with printed diffusion. On this last issue a decision must soon be reached,
since the purist approach to defining and collecting folktales
by the touchstone of oral currency is gradually being refuted
by poaching literary historians. I suggest that, because of the
special and even unique conditions of United States history,
folklorists acknowledge the function of print in spreading,
perpetuating, and preserving American popular tales, and
the value of printed sources as repositories of folktale. The

©1945 by the California Folklore Society. Reprinted by permission of the
Society from *California Folklore Quarterly* (now *Western Folklore*) 4,
no. 3 (1945) : 207–15.

problem of deciding when a printed tale is a folktale must then of course be met and vanquished.

Obviously the circumstances of American birth and growth offer basic divergences from the customary evolution of cultures. One notes first the lack of a direct ancient past, with its accumulated heritage of primitive myth and family saga and household tales—fountainheads of much of the world's folk story. One notes again the emphasis on schooling and the high level of literacy and the many popular printed circuits of communication—penny newspapers, almanacs, family weeklies, monthly magazines, annuals, joke books, compendiums, digests. Further, one thinks of the vigor, the exuberance, the expansiveness of frontier America, so striking and so confusing to foreign travelers, and how her confidence in an economic and political Manifest Destiny found reflection in a cocky humor of extravagance. Take away pagan divinities, chivalric aristocracy, an animistic universe, rigid and static societies, substitute physical mobility, social democracy, scientific explanations, and the historian finds reason for the different folklore expression of American civilization.[1]

One especial difference, the influence of printing in American life, upsets cherished convictions and established methods of the folklorist. For the ubiquitous printed page becomes an instrument to diffuse and a table to record folktales. Stories in the United States travel interchangeably through the spoken and the printed word; if communities are scattered and fluid and culturally advanced beyond the cement of purely oral tradition, a cohesive force is supplied by commonly read printed matter. Generally speaking, diffusion by print takes two broad directions, a lateral spread of popular tales over a considerable area within a limited time-span— particularly the pre–Civil War decades—and a vertical descent of popular legends through an extended period of time within a circumscribed locale. What collectors today gather directly from the folk as living tradition may well have drained

1. Actually a *folk* does not exist in the United States in the Old World sense of a rooted, tightly knit, traditionally minded community. In 'this connection see Margaret Marshall's remarks in *The Nation*, April 21, 1945, pp. 447–48.

through subliterary conduits—the sprouting mid-nineteenth-century newspapers which clipped one another's anecdotal humor unceasingly, the continuous chronicles of township *Sagen* periodically repeated from the seventeenth-century providential histories through town and county and regional histories.[2]

If tales lodge in print, then the logical combing of printed sources for new texts and variants should proceed no less actively than search among the living folk. A virtually unexplored country opens for folklore hunting, the contours of which are already roughly discernible. Early newspapers, especially in the first half of the nineteenth century, when directed by breezy editors, may abound with yarns and other folk stuff.[3] Literary, family, and sporting weeklies, in vogue in the pre–Civil War years, often contain narratives grounded in folk tradition. Regional periodicals in any period frequently prove reservoirs of local legend and anecdotage. Purveyors of popular humor, from Joe Miller to Laughter Libraries, snare floating fictions. In the formidable storehouse of local and antiquarian history, much traditional matter lies

2. For evidence of horizontal diffusion, see e.g., the list of over three hundred newspapers from which one Vermont paper clipped humorous fiction during the years 1848 to 1858, cited in the *Index to the Burlington Free Press in the Billings Library of the University of Vermont* (Historical Records Survey, Montpelier, Vt., 1940), Vols. 1 to 3, under the classified items "Anecdotes," "Humor," and "Sketches." For an example of vertical perpetuation, consider the legend of the Indian wizard Passaconaway, first publicized by the colonial reporters William Wood and Thomas Morton, reprinted in New Hampshire town histories of Barnstead, Concord, and Manchester, versified in John Farmer and Jacob B. Moore, *Collections, Historical and Miscellaneous* (Concord, 1823), 2: 89–90; revived in Charles F. Beals, *Passaconaway in the White Mountains* (n.p., 1916), pp. 26–51—not to mention popular accounts by Charles M. Skinner, Samuel A. Drake, and G. Waldo Browne.

3. Some instances of recent scholarship that has uncovered folklore in the mid-nineteenth-century press are Levette J. Davidson, "Colorado Folklore," *The Colorado Magazine* 18 (January 1941): 1–13; Philip D. Jordan, "Humor of the Backwoods, 1820–1840," *Mississippi Valley Historical Review* 25 (June 1938): 25–38: Eston E. Ericson, "Folklore and Folkways in the Tarboro (N. C.) *Free Press*, 1824–1850," *Southern Folklore Quarterly* 5 (June 1941): 107–25; Donald Day, "Leaves of Mesquite Grass," in *From Hell to Breakfast* (Austin and Dallas: Texas Folk-Lore Society, 1944), pp. 63–81.

buried. Literature itself, local color or regional in character, provides surprising caches of traveled tales transferred from oral to written narration with few marks of internal injury.

What advantages do printed sources offer the folktale collector that the present-day folk cannot supply? Since the collection of United States tradition has firmly begun only in the twentieth century, opportunity for comparison and analysis of texts over a protracted time interval must depend upon harvests from these older sources. From the irradiating web of nineteenth, and even eighteenth and seventeenth, century printed mediums, earlier instances of tales now gathered orally may be culled, the life history of which is thus extended. Some kinds of folktale appear most capable of detection, or most fully recorded, in printed form, perhaps because the traditional impulse has largely died (for example, the Crockett cycle) or because the stories are too detailed for casual oral rendering (for example, Indian tragedies and Yankee yarns). Still another, if heretical, argument for print adduces the aesthetic superiority of the literary over the verbatim transcript. The rendition of a popular tale by a *Spirit of the Times* correspondent or a local-color writer like Rowland Robinson reproduces the tones and emphases and settings of narrative art more faithfully than the literal transcript divorced from mood and audience, so that the freer translation becomes the more realistic. Finally, the existence of printed texts may well indicate the vitality, persistence, and range of a given tale that eventually forces its way into some avenue of publication. The investigator of United States folk story who restricts himself to what he can gather today cuts himself off from the profitable heritage of the congealed past. Even today printed sources can be profitably used.[4]

4. Although the twentieth-century press defies combing in any manner comparable to that fruitful for the eighteenth and nineteenth, it still continues the journalistic function of disseminating folklore. Clipping books in the Maine State Library at Augusta contain many local legends printed in the weekly feature sections of large city newspapers with rural readers, and woods guides' tall tales collected in lying contests. Locally published booklets today replace the comic almanacs and American Joe Millers as purveyors and conduits of folk humor. Some random examples are: *Jim Bridger's Yarns of the Yellowstone* (n.p., Northern Pacific Railway, 1931); *The 25 Best Lies of 1933* (Burlington, Wis., 1934); *Ed*

If printed texts present certain advantages, they also introduce perplexing problems. How will the folklorist know whether a narrative is folk or literary? In attempting to frame a clear distinction the appraiser soon discovers a sequence of borderline shadings between the polar boundaries.

Some printed texts fulfill all possible folklore criteria. "The Ill-Looking Horse" is a short yarn concerning a sharp Yankee trader who sells a horse to an eager purchaser with the admonition "He don't look very good"; subsequently the buyer discovers the horse is blind. This tale appeared, in a fixed text, in many newspapers in the 1850s. It also turns up in different forms, verse and prose, at later dates, and was orally told to the writer in 1943. Its motif, the horse swap based on a literal statement, dates back to medieval times. On all counts "The Ill-Looking Horse" must pass as folktale.[5]

More challenging is the more elaborate literary tale, not at first sight readily convertible into, or from, oral currency. "How Big Lige Got the Liquor" looks like the typical *Spirit of the Times* Southwestern narrative, complete with steamboat characters, successful saw, exaggerated idiom, and salty detail. The saw involves the securing of whiskey by a penniless customer who asks to have his keg half filled with liquor and then, when refused credit, reluctantly pours the liquor back into the barrel; but since the keg had originally been half filled with water, and the customer had turned it upside down and shaken it vigorously, ostensibly to test the bung, he takes away with him a liquid considerably stronger than what he brought. Was this scene actually witnessed, or simply

---

*Grant's Backwoods Fairy Tales* (Farmington, Me., 1941); Ernest E. Bisbee, *The State o' Maine Scrap Book* (Lancaster, N. H., 1940); the Red River Lumber Company's Paul Bunyan advertising pamphlets.

5. The fixed text of "The Ill-looking Horse" is in *The Yankee Blade* August 2, 1851, credited to the *Boston Post;* the *Burlington Daily Free Press,* May 29, 1868; the *Portland Transcript,* Aug. 9. 1851. Variants can be found in "Pete's Bargain Horse," *The Northern* 2 (March 1923): 16; Marion Blake, "A Hopeless Plight," *The Burlington Free Press and Times,* January 27, 1936; "Defense," *Yankee* 3 (July 1937): 15. See Stith Thompson, *Motif-Index of Folk-Literature,* K 134, "Deceptive horsesale"; Harold W. Thompson, *Body, Boots and Britches* (Philadelphia, 1940) pp. 158–59; Cornelius Weygandt, *November Rowen* (New York and London, 1941), p. 251, for variations on the motif.

imagined, or perhaps drawn from floating lore by the *Spirit* correspondent? Examination discloses that the same trick forms the core for two other mid-nineteenth-century newspaper yarns, for twentieth-century oral tales collected by Cornelius Weygandt in New Hampshire and Harold W. Thompson in New York, for a Berkshire local item, and for an anecdote told by one of Rowland Robinson's Vermont characters[6]—in every case perpetrated by some locally celebrated scapegrace. Clearly then the Big Lige story is a traveling fiction, brother-variant to the bald brief tales orally captured. Other examples of literary folktales can be cited; a *Spirit* piece entitled "The Toughest Gamecock on Record," and Antoine's "windy" in *Danvis Folks* of the pulsating rock, both arch about well-known tall-tale motifs, the aged fowl that defies cooking and the hollow tree that expands and contracts with the breathing of animals inside.[7]

In such tales the narrator uses literary effects to simulate oral art. Newspaper folk humorists in the 1840s and local colorists somewhat later indulge in this kind of transcription: Rowland Robinson and George Wasson employ a liars' bench backdrop to introduce comic yarns and supernatural legends they overheard in Ferrisburgh, Vermont, and Kittery Point, Maine; the jingling ballads of Holman Day and the casual

6. New York *Spirit of the Times,* January 25, 1845, p. 569; ibid., July 27, 1850, p. 266; New York *Atlas,* May 20, 1860; *The Berkshire Hills,* April 1, 1902; Cornelius Weygandt, *The White Hills* (New York, 1934), pp. 144–47, and *New Hampshire Neighbors* (New York, 1937), p. 213; Rowland E. Robinson, *Uncle Lisha's Outing* (Rutland, Vt., 1934), p. 132; Harold W. Thompson, *Body, Boots, and Britches,* pp. 281–82.
7. "The Toughest Gamecock on Record," New York *Spirit of the Times,* April 29, 1848, p. 116; Jonathan F. Kelley, *Dan Marble: A Biographical Sketch* (New York, 1851), pp. 58–60. For other uses of the same motif, see the *Spirit,* June 11, 1836, p. 134; T. R. Hazard, *The Jonny-Cake Letters* (Providence, 1882), pp. 33–36; John A. and Alan Lomax, *Negro Folk Songs as Sung by Lead Belly* (New York, 1936), pp. 108–10.
   Antoine's coon-hunt story of the breathing rock is in Rowland E. Robinson, *Uncle Lisha's Shop* (Rutland, Vt., 1933), pp. 220–21. Cf. "Cale Lyman's Coon Story," New York *Spirit of the Times,* October 10, 1846, p. 389; "Major Brown's Coon Story," clipping in Scrapbook AC 040. I: P873g in the Vermont Historical Society, Montpelier. For twentieth-century oral variants of the breathing tree, see the *Hoosier Folklore Bulletin* 1 (1942): 14, 52–53, 66; *Tennessee Folklore Society Bulletin* 5 (October 1939): 57–58.

free verse of Walter Hard readily lend themselves to village
folk story. These authors, knowing traditions as an integral
part of Maine and Vermont rural life, arrest tales in flight and
permanently record them in aesthetic form.[8]

Where the writer embroiders the folk yarn with added
plot and character portrayal, it draws away from the realm of
folklore and approaches that of pure literature. In "How
Sharp Snaffles Got his Capital and Wife," William Gilmore
Simms has Sharp, a Tennessee mountaineer, ask Mary Ann's
father for her hand and receive a cruel snub because he lacks
capital. So he goes hunting; a flock of geese, caught in a net
he has spread, pull him up in the air as he tries to land them;
the net tangles with the branches of a hollow tree, causing
him to fall into the trunk; he clambers out by hanging onto
the tail of a bear that backs into the hollow; he kills the
bear, finds honey in the tree, and sells bear, geese, and honey
at the market for a substantial sum. He thus becomes a man
of capital and claims Mary Ann. Two familiar American adventures dovetail here, the marvelous hunt and the bear on
the stump.[9] Simms even provides the account with a campfire
yarn-spinning background and faithfully describes the back-
mountain practice of drawing the long bow, presided over
by the "Big Lie," who strictly regulates the storytelling to
see that no raconteur lapses into unvarnished truth. Counter-

8. Storytelling sessions are used as background for folktales by Rowland
Robinson in *Uncle Lisha's Shop* (1887), *Danvis Folks* (1894), and *Uncle
Lisha's Outing* (1897); by George Wasson in *Cap'n Simeon's Store* (1904)
and *Home from Sea* (1908); by Holman Day in "Cy Nye, Prevaricator,"
"Grampy's Lullaby," and "Zek'l Pratt's Hurrycane" in *Up in Maine*
(1900); by Walter Hard in "A Good Investment," "A Romanticist," and
"Weather Change" in *Walter Hard's Vermont* (1941), and *A Mountain
Township* (1933).

9. William Gilmore Simms, "How Sharp Snaffles Got His Capital and
His Wife," *Harper's New Monthly Magazine* 41 (October 1870), 667–87.
Dr. Carvel E. Collins brought this story to my attention. For the marvelous
bag of game, see R. M. Dorson, "Jonathan Draws the Long Bow," *New
England Quarterly* 16 (June 1943): 253–59; and the *Hoosier Folklore
Bulletin* 1 (1942): 20–21, 41–42, 53–54. For the bear, man, and hollow
tree see Antti Aarne and Stith Thompson, "How the Man Came Out of
a Tree Stump," *The Types of the Folk-Tale* (Helsinki, 1928), type 1900;
Thomas C. Haliburton, ed., "Col. Crockett, the Bear and the Swallows,"
*Traits of American Humor* (London, 1852), 1: 301–4; *The Westerners
Brand Book*, no. 9 (December 1944): 7–8.

balancing the folktale elements are the length and the additions encasing the yarn, the beginning and the end, that contrive the plot to secure capital for a wife. In this instance the genre might be termed a literary embellishment or elaboration of a popular tale. The way in which Mark Twain worked up "The Jumping Frog of Calaveras County" from a current hoax-yarn illustrates this literary-folk relationship.[10]

Frequently the writer working close to the fertile mold of American story lore leans more on imagination than on tradition for his composition. That Southwestern classic, "The Big Bear of Arkansas," displays many earmarks of United States folktale: it enjoyed wide exchange popularity; it presents a Mississippi screamer telling large fictions to an awed assembly; its main theme, an extraordinary bear hunt, is a favorite backwoods story-topic; several minor "windies" tossed off by Jim Doggett are common tall tales. Nevertheless the piece as a whole seems to belong to creative literature. It has circulated only in one set text, under the known authorship of Thomas B. Thorpe. Its fame derives from literary qualities —the lushly painted backdrop of a Mississippi River steamboat crowd, the subtly recorded give-and-take of yarner and audience, the effervescence and Chaucerian poetry in Doggett's narrative. If this is a fine depiction of the method and manner of frontier fictionizing, the scene is generalized, the type characters (the half-horse half-alligator, the English traveler, the contentious Hoosier) fall close to caricature, and the climactic yarn of the bear hunt appears deliberately conceived. Before launching into his major Arkansas wonder, Jim lets fly preliminary marvels that are traveled tales—the turkey so fat it bursts open; the fast-growing corn that kills a sleeping sow—but until variant texts of the "unhuntable b'ar" fiction turn up, Thorpe's writing remains an individual property, sown with traditional elements.[11]

10. For precursors of "Jim Smiley and His Jumping Frog," see "Frogs Shot with Powder," New York *Spirit of the Times*, May 26, 1855, p. 170; Oscar Lewis, *The Origin of The Celebrated Jumping Frog of Calaveras County* (San Francisco, 1931).
11. Actually a case can be made for resemblances between Thorpe's story and the well-known folktale "The Bear's Son," the most famous rendering of which is in "Beowulf," but which appears all over the world.

If folktales ascend into literature, so literary stories descend into popular tradition, when they suit the needs of oral narration and folk fancy. Let the composed tale employ congenial motifs, avoid description, abstraction, stylistic peculiarities, offer attractive horror or humor, and it well may lose its identity in folk retellings. This kind of process affected at least one Southwestern journalistic story, "Cousin Sally Dilliard," the literary introduction of which was sloughed off in the oral rendering.[12] William Austin employed the recurrent supernatural motif of the retributive curse in "Peter Rugg, the Missing Man," so convincingly that it passed immediately into New England local legendry, varying in its details but consistent in the report of a frenzied traveler whipping his horses in a ceaseless search for the road to Boston.[13] Yet another composition by Austin purporting to be traditional failed to fool the folk; "The Man with the Cloaks: A Vermont Legend," in its conceit of the stony-hearted miser who could not warm himself with three hundred and sixty-five cloaks until he had performed an act of kindness, did not accord with American experience. Tall tales embroider facts, supernatural legends explain natural mysteries, but Märchen and myths describe a magical universe that strikes little response in United States folk wisdom, which accordingly

---

See Friedrich Panzer, *Beowulf* (Munich, 1910). Both plots have the following motifs in common: a greatly feared monster; attack by a superior hunter; his underwater descent, via a rope, in order to grapple with the monster; the appearance of a second, she-monster which he kills; his return above to find himself deserted by his companions.

12. Upon the modern reprinting of "Cousin Sally Dilliard" by Franklin J. Meine in his *Tall Tales of the Southwest*, he received the following comment from Ed Carter, a septuagenarian of Keokuk, Iowa: "My grandmother used to recite a long rigamarole beginning 'Captain Rice he gin a treat and asked Cousin Sally Dilliard if she won't go' and ending 'my wife, like a dam fool, just histed her skirts and waded across.' I always thought it was a true story of her girlhood days in southern Indiana. Imagine the thrill I got in reading it in *Tall Tales*. So she must have read it down at Greenville, across the river from Louisville, when it was a popular story, and committed it to memory, to be recited to her grandchildren years after."

13. See Amy Lowell, *Legends* (Boston and New York, 1931), pp. 13, 238–52. "A true legend it was to me, however, long before I knew its origin and as such I have treated it, with the result that my version is quite unlike Mr. Austin's" (p. xiii)

accepts Munchausen and rejects Grimm. Those literary writings that descend, like Irving's "The Devil and Tom Walker," apparently must fit a preconceived pattern of American yarning.[14] Where this process occurs, the original narrative can be described as the literary parent of a folktale, but the offsring must be accounted live folklore.

When the germinal folklore dwindles and the created elements of drama and characters, symbolism and descriptive settings, completely dwarf it, the battle of invention over tradition, of the literary over the folk, may fairly be said to have been won. Still connections remain, and James Hall, Stephen Vincent Benét, and Nathaniel Hawthorne all draw inspiration, at any rate, from the fiction of legend. Hall, the early Midwestern writer, elaborates upon well-founded motifs: the deathless White Steed of the Prairies, the location of buried treasure by a hazel divining rod, and in a particularly authentic manner, the breaking of a witch spell by a backwoodsman shooting a silver bullet. In such pieces, which consciously preserve historical accuracy, Hall intrudes personal commentary, strives jerkily for style, and forces romantic plots in an Irvingesque way that quite rends the fabric of legend. For example, the backwoodsman Pete Featherton is genuine Crockett, and the witch-spell incident good local superstition, but their combination in one story juxtaposes incongruously the comic saga hero with village supernaturalism.

Although Benét takes even more creative liberties, he simulates far more convincingly the manner of folk yarn in his fluent, conversational delivery. In "Daniel Webster and the Sea Serpent," the luster given Webster savors of American comic myth making, and the activities of the sea serpent follow an honored New England hoax. So the statesman's unintentional amorous conquest of the creature, which swims up the Potomac when Daniel leaves New Hampshire for Washington and coos for him nightly, until bought off with a commission in the United States navy, smacks mightily of tall-tale fiction. But the piece is replete with sly political innuendo; it is too long, too subtle, too devious, too elegant, for folk ren-

14. Notice how readily Irving's tale fits into the collection of local legends made by Charles M. Skinner, *Myths and Legends of Our Own Land* (Philadelphia and London, 1896), 1: 275–79.

dition; in particular, the characters neither of Webster nor of
the sea serpent fit into established myth, for the one has never
been a folktale hero, and the other is never endowed with
anthropomorphic qualities. Similarly an analysis of Benét's
well-known story of "The Devil and Daniel Webster" shows
a nugget of genuine folklore—the covenant between the Fiend
and a sinner who trades his soul for gold—wrenched from tradition and turned into a pivot for a literary fantasy.

None of the moralistic romances of Hawthorne can be
mistaken for legends, although he retains local roots and
supernatural phenomena. What folk transcription could reproduce the symbolism of "The Great Carbuncle" or "Young
Goodman Brown"? For the long-time resident of Concord,
Lenox, and Salem, the attraction of regional legends lay in
their blend of the prosaic with the intangible and the conse-
quent opportunity they afforded to "frame a tale with a deep
moral" rooted in disturbing human experience.[15] This genre,
exemplified by these authors, might be categorized simply as
literature that incorporates traditional themes or incidents,
but remains in its art form. Such usage should not affect one
way or other the belletristic achievement, although obviously
the writer is trying to extract certain appeals of folklore for
his own offering. For the literary historian this last relationship has particular interest in indicating one aspect of literary
nationalism, the deliberate use of regional lore as materials
for creative prose, poetry, and drama—as well for the other
fine arts.[16]

15. Good examples of his short stories that expand New England fictional legends into "philosophic romances" (his own description of "The
Maypole of Merry Mount") are "The Minister's Black Veil," "The Great
Carbuncle," and "The Gray Champion," based on local traditions about
the Reverend Joseph Moody of York, Maine, the mysterious gem of the
White Mountains, and the regicides Goffe and Whalley. "Young Goodman Brown" differs in employing generalized witchlore, and "The Ambitious Guest" in elaborating upon historical tradition. Hawthorne's
acquaintance with rural Munchausens is shown in "The Village Uncle."
16. Foreign literatures with roots in romances, sagas, *volkslieder*, popular
ballads, *fabliaux*, *novelle*, Märchen and *Sagen* present similar problems
in far more intensified form. For some revealing comments on the art
fairy tale, for example, see Robert M. Waerner, *Romanticism and the
Romantic School in Germany* (New York and London, 1910), pp. 252–79,
which discusses the literary Märchen of Ludwig Tieck and Friedrich
Novalis.

One need only to consider the better-known collections
of folklish literature from the United States to appreciate the
need for adequately defining the popular tale. In his *Tall
Tales of the Southwest* (1930), Franklin J. Meine gathers
the cream of Southwestern antebellum journalistic humor;
the selections invariably lie close to folk tradition, in their
portrayal of backwoods types, customs, roguery, eccentricities,
but only specific case studies can determine which are floating
yarns. A different complex of material is mined for virtually
the same region and period by Arthur Palmer Hudson in
*Humor of the Old Deep South* (1936), which rifles all manner
of writings, subliterary and subhistorical, depicting frontier
society without, however, attempting to isolate fact from fiction, or fiction from folklore. The *Body, Boots and Britches*
(1940) of Harold W. Thompson consciously seeks traditional
narrative but largely bypasses printed sources, thus avoiding
the troublesome queries, and ample rewards, involved in their
use.[17] At the other pole, a recent ambitious approach accepts
the most varied printed literature as folk stuff, without achiev-
ing the most rudimentary synthesis. B. A. Botkin's *A Treasury
of American Folklore* (1944) observes an extreme eclecticism,
discarding any restrictions by period, region, genre, culture
group, or source type. Since the editor expressly disclaims
any intention to distinguish between tradition and invention, the book belies its title, and presents fictions wrenched
from, or unconnected with, a context of community life.[18]
These treasuries offer riches of frontier, oral and popular

17. For one example, Thompson presents current tall tales about Joe
Call, the Keeseville strong man, but these can be found in old newspapers (*Burlington Daily Free Press*, January 6, 1849: "Joe Call, the
modern Hercules"). Frontier humor in the ante-bellum press exhibits
Yorkers; the *Spirit of the Times* contains some fine York State yarns.
18. Types of non-folklore or dubious material that Botkin includes are:
embroidered hero stories (Carl Carmer, Jeremiah Digges, Glen Rounds);
ante-bellum journalism (Crockett almanacs, J. M. Field, C. F. M.
Noland); individual authors (Alfred Henry Lewis, Washington Irving,
William Austin); sober accounts of historical characters (Johnny Appleseed, Buffalo Bill, Wild Bill Hickok) unsound collectors (Elizabeth F.
Reynard, Charles M. Skinner); biographical anecdote, local puffery, urban
jokes.

literature, but sifted too loosely or too finely for the American folklorist.

That a beginning may be made toward delimiting the province of United States folk narrative, agreement must come on usable definitions and acceptable evidence. To determine whether the printed tale belongs to folklore, the searcher can apply certain tests. Is the tale readily convertible into an oral version? Does it provide internal evidence of previous traditional life? Does external evidence, in the form of known variants or data on its circulation, indicate that this is a floating story? Do its structural traits resemble the persistent motifs of world folk literature? By such checks he may succeed in wresting twice-told tales from their printed crannies, and separate folk soil from its literary flowering. But at all odds let us recognize that in the United States the electric currents of tradition flow through a grid of mechanical as well as human circuits.

# 11

## The Identification of Folklore in American Literature

Folklore can no longer be gainsaid as an instrument of literary analysis. Some forty articles have appeared since 1937 in American folklore journals discussing relationships of folk material to literary works. Similar studies occasionally appear in literary quarterlies and in book-length studies of individual authors. American writers credited with using folklore include Conrad Aiken, Bill Arp, James Fenimore Cooper, Stephen Crane, Emily Dickinson, Ralph Waldo Emerson, William Faulkner, Benjamin Franklin, Robert Frost, George Washington Harris, Joel Chandler Harris, James Hall, Bret Harte, Nathaniel Hawthorne, Washington Irving, Sylvester Judd, John Pendleton Kennedy, Henry Wadsworth Longfellow, Herman Melville, Eugene O'Neill, James Kirke Paulding, Julia Peterkin, Marjorie Kinnan Rawlings, Conrad Richter, Irwin Russell, Carl Sandburg, Harden E. Taliaferro, John Greenleaf Whittier, Thomas Wolfe. In her seminal work, *American*

From *Journal of American Folklore*, 1957.

*Humor,* Constance Rourke analyzed the impact of American popular lore on such major artists as Walt Whitman, Edgar Allan Poe, and even Henry James. Other students of American humor have called attention to both the literary and the folklore qualities in the antebellum Southern humorists. My own *Jonathan Draws the Long Bow* considers seven New England writers, besides Whittier, who drew upon folk themes. Some scattered articles in the folklore journals deal with Byron, Chaucer, Milton, Southey, Spenser, and Yeats, but these journals are primarily devoted to American folklore, and studies of folk elements in foreign, classical, or medieval literatures must be sought elsewhere.

While the mere bulk of this recent scholarship must impress the observer, a closer scrutiny soon dispels the idea that a substantial case has been made for the thorough impregnation of American literature by an indigenous folklore. Too many of these studies fail to demonstrate the presence of folklore in creative writings. They employ the concept of folklore in so fuzzy and loose a fashion that it soon loses any precise meaning. A more successful group of these analyses adequately perceives folklore in literary dress, but then fails to render any meaningful judgment about this discovery. So what if an author does employ proverbs or similes or lyrics known to folklore collectors?

The first need, then, is to establish clearly and demonstrably that novels, short stories, poems or plays incorporate folk materials. The second desideratum is to show that this folklore offers new insights into our understanding of creative writing.

Three flaws impair the attempts hitherto made to identify the oral traditions used by American authors. Some critics confuse *folk* with *folklore,* and convey the impression that any writer dealing with the people of a distinctive region, say the deep South or the Middle Border, or even the ethnic groups in a metropolis, therefore describes *folkways* or *folk culture,* or *folklore.* This confusion mars the flimsy survey-articles by Leisy and Davidson, and the giant bibliography of Haywood. Davidson equates *the people* with the *folk,* and regards such naturalistic novelists as Farrell and Steinbeck, or realistic poets like Sandburg and Frost, who concentrate on the common man, as somehow indebted to folklore. Only those artists who weave tales about high society, or about animals, would on this reasoning fail to include folk elements. Leisy carries the same viewpoint to even more lengths. Cooper "created our first folk hero in Leatherstocking"; Longfellow's poem *Evangeline* "introduces enough Acadian folk beliefs to make the reputation of an ordinary folklorist"; *The Grapes of Wrath* "truly is a folk book if ever there was one"; "Robert Frost has written about folks all his life. . . . It is not unnatural that he has made out of the legend of Paul Bunyan a story as beautiful as a Greek legend." Must we explain that a novelist does not create folk heroes, unless his characters pass into oral tradition? And so far no one has collected tales about Leatherstocking. Steinbeck's novel is as literary and nonfolk a work as any ever written. Longfellow draws upon purely literary sources for his conventional folk motifs. Frost also went to print for his Paul Bunyan poem, and in this case he selected an artificial episode about a character more fake than folk. Holmes, according to Leisy, "was not the stuff out of which folk writers are made"; actually in one poem Holmes retells a plot familiar in Yankee humor, and in another utilizes a romantic legend of Marblehead.[1]

A series of essays in the *Southern Folklore Quarterly* by John M. Maclachlan purports to consider folk concepts in the novels of Faulkner, Caldwell, and Wolfe. They belong in a sociological rather than a folklore journal, for they say nothing about the familiar categories of folk tradition and deal tortuously with aspects of Southern society reflected in the fiction of the three authors.

A second criticism of methods presently used to analyze folklore in literature concerns more sophisticated treatments, which do isolate folk items. In these treatments, proverbial sayings, expressions, and similes rank first among the types of folklore extracted, probably because they are easiest to cull. Customs and folkways, superstitions and beliefs, come next;

1. See the comparative references to Holmes's poems, "How the Old Horse Won the Bet" and "Agnes," in Dorson, *Jonathan Draws The Long Bow* p. 8, n. 7; p. 22, n. 10.

frontier humor, in the form of tall tales, boasts, hoaxes, and comic folktypes, follows; the use of folkloristic themes, like the Devil, receives occasional attention; and at the bottom, surprisingly, fall the categories of folktale and folksong. Too many of these articles, however, simply list supposedly traditional items with no attempt to prove their folk quality. Figh sets down a number of "folk sayings" found in Bill Arp's writings, with the comment that their frequent recurrence in his humorous prose indicates Arp heard them in daily talk. Perhaps so, but the folksy sound and feel of a phrase cannot justify a claim for traditional usage. Ivan Walton asserts the presence of folklore and folkways of the sea in the plays of Eugene O'Neill, simply by quoting passages from the plays relating to nautical matters. Anything that a sailor does, whether grumble, drink, or fornicate, is a "folkway." Walton fails to provide a solitary reference to any collection of sailor folklore, and his article actually demonstrates the paucity of seafaring traditions in O'Neill's work.

Collectors as well as critics publish materials without providing the necessary annotation that involves tedious search through glossaries, indexes, field reports, town histories, and any other available sources. But at least the field collector knows that his contributions come from speakers, while the library collector can never be sure, without proper documentation, that his author has not invented, improved, or adapted from other authors his proverbs, tales, and songs. In an intriguing study, involving correspondence with a number of contemporary Southern writers, Arthur Palmer Hudson has shown how they have frequently made up "traditional" ballads, or even borrowed them from scholarly sources, to supply local color. A careful inquiry into the proverbs Benjamin Franklin set down in *The Way to Wealth* revealed two classes, traditional and created. Gallacher then analyzed the success of Poor Richard in coining pithy saws, by tracing their subsequent history, to see which caught the folk fancy and themselves became traditional. Only this kind of comparative documentation can separate folk property from literary productions. The catalog of plots, songs, riddles, and beliefs in the Uncle Remus stories, compiled by Stella Brookes in her

study of *Joel Chandler Harris: Folklorist,* or the list of superstitions in Mark Twain made by Victor West, amount to little
more than clerical exercises. When the Uncle Remus tales
are evaluated against the collected repertoire of American
Negro folk narrative, the observer soon sees that Harris has
portrayed only one segment of a richly diversified lore. Since
collectors themselves followed the lead of Harris and sought
for Brer Rabbit stories, the critic may here easily be misled
even by the field records, and must know the entire bibliography of Negro folktales.

A third fault in the studies under consideration arises
from too ready an accepance of the Rourke thesis. Constance
Rourke ingeniously traced the vogue of the spare Yankee and
the Western roarer in nineteenth-century almanacs, jokebooks, newspapers, periodicals, and plays, and she maintained
that the two figures worked their way from the humble layers
of popular literature up into the fiction of masters. Later
scholars have expanded her interpretation. Richard Chase
finds Melville steeped in frontier humor, a revelation Bernard
DeVoto had earlier reported for Mark Twain. Ahab's quest
for Moby Dick raises to an epic level the frontiersman's hunt
for fabulous game; *The Confidence-Man* brilliantly fuses the
down-East pedlar and the Mississippi screamer in its title
character. Daniel G. Hoffman argued for the appearance of the
two character types in Washington Irving's "The Legend of
Sleepy Hollow" as early as 1819; Ichabod Crane is the pawky
Yankee, and Brom Bones the blustery frontiersman. Several
commentators emphasize the close relationship of the Southwestern humorists, George W. Harris, Johnson J. Hooper,
William T. Thompson and their fellows, to oral comic traditions of the backwoods.[2]

A major misconception has sprouted in this body of
folk-criticism. The humorous vein of the Crockett almanacs,
Jack Downing and Sam Slick, the New York *Spirit of the
Times,* Simon Suggs and Sut Lovingood, belongs to popular
literature and not to folklore. To say that the spirit of Davy
Crockett and Sam Slick breathes in *The Confidence-Man* or in

2. James H. Penrod has most recently pursued this thesis in articles in
the *Tennessee Folklore Society Bulletin.*

"The Legend of Sleepy Hollow" is not to say that Melville and Irving therefore have assimilated American folklore. The almanac tales of Davy Crockett, the comic letters by Seba Smith and Thomas Haliburton, and the picaresque narratives by Hooper and Harris are sophisticated compositions, written for and responsive to a popular audience, but nevertheless literary products, striated with oral folk humor. A recent attempt by Penrod to pin down the folk elements in *Sut Lovingood* reveals the difficulty of isolating those strains. Some samples of mountaineer speech, of rough pranks of the backwoods, of tall-tale hyperbole, and the case is ended. Several antebellum writers of the Longstreet group do display a provable debt to folk sources, but each author, and even each sketch, needs to be judged individually. Taliaferro in his book of North Carolina scenes includes tall tales and proverbial sayings set in a storytelling frame, clearly in the oral style, and known in variant forms to collectors. No other journalist of the Old Deep South, however, contains so many nuggets of nearly pure folklore. Before a rough practical joke or hoax performed in the backwoods can qualify as a folk tradition, a pedigree of oral and popular repetition must be supplied, in the manner that Whiting has rendered for the Royal Nonesuch episode in *Huckleberry Finn*.

The whole literature of early American humor needs far closer scrutiny before this humor can be equated with folklore. Many of the tales and sketches which first appeared in the New York *Spirit of the Times* and were subsequently published in book form are composed pieces. Many other tales, these chiefly uncollected and buried in library files, are traditional. They can be easily recognized as folktales, in spite of some literary touches, and assigned to types and motifs.[3] We know that the doctors, lawyers, travelers, and other educated Easterners in the backcountry wrote up comic and eccentric scenes they witnessed, but whether they wrote fiction or folk-

3. See e.g., Arthur K. Moore, "Specimens of the Folktales from Some Antebellum Newspapers of Louisiana," *Louisiana Historical Quarterly,* 32 (1949) : 723–58; and Dorson's "Jonathan Draws the Long Bow," *New England Quarterly,* 16 (1943) : 244–79, and "Yorker Yarns of Yore," *New York Folklore Quarterly,* 3 (1947) : 5–27.

lore, humor or tragedy, cannot be determined with any one sweeping answer.[4]

Constance Rourke and such able scholars as Meine and Blair and Hudson unearth popular and folk humor so successfully that other strands of early printed folklore are now neglected. The dark and somber theme of supernatural legends merits as much attention as the current of humorous exaggeration in our literary and subliterary history. To revert to "The Legend of Sleepy Hollow," we can see this darker tradition clearly revealed, and with an evident appreciation of its vitality in chimney-corner and village-store gossip, in the following passage.

But all these were nothing to the tales of ghosts and apparitions that succeeded. The neighborhood is rich in legendary treasures of the kind. Local tales and superstitions thrive best in these sheltered long-settled retreats; but are trampled under foot by the shifting throng that forms the population of most of our country places. Besides, there is no encouragement for ghosts in most of our villages, for they have scarcely had time to finish their first nap, and turn themselves in their graves, before their surviving friends have travelled away from the neighborhood; so that when they turn out at night to walk their rounds, they have no acquaintance left to call upon. This is perhaps the reason why we so seldom hear of ghosts except in our long-established Dutch communities.

The immediate cause, however, of the prevalence of supernatural stories in these parts, was doubtless owing to the vicinity of Sleepy Hollow. There was a contagion in the very air that blew from that haunted region; it breathed forth an atmosphere of dreams and fancies infecting all the land. Several of the Sleepy Hollow people were present at Van Tassel's, and, as usual, were doling out their wild and wonderful legends. Many dismal tales were told about funeral trains, and mourning cries

4. Louis J. Budd has emphasized the genteel aspects of Southern antebellum humor in "Gentlemanly Humorists of the Old South," *Southern Folklore Quarterly* 17 (1953): 232–40.

and wailings heard and seen about the great tree where the unfortunate Major André was taken, and which stood in the neighborhood. Some mention was made also of the woman in white, that haunted the dark glen at Raven Rock, and was often heard to shriek on winter nights before a storm, having perished there in the snow. The chief part of the stories, however, turned upon the favorite spectre of Sleepy Hollow, the headless horseman, who had been heard several times of late, patrolling the country; and, it was said, tethered his horse nightly among the graves in the churchyard.[5]

No one unfamiliar with village storytelling habits could have written those lines. Hawthorne, Whittier, and James Hall similarly draw from the rich reservoir of supernatural place legends. We have as yet no studies demonstrating the influence of legendry on American literature.

How can the literary critic satisfactorily establish the relationship of a given work to folk tradition? Three principal kinds of evidence can be afforded.

An author may be shown through *biographical evidence* to have enjoyed direct contact with oral lore. In his notebooks Hawthorne records conversations with old residents on Star Island who told him legends about buried treasure and haunted spots.[6] In one informative preface Joel Chandler Harris describes his experience at a Southern railroad station where he found himself suddenly in the midst of a storytelling Negro circle.[7] By contrast, Longfellow never lived among Indians, and read the improved narratives Schoolcraft had set down in his noteooks. Both Harris and Longfellow treated their materials artistically, but the stories of Harris are vitally related to Negro folklore and indeed are cited in the comparative notes of collectors, while the Indian legends in *The Song of Hiawatha* possess no ethnographic value, if considerable literary interest. The lives of Melville and Mark Twain,

5. In *Washington Irving*, ed. Henry A. Pochmann (New York, 1934), pp. 163–64.
6. *The American Notebooks by Nathaniel Hawthorne*, ed. Randall Stewart (New Haven, 1932), pp. 261–62, 267.
7. *Nights with Uncle Remus* (Boston and New York, 1883), pp. xii-xiv.

now richly documented, touch oral lore at many points. Daniel G. Hoffman has recently shown that Stephen Crane pursued New Jersey legends for newspaper articles.

A curious sidelight in American literary history involves the relationship of various American authors to the old Chicago Folklore Society. This organization, founded by Lieutenant Fletcher Bassett of the United States Navy, flourished briefly but vigorously in the 1890s, and invited leading local color writers to present papers and to become members. The files of the society contain letters from Hamlin Garland, George Washington Cable, Joel Chandler Harris, Mary Hartwell Catherwood, Joseph Kirkland, Harriet Monroe, Harry Stillwell Edwards, Will N. Harben, and Will Allen Dromgoole. Harris writes he is too shy to speak publicly, Cable knows no Negro folklore, Whittier refers to the specter ship of Salem, Catherwood states her use of oral legends from Mackinac Island, Kirkland and Edwards promise to give papers, Garland says he has spoken on the Indian Acoma dance. This correspondence proves that some late-nineteenth-century authors understood the concept of folklore and its usefulness for their craft.

By chance, I can offer several case examples of contemporary fiction writers who seek oral traditions in their localities. Paul Green, whose plays, pageants, and short stories show a perceptive interest in folk life, has driven around his state on collecting trips and donated his materials to the Frank C. Brown Archives of North Carolina Folklore. One evening in Chapel Hill, where Green lives, I heard him deliver a cascade of local tales, picked up from the county clerk or a Negro farmer or a fishing companion. With growing amazement I tape-recorded the humorous and pithy yarns that Green poured forth in a silvery flow. Some were recognizable folktales—one indeed is the only variant I know for a Negro preacher jest I collected in Mississippi—but Green made no distinction between the traveling fiction and the actual or embroidered incident; he listened to his townsmen with the ear of the artist, not of the classifier. On my tape lies the most splendid proof for the immersion of a talented writer in the wells of folk tradition. Yet the next steps in my proposed method will show that folklore does not strongly shape Green's genius.

During my field trip into the Upper Peninsula of Michigan in 1946, I met John Voelker, a lawyer in Ishpeming who has written two fine collections of short-story sketches about his country. He knew the notorious legends and fabulous characters of the Peninsula and took me calling on an effervescent Cousin Jack, Dave Spencer, who erupted tales, songs, and rhymes before us in a local tavern. Subsequently I included a ballad Dave sang in my book of Upper Peninsula folklore, and Voelker wove it into one of his sketches.[8] A good deal of lore creeps into his fiction, the genuine, rugged, turbulent lore of this bypassed frontier, but few readers outside the Peninsula recognize this strain in Voelker's work, and continue to associate northern Michigan folklore with insipid and sentimental Indian legends. So little did publishers understand his purposes that they suggested he rework his lively episodes into a streamlined novel.

Where Green and Voelker drench themselves in the traditional history of their land, without wondering in academic fashion whether they are hearing folklore, Julian Lee Rayford actually set out to collect in the field and transmute his collectanea into literary pieces. Rayford had already written one novel about his birth city, Mobile, Alabama, and another on Mike Fink, the king of the Mississippi keelboatmen, that drew from oral data he secured on a trip down the Mississippi.[9] Becoming consciously aware of folklore, Rayford settled down for a summer in the fishing port of Bayou la Batre on the Gulf coast in 1947 and filled his notebook with tales and beliefs. This material he used as the basis for literary

8. See Robert Traver (Voelker's pen name), *Danny and the Boys* (Cleveland and New York, 1951), p. 176, and my *Bloodstoppers and Bearwalkers* (Cambridge, Mass., 1952), pp. 106–7. Voelker's other work is *Troubleshooter* (New York, 1944).

9. Rayford's novels are *Cottonmouth* (New York, 1941) and *Child of the Snapping Turtle, Mike Fink* (New York, 1951). The latter work was issued with a recording of Mississippi songs and chants collected and sung by Rayford. He also has published "An Incident of the Nativity as It Might Be Seen through the Eyes of a Negro Preacher," *The First Christmas Dinner* (Mobile, 1947).

stories he sent off to magazines, but their editors showed little sympathy or interest in fiction based on folklore.

Besides biographical information, a second technique available to the folk critic proceeds from *internal evidence* in the literary composition itself, that indicates direct familiarity of the author with folklore. This evidence includes the alleged folktales, folksongs, folk sayings, or folk customs imbedded in literature, and their settings as well. A bookish writer may easily incorporate folk materials into his productions from his reading, but he can never plausibly describe a storytelling scene without having known and observed it at firsthand. Collectors almost invariably concentrate on texts and omit accounts of informants or the milieu, and in any case they lack the skill of novelists in depicting the folk background. The novelist may draw upon their hoard, but he cannot borrow their eyes. For skillfully etched pictures of American rural raconteurs and their audiences, read William Gilmore Simms's Tennessee mountain story of "How Sharp Snaffles Got His Capital and His Wife," or the Vermont sketches of Rowland Robinson in *Uncle Lisha's Shop,* or the Maine coastal vignettes George S. Wasson unfolded in *Cap'n Simeon's Store,* or certain Pine Tree Ballads of Holman Day, or Hawthorne's New England tale of "The Village Uncle." The very titles of their volumes reveal the focus of Robinson and Wasson on a favorite gathering place where villagers gossip and yarn and drift irresistibly into narrative jousts, with one longbow topping another. Early humorists continually employed the framework device to introduce a tale within a tale; in the frontier classic by T. B. Thorpe, "The Big Bear of Arkansas," a garrulous backwoodsman launches into his hunting epic before an entranced steamboat audience. The writings of Mark Twain, who had an especially keen ear for the rhythms and inflections of oral tales, are strewn with yarnspinners.

This internal evidence can take other forms besides that of storytelling scenes. The passage already quoted from "The Legend of Sleepy Hollow" Irving must have based upon personal observation. His comments that only the long-inhabited Dutch homes possessed ghosts, and that a mobile culture rends the fabric of community tradition, show keen insight into folklore processes. A century later a treatise on "The Ghosts of New York" would confirm his inductions.[10] The novels about Gullah Negro life by Julia Peterkin contain so much intimate detail of the sort cultural anthropologists have since reported, that we are ready to credit her primary knowledge of Negro folk beliefs in hoodoo, "cunjers," signs, and spirits.

Finding a likely piece of folklore properly set in an authentic social situation, or woven naturally into the speech and manners of regional characters, does not terminate the quest of the folk critic. He must prove that the saying, tale, song, or custom inside the literary work possesses an independent traditional life. In other words, our critic must present *corroborative evidence* to supplement his proofs from biographical and internal evidence. We can say, for example, that Rowland Robinson grew up in Vermont and knew the village folk intimately, and that he has adeptly protrayed in fiction the down-East mode of storytelling. But Thorpe's "The Big Bear of Arkansas" describes a frontier fabulist, and yet the tale he tells is no folktale, but a literary invention. Jim Doggett's elaborate narrative has no counterparts among our thousands of field-collected texts, although curiously it shows some parallelism with Beowulf. The windies spun by Uncle Lisha, Sam Lovel, Antoine Bassette and the lesser members of Robinson's yarnspinning circle follow the main themes, types, and motifs of indigenous American and especially New England traditions: hunting and fishing tall tales, local legends of buried treasure and haunted crime-spots, anecdotes of eccentric characters. The French-Canadian wag, Antoine Bassette, speaks in dialect and narrates *contes* about the *loup-garou* strangely at variance with Yankee yarns, but firmly consistent with his own tradition. Indeed, Robinson has caught the mingling of folktale repertoires that flourishes along national borders, a phenomenon rarely observed by folklorists in the field. In northern New England and the Great Lakes states, French-Canadian folk culture, nourished from the province of Quebec, has spilled over into the United

10. By Louis C. Jones in *Journal of American Folklore* 57 (1944) : 249, who concludes, "For ghostlore to thrive one needs a section that has been settled for a considerable length of time, where the houses are old, and at least a fair share of the population is permanent."

States. We can document Robinson's tales with extensive parallels from the New England area, lodged in obscure printed sources and recent field collections which he could never have seen. Irresistible evidence demonstrates the presence of valid folklore in the Green Mountain sketches of blind Rowland Robinson.

On the other hand, internal and corroborative evidence fail to support the inference that Paul Green, immersed in North Carolina oral traditions, therefore incorporates much folklore in his Southern stories. In two volumes of these stories, *Dog on the Sun* and *Salvation on a String,* Green looks into the lives of Negro laborers and white sharecroppers, with passion and pity and powerful insight. Unlike say Voelker, he sees few comic legends growing in his country, and many harsh and hopeless realities. A mere handful of touches suggests folk tradition. The renowned strong man, who intimidates a challenging bully by striding up the road with a cow under one arm and a calf under the other, recalls equivalent figures in both Negro and white folktales. Sometimes the hero bluffs his opponent by casual reference to his forthcoming feats of strength, and again he actually tosses a horse and his rider over a fence.[11] This incident plays only a passing part in Green's plot, but the main episode too, where Zeke Broadhuss loses his britches on the point of testifying at the height of the revival, smacks of many village yarns about local eccentrics. Corroborative and internal evidence both indicate "The Ghost in the Tree" as an historical legend dating back to Civil War times. A noted raconteur tells a fireside circle a revolting tradition, of how Yankee soldiers hung to a persimmon tree the little son of their host; ever after the boy's ghost was seen shinning up the tree.[12] Negro hoodoo and ritual magic underlie the macabre fantasy of "Supper for the Dead."

11. Compare the title story in *Salvation on a String and Other Tales of the South* (New York and London, 1946), pp. 5–6, with "The Fight" in Dorson's *Negro Folktales in Michigan* (Cambridge, Mass., 1956), pp. 55–56, 210, n. 23.

12. The internal evidence lies in the plausibility of the story-telling scene within the story, and of the localized Confederate legend; the corroborative evidence lies in the familiar motif at the heart of the legend, E275, "Ghosts haunts place of great accident or misfortune."

These examples virtually exhaust the instances in which Green relies on folk narratives. I suspect that other celebrated community traditions assimilated by Green might qualify as folklore, if collectors would spread a wider net, and record oral history as well as oral fiction.

The method outlined here should serve to identify reasonably and clearly the presence of folklore in literature. Once we can prove that authors have directly dipped into the flowing streams of folk tradition, we are then in a position to discuss whether or not this folklore contributes to a given literary work in any important way.

## Additional References

Other works consulted in the preparation of this essay include the following:

### General

Brown, Sterling. "In the American Grain." *Vassar Alumnae Magazine* 36 (1951): 5-9.

Leisy, Ernest E. "Folklore in American Prose." *Saturday Review of Literature* 34 (21 July 1951): 6–7, 32.

———. "Folklore in American Literature." *College English* 8 (1946): 122–29.

———. "Literary Versions of American Folk Materials." *Western Folklore* 7 (1948) : 43–49.

Matthiessen, F. O. "American Demigods." In *American Renaissance,* pp. 635–45. New York, 1941.

Rourke, Constance. *American Humor* New York, 1931.

### Regional

Davidson, Levette J. "Folk Elements in Midwestern Literature." *Western Humanities Review* 3 (1949): 187–95.

Dorson, Richard. "Literary Folktales." In *Jonathan Draws the Long Bow,* ch. 6. Cambridge, Mass., 1946.

Hudson, Arthur P. "The Singing South, Folksong in Recent Fiction." *Sewanee Review,* July 1936; reprinted for North Carolina Folklore Council, Chapel Hill, pp. [3]–30.

Johnson, Guy B. "Folk Values in Recent Literature on the Negro." *Folk-Say, A Regional Miscellany* (1930) : 359–72.

Law, Robert A. "Notes on Some Recent Treatments of Negro Folk-Lore." *Texas Folklore Society Publication* 7 (*Follow de Drinkin' Gou'd,* 1928) : 140–44.

Penrod, James H. "The Folk Hero as Prankster in the Old South-
western Yarns." *Kentucky Folklore Record* 2 (1956) : 5–12.
———. "The Folk Mind in Early Southwestern Humor." *Tennessee
Folklore Society Bulletin* 18 (June 1952): 49–54.
———. "Folk Motifs in Old Southwestern Humor." *Southern Folk-
lore Quarterly* 19 (1955) : 117–24.
Yates, Irene. "A Collection of Proverbs and Proverbial Sayings from
South Carolina Literature." *Southern Folklore Quarterly* 11
(1947): 187–99.

## Individual Authors
### Aiken
Hoffman, Daniel G. "Poetic Symbols from the Public Domain."
*Southern Folklore Quarterly* 12 (1948) : 293–97.

### Arp
Figh, Margaret G. "Tall Talk and Folk Sayings in Bill Arp's
Works." *Southern Folklore Quarterly* 13 (1949) : 206–12.
———. "A Word-list from 'Bill Arp' and 'Rufus Sanders'," *Publica-
tion of the American Dialect Society*, no. 13 (1950) , pp. 3–15.

### Caldwell
Maclachlan, John M. "Folk and Culture in the Novels of Erskine
Caldwell." *Southern Folklore Quarterly* 9 (1945): 93–101.

### Cather
Ericson, Eston E. "Burial at the Cross-Roads." *Folk-Lore* 47 (1936) :
374–75 [a Bohemian folk-custom in *My Antonia*].

### Cooper
Walker, Warren S. "Proverbs in the Novels of James Fenimore
Cooper." *Midwest Folklore* 3 (1953) : 99–107.

### Crane
Hoffman, Daniel G. "Stephen Crane's New Jersey Ghosts: Two
Newly-Recovered Sketches." *Proceedings of the New Jersey His-
torical Society* 71 (1953) : 239–53.

### Dickinson
Whicher, George F. "American Humor." In *This Was A Poet, A
Critical Biography of Emily Dickinson,* ch. 10. New York and
London, 1939.

### Emerson
Anderson, John Q. "Emerson and the Language of the Folk." *Texas
Folklore Society Publication* 25 (*Folk Travelers,* 1953): 152–59.

### Faulkner
Maclachlan, John M. "William Faulkner and the Southern Folk."
*Southern Folklore Quarterly* 9 (1945) : 153–67.

## Franklin

Gallacher, Stuart A. "Franklin's *Way to Wealth:* A Florilegium of Proverbs and Wise Sayings." *Journal of English and Germanic Philology* 47 (1949): 229–51.

Meister, Charles W. "Franklin as a Proverb Stylist." *American Literature* 24 (1952–53) : 157–66.

## Frost

Hoffman, Daniel G. "Robert Frost's Paul Bunyan: A Frontier Hero in New England Exile." *Midwest Folklore* 1 (1951) : 13–18.

## Hall

Flanagan, John T. "Folklore in the Stories of James Hall." *Midwest Folklore* 5 (1955): 159–68.

## G. W. Harris

Penrod, James H. "Folk Humor in *Sut Lovingood's Yarns.*" *Tennessee Folklore Society Bulletin* 16 (December 1950) : 76–84.

## J. C. Harris

Brookes, Stella B. *Joel Chandler Harris—Folklorist* Athens, Ga., 1950.

Ives, Sumner. "Dialect Differentiation in the Stories of Joel Chandler Harris." *American Literature* 27 (1955) : 88–96.

## Harte

Loomis, C. Grant. "Bret Harte's Folklore." *Western Folklore* 15 (1956) : 19–22.

## Hawthorne

Cohen, Bernard. "Hawthorne and Legends." *Hoosier Folklore* 7 (1948) : 94–95.

## Hurston

Byrd, James W. "Zora Neale Hurston: A Novel Folklorist." *Tennessee Folklore Society Bulletin* 21 (June 1955): 37–41.

## Irving

Hoffman, Daniel G. "Irving's Use of American Folklore in "The Legend of Sleepy Hollow." *PMLA* 68 (1953) , 425–35.

## Irving, Hawthorne, Poe

Lynch, James J. "The Devil in the Writings of Irving, Hawthorne, and Poe." *New York Folklore Quarterly* 8 (1952) : 111–31.

## Judd

Loomis, C. Grant. "Sylvester Judd's New England Lore." *Journal of American Folklore* 60 (1947): 151–58.

## Kennedy

Roberts, Warren E. "Some Folksong References in Kennedy's 'Swallow Barn.' " *Southern Folklore Quarterly* 27 (1953) : 249–54.

## Lewis

Anderson, John Q. "Folklore in the Writings of 'The Louisiana Swamp Doctor'" [Henry Clay Lewis]. *Southern Folklore Quarterly* 19 (1955): 243–51.

## Longfellow

Moyne, Ernest J., and Mustanoja, Tauno F. "Longfellow's 'Song of Hiawatha' and 'Kalevala.'" *American Literature* 25 (1953): 87–89.

Osborn, Chase S., and Osborn, Stellanova. *Schoolcraft—Longfellow—Hiawatha*. Lancaster, Pa., 1942.

## Mark Twain

DeVoto, Bernard. *Mark Twain's America*. Boston, 1932.

Cuff, Roger P. "Mark Twain's Use of California Folklore in His Jumping Frog Story." *Journal of American Folklore* 65 (1952): 155–58.

Whiting, B. J. "Guyuscutus, Royal Nonesuch and Other Hoaxes." *Southern Folklore Quarterly* 8 (1944): 251–75.

McKeithan, D. M. "Mark Twain's Story of the Bull and the Bees." *Tennessee Historical Quarterly* 11 (1952): 246–53.

——. "Bull Rides Described by 'Scroggins,' G. W. Harris, and Mark Twain." *Southern Folklore Quarterly* 17 (1953): 241–43.

West, Victor R. "Folklore in the Works of Mark Twain." *University of Nebraska Studies in Language, Literature, and Criticism*, 87 pp. (1930).

## Melville

Babcock, C. Merton. "The Language of Melville's 'Isolatoes.'" *Western Folklore* 10 (1951) : 285–89.

——. "Melville's Backwoods Seamen." *Western Folklore* 10 (1951) : 126–33.

——. "Melville's Proverbs of the Sea." *Western Folklore* 11 (1952) : 254–65.

——. "Melville's World's-Language." *Southern Folklore Quarterly* 16 (1952): 177–82.

Chase, Richard. *Herman Melville, A Critical Study*. New York, 1949.

Hoffman, Daniel G. "Melville in the American Grain." *Southern Folklore Quarterly* 14 (1950) : 185–91.

## O'Neill

Walton, Ivan. "Eugene O'Neill and the Folklore and Folkways of the Sea." *Western Folklore* 14 (1955): 153–69.

## Paulding

Watkins, Floyd C. "James Kirke Paulding's Early Ring-Tailed Roarer." *Southern Folklore Quarterly* 15 (1951): 183–87.

## Peterkin
Yates, Irene "Conjures and Cures in the Novels of Julia Peterkin." *Southern Folklore Quarterly* 10 (1946) : 137–49.

## Rawlings
Figh, Margaret G. "Folklore and Folk Speech in the Works of Marjorie Kinnan Rawlings." *Southern Folklore Quarterly* 11 (1947) : 201–9.

## Richter
Flanagan, John T. "Folklore in the Novels of Conrad Richter." *Midwest Folklore* 2 (1952) : 5–14.

## Russell
Webb, James W. "Irwin Russell and Folk Literature." *Southern Folklore Quarterly* 12 (1948): 137–49.

## Sandburg
Hoffman, Daniel G. "Sandburg and 'The People': His Literary Populism Reappraised." *Antioch Review* 10 (1950): 265–78.

## Taliaferro
Whiting, B. J. "Proverbial Sayings from Fisher's River, North Carolina." *Southern Folklore Quarterly* 11 (1947) : 173-85.

## Wolfe
Maclachlan, John M. "Folk Concepts in the Novels of Thomas Wolfe." *Southern Folklore Quarterly* 9 (1945) : 175–86.

# 12

# Folklore in American Literature
# A Postscript

In our symposium on "Folklore in Literature" in last year's *Journal,* I commented on the problem of "The Identification of Folklore in American Literature."[1] Meanwhile, the flood of articles describing the debt of American authors to folk materials rolls on. For the record I add the references to these new studies on Bacheller, Eggleston, Faulkner, Irving, Caroline Kirkland, Kroll, Longfellow, Taliaferro, Thoreau, and Twain, to supplement my bibliographical note in the *Journal of American Folklore.*[2]

Several of the present studies follow the course I attacked of relying exclusively on unsupported internal evidence to make their case. A would-be authority picks up *Huckleberry Finn* or *The Sketch Book,* turns its pages, notes when an owl hoots or the word *ghost* occurs, and strings the page references

From *Journal of American Folklore,* 1958.
1. See ch. 11 above.
2. See p. 199, "Additional References."

together to compose a learned article. If not overcome by the rigorous demands of such research, our folk critic may reach for a Botkin treasury to furnish a footnote. As a clinching technique, he concludes the essay with a sonorous paragraph reiterating half a dozen times or more the dependence of his author upon folklore. Yet he has never done any field work, has read no field collections, and knows nothing of type or motif indexes.

I refer particularly to the articles by Frantz on Mark Twain, and by Rodes on Washington Irving. There is plenty of folk matter in *Huckleberry Finn,* but Frantz judges folklore purely by instinct. One reference to the *Standard Dictionary of Folklore, Mythology and Legend*—a poor place to go for regional American folklore—is his sole folkloristic documentation. Not even so familiar a work as N. N. Puckett's *Folk Beliefs of the Southern Negro*[3] appears in a footnote to save him from the egregious error of saying that all Nigger Jim's folk-knowledge—like telling the bees!—comes straight from Africa. Actually, Nigger Jim's beliefs are mostly English.[4] A splendid example of Southern Negro lore occurring at the outset, the belief in witch-riding, Frantz passes by. When Tom Sawyer hangs Nigger Jim's hat on a limb above the sleeping slave, Jim awakes to believe himself witch-ridden, and enlarges on his experience to gaping fellow slaves, thus giving himself special status.[5] At his most ridiculous, Frantz declares that Twain delineates the character of Mrs. Loftus through folklore, because she detects Huck as a boy in woman's dress by watching him thread a needle and throw a lump of coal at a rat. Observation of motor behavior is thus folklore. Finally Frantz asserts that the King, the Duke, and Huck continually talk in proverbs, and gives a number of examples with no reference material whatsoever, apparently on the theory that any unorthodox utterance constitutes a proverb. When Huck says a cave looks as "big as two or three rooms bunched together," this is proverbial. Obviously the editors

3. (Chapel Hill, N. C., 1926) .
4. Puckett, *Folk Beliefs of the Southern Negro,* p. 82.
5. Chapter 2. For current examples of the tradition, see my "Negro Witch Stories on Tape," *Midwest Folklore* 2 (1952) : 229–41.

of *American Literature* do not demand the same documentation for folklore they insist on for literary history.

The Rodes article commits similar faults, and the wonder is that it should be printed as a lead article in one folklore journal and reprinted as such in another. A series of naive assertions states that Irving was drenched in New York folklore. When Rodes surmises that Irving could well have taken *The Devil and Tom Walker* straight from the lips of the folk, we surmise that she never heard or read an oral folktale text. When she declares that so sophisticated a satirical writing as Knickerbocker's *History of New York* is near the "folk level," we can simply gasp. She could have benefited from Hoffman's authoritative piece on "Irving's Use of American Folklore in "The Legend of Sleepy Hollow' " in *PMLA* in 1953.

Still other essays rely wholly or largely on internal evidence. The article on folkways in Caroline Kirkland's minor classic of Michigan pioneer life, *A New Home—Who'll Follow?*, excerpts her references to dress, travel, inns, log houses, breadmaking, borrowing, churches, lawsuits, and personalities in backcountry Michigan of the 1830s. There is no comparative material. Nor is there in the brief comment on "Folklore in Eben Holden," but this is an unpretentious and useful note simply calling the attention of folklorists to the yarns of Uncle Eb in Irving Bacheller's novel. Penrod could make a still stronger case for folk humor in Taliaferro, for alone of the Southern humorists he describes informants and presents tale texts in a manner suggestive of a modern collector. Penrod gives specific examples of folk humor in Taliaferro, while Hoadley applies the phrase *folk humor* or its equivalent (*regional, frontier, tall tale humor*) twenty-two times in seven pages to the novels of Faulkner without any illustration of what he has in mind.

Turning from the guesswork method of internal evidence to the use of biographical evidence, we find valuable contributions. Reichart fully documents Irving's contacts with German legends in an article that points up all Rodes fails to do. Loomis uncovers the journal notes of Thoreau which show his live interest in local legends, customs, and expressions. The prize illustration of biographical evidence is written by a novelist on his own work. After Archer Taylor employed the corroborative method to document proverbial material in the novels of Harry Harrison Kroll, Kroll himself came forward to explain where he learned and how he used proverbs. He provides a splendid statement of the manner in which the creative writer draws from his fund of subconscious memories and experiences for traditional matter that may shape his characters and clothe his story. Kroll describes the sharecroppers living outside Dyersburg, Tennessee, and the "middleclass two-mule family" at Dixon Mills, Alabama, from whom he heard "simple strong words, earthy metaphors, barnyard vulgarity, and proverbs." But he also says—and let the folklorists take note—that some odd sounding twists of old proverbs which Taylor could not locate were simply his mother's peculiar phrases.

The only example, and a successful one, presenting all three kinds of evidence I suggested—internal, biographical, and corroborative—is the fully documented study by Davis on *Hiawatha*. One would prefer that she had relied more on original collections of Ojibwa tales, and less on Stith Thompson's anthology. But the analysis of poetic mood and structure, the investigation of Longfellow's sources, and the comparison of Indian tales with his poetic treatment support a convincing thesis. Davis concludes that Longfellow missed the deeper tragic view of Indian animistic myths in settling for a happy primeval poem directed toward white readers.

Reading these studies strengthens in my own mind the views I expressed in the symposium. I must enter my disagreement with Daniel G. Hoffman's assertion there that my demands for evidence will limit the folklore critic of literature to regional and provincial authors and deny him access to the mainstreams. For one thing I do not understand this big-city criterion of literary importance, even recognizing that Hoffman resided in New York when he expressed his views. Nor do I share his definition of folklore in terms of remoteness from the cosmopolis. Ethnic folk traditions flourish in urban centers and serve the writer. We can certainly document the debt of major American authors like Mark Twain, Melville, and Hawthorne to living folk traditions. The term *provincial* strikes me as unhappy, reflecting the literary reputation of the moment. Rowland Robinson deserves recognition not because

he describes cracker barrel storytelling, but because he caught
the moods, the country characters, the leisurely rhythm, the
focal points of village interest, and the accents of "idlesome
talk" (as Kroll puts it) in a Vermont hillside town. There
is humor in the speech and behavior of his Danvis folk
delicious as anything in Mark Twain. But Hoffman errs when
he says Robinson is simply faithfully recording folkways. Let
him just compare a tape recorded transcript of a tale telling
session with one of Robinson's artistically drawn yarnfests,
building up through point and counterpoint to a striking
climax. Fourteen critics wrote prefaces and introductions to
the centennial edition of Robinson's works in 1937, each pay-
ing tribute to Robinson as a writer, but not one recognized
his use of folklore. The folklore critic can considerably deepen
our awareness of Robinson's materials and techniques.

If we fail first to identify and document as accurately as
possible the contact of authors with folk traditions, we cannot
make critical judgments on their use of folklore motifs and
structural patterns. Poet and novelist and playwright fit to
their own imaginative purposes the folk materials they know,
and critics must tread warily to distinguish folk from literary
or personal inspiration. There is a danger that the search for
structural symbols may become as seductive as the quest for
ritual myths.

## Additional References

Works consulted in the preparation of this essay include the following:

*Individual Authors*

### Bacheller
Samuels, Charles E. "Folklore in Eben Holden." *New York Folklore
Quarterly* 13 (1957): 100–103.

### Eggleston
Taylor, Archer. "Proverbial Materials in Edward Eggleston, *The
Hoosier Schoolmaster.*" *Studies in Folklore,* ed. W. Edson Rich-
mond, pp. 262–70. Bloomington, Ind., 1957.

### Faulkner
Hoadley, Frank M. "Folk Humor in the Novels of William Faulkner." *Tennessee Folklore Society Bulletin* 23 (1957) : 75–82.

## Irving

Reichart, Walter A. "Washington Irving's Interest in German Folklore." *New York Folklore Quarterly* 13 (1957): 181–92.

Rodes, Sara P. "Washington Irving's Use of Traditional Folklore." *Southern Folklore Quarterly* 19 (1955): 143–53; reprinted in *New York Folklore Quarterly* 13 (1957) : 3–15.

## Kirkland

McCloskey, John C. "Back-Country Folkways in Mrs. Kirkland's *A New Home—Who'll Follow?*" *Michigan History* 11 (1956): 297–308.

## Kroll

Kroll, Harry Harrison. "How I Collect Proverbial Materials for My Novels." *Tennessee Folklore Society Bulletin* 23 (1957) : 1–5.

Taylor, Archer. "Proverbial Materials in Two Novels by Harry Harrison Kroll." *Tennessee Folklore Society Bulletin* 22 (1956): 39–52.

———. "Proverbial Material in Two More Novels by Harry Harrison Kroll." Ibid., 73–84.

## Longfellow

Davis, Rose M. "How Indian is Hiawatha?" *Midwest Folklore* 7 (1957) : 5–25.

## Taliaferro

Penrod, James H. "Harden Taliaferro, Folk Humorist of North Carolina." *Midwest Folklore* 6 (1956) : 147–53.

## Thoreau

Loomis, C. Grant. "Henry David Thoreau as Folklorist." *Western Folklore* 16 (1957) : 90–106.

## Twain

Frantz, Ray W. "The Role of Folklore in *Huckleberry Finn.*" *American Literature* 28 (1956): 314–27.

# Index

Aarne, Antti, folklorist, 17; *Types of the Folktale*, 83; *Vergleichende Märchenforschung*, 18n
Aaron, Daniel, historian, 79
*Abby Aldrich Rockefeller Folk Art Collection*, 126
Abrahams, Roger D., folklorist, *Deep Down in the Jungle*, 61, 71–72
*Account of Two-Voyages to New England* (Josselyn), 30
Adams, Percy G., historian, *Travelers and Travel Liars 1660–1800*, 64–65
Adario motif, 65–66
Addison, Joseph, 172
*Aeneid*, 140
Aesop's *Fables*, 139
Africa, oral history in, 131
*Age of Reform, The* (Hofstadter), 135

Aiken, Conrad, 186
Alabama, 40, 195, 207
Alamo, 104–65
Albemarle Sound, 122
Alfred E. Packer Cafeteria, 168
Allegheny River, 84
Allen, Ethan, 170
Alley, Judge Felix E., *Random Thoughts and Musings of a Mountaineer*, 132
Allsopp, Fred W., *Folklore of Romantic Arkansas*, 163, 164
Almanacs, 118; Crockett, 104, 135; Massachusetts, 30
*America Begins* (Dorson), 31n
*American Adam, The* (Lewis), 61
American Anthropological Association, 12, 112
*American Anthropologist*, 51
American Antiquarian Society, 115

"American Circus as a Source
  of Folklore," 92
American Diaries (Matthews),
  119
American Dictionary of the
  English Language (Webster),
  99
American Folk Art in Wood,
  Metal and Stone (Lipman),
  125
American Folklore (Dorson),
  49, 62, 66; reviews of, 51–54
American Folklore Society, 15,
  16, 49, 110, 111, 112; and
  fakelore, 11–13
American Heroes: Myth and
  Reality (Fishwick), 27
American Historian's Raw
  Material, The (Jameson), 129
American Historical Association,
  96, 131
American historical personalities,
  folkore of, 44–45
American Humor (Rourke),
  24–25, 27, 186–87
"Americanism," 99
American Liberty (American
  symbol), 64
American Literature, 26, 206
American Mercury, 6–7
American Murder Ballads and
  Their Stories (Burt), 170
American Myths and Legends
  (Skinner), 161
American Philosophical
  Society, 95
American Quarterly, 79
American Renaissance
  (Matthiessen), 80
Americans, The: The Colonial
  Experience (Boorstin), 48n
Americans, The: The National
  Experience (Boorstin), 96, 97
American Studies Association, 15
Anatomy of American Popular
  Culture, 1840–1861 (Bode),
  91

Anatomy of a Murder (Voelker),
  87
Anderson, John Q., Tales of
  Frontier Texas 1830–1860, 67
Anecdotes, in newspapers, 117
Angoff, Charles, 6–7
Annie Christmas, manufactured
  folk heroine, 9–10
Anthropologists, and folklore
  theory, 18–21
Antoine Bassette, 197
Appalachians, 21, 23, 42, 111
Appleseed, Johnny. See Johnny
  Appleseed
Archive of American Folksong,
  112
Arizona and the West, 52
Arkansas, 180
Arkansawyer, regional character
  type, 121
Armenian-American folklore,
  123
Arnold, George W., 84
Arp, Bill, 186, 189
Asbury, Herbert, 10
Austin, Stephen F., 165
Austin, William, 181


Baal Shem Tov, 71
Bacheller, Irving, 204, 206
Baez, Joan, 92
Baldwin, James, 75
Bales, Robert, 76
Ballads, American: collecting of,
  111–12; patriotic, 43, 45;
  texts in printed sources, 118
Ballads, English and Scottish,
  22, 110
Balys, Jonas, folklorist, 123–24;
  Lithuanian Folksongs in
  America, 124
Bambakou, Greece, 36, 143
Bancroft, George, historian, 96
Bank War, symbolic
  interpretation of, 54
Banta, R. E., 117

Baring-Gould, Sabine,
  folklorist, 26
Barney Beal, Maine folk hero,
  43
Barrett, W. H., narrator, 88
Barry, Phillips, folklorist, 21,
  111, 113
Bartlett, John Russell,
  *Dictionary of Americanisms*,
  99
Bascom, William R., 18–19
Basque-American folklore, 123
Bass, Sam. *See* Sam Bass
Bassett, Fletcher S., folklorist,
  111, 194
Bassette, Antoine, 197
Battle of Camden, legend of, 45
Battle of Lundy's Lane, 137
Baughman, Ernest W., 139;
  *Type and Motif-Index of the
  Folktales of England and
  North America*, 85
Bayard, Samuel P., folklorist,
  19n, 29
Bayou la Batre, 195
Beaver, Tony. *See* Tony Beaver
Beal, Barney. *See* Barney Beal
Beal's Island, Maine, 161
"Bear's Son, The," 180n
Beaver Island, 165
Beck, Horace, folklorist, *The
  Folklore of Maine*, 42
Becker, Carl, historian, *The
  Heavenly City of the
  Eighteenth Century
  Philosophers*, 58
Belden, H. M., folksong
  collector, 21, 111
Bell family, haunted family in
  Tennessee and Mississippi,
  159
Benedict, Ruth, 12
Benet, Stephen Vincent, 25,
  182, 183
Benton, Senator Thomas Hart,
  136
Beowulf, 180n, 197

*Bibliography of American
  Folklore and Folk Song*
  (Haywood), 113
*Big Bear of Arkansas, The*, 180,
  196, 197
Biglow, Hosea, 84
Billy the Kid, folk hero, 33,
  136, 137, 159
Blair, Walter, folklorist, 10, 25,
  119, 192
Bland, Big Bobby Blue, 74
Blason populaire, 63
Blegen, Theodore, historian,
  34, 150; *Grass Roots History*,
  87–88, 128, 148–49
*Bloodstoppers and Bearwalkers*
  (Dorson), 85–87, 138, 154, 166
Boas, Franz, anthropologist, 12,
  20, 27; *Tsimshian Mythology*,
  18
Boatright, Mody C., folklorist,
  158; *Folklore of the Oil
  Industry*, 73–74
Bode, Carl, *The Anatomy of
  American Popular Culture,
  1840–1861*, 91
*Body, Boots, and Britches*
  (Thompson), 8, 184
Boggs, Ralph Steele, folklorist,
  4, 183
Bolte, Johannes, folklorist, 17
*Book of New England Legends
  and Folklore, A* (Drake),
  159–60
*Book Review Digest*, 6
Boone, Daniel, as mythical
  hero, 98
Boorstin, Daniel J., historian,
  *The Americans: The
  Colonial Experience*, 48n;
  *The Americans: The National
  Experience*, 96, 97; *The
  Image, or What Happened
  to the American Dream*, 135
Borski, Jim, 165
Bossu, J. -B., 65
Boston, 104, 110, 123

*Boston Evening Post,* 66
Botkin, Benjamin A., folklorist,
    27, 62, 205; curator of the
    Archive of Folksong, Library
    of Congress, 5; and *New
    York Folklore Quarterly,* 12,
    26; *Folk-Say* volumes, 13–14;
    *Lay My Burden Down,* 88;
    *A Treasury of American
    Folklore,* 5–6, 184; *A
    Treasury of Mississippi
    Folklore,* 10; *A Treasury of
    New England Folklore,* 6;
    *A Treasury of Railroad
    Folklore,* 72
Boulder, Colorado, 168
Bowery, New York, 101, 105
Bowie, Jim, 165
Bowleg Bill, manufactured folk
    hero, 10
Bowman, James Cloyd, 10
*Boyhood of Abraham Lincoln,
    The* (Gore), 133
Boykin, Carol, 66
Bradford, William, 160
Brandeis, Louis D., money trust
    attacked by, 56–57
Breasted, J. H., historian, 131
Brer Rabbit, 40, 72, 190
Brewer, J. Mason, folklorist, 23
Brimley, Michigan, 39
Brinton, Daniel, 18
Broadhuss Zeke, 198
Brookes, Stella, *Joel Chandler
    Harris: Folklorist,* 189–90
Brooklyn, New York, Hasidic
    culture in, 69–71
*Brooklyn Eagle,* 161
Brother Jonathan (American
    symbol), 64
Brown, Frank C., folklorist,
    21, 113
Browne, G. Waldo, 175n
Browne, Ray B., folklorist, 66
Brunvand, Jan, folklorist,
    *Dictionary of Proverbs and
    Proverbial Phrases from*

*Indiana Books Published
    before 1880,* 117–18; *The
    Study of American Folklore:
    An Introduction,* 50
Bryan, William Jennings, and
    the money issue, 56
Buck, Paul, historian, 79
Buckle, Thomas Henry,
    historian, *History of
    Civilization in England,* 130
Buckley, Bruce, folklorist, 51,
    168
Buffalo Bill, 136
Buffon, Comte de, *Histoire
    Naturelle,* 65
Bunyan, Paul. *See* Paul Bunyan
Burke, Kenneth, 7i
*Burlington Free Press,* 116
Burne, Charlotte, folklorist, 24
Burt, Olive Wooley, *American
    Murder Ballads and Their
    Stories,* 170
"Business Man in American
    Folklore, The" (Porter), 45
*Buying the Wind* (Dorson),
    169
*Byliny,* Russian epic songs, 109
Byron, Lord George Gordon,
    187

Cable, George Washington, 111;
    and Negro folklore, 194
Cajun folklore, collector of, 23
Caldwell, Erskine, 188
*Calendar History of the Kiowa*
    (Mooney), 142
Calhoun, John C., 133
California, 34, 36, 106, 136,
    154, 155, 165
California, University of, at
    Los Angeles, 13, 112
*California Folklore Quarterly,* 5
Calvin, Michigan, 88
Cambridge, Massachusetts, 110
Cambridge University, 80

Camingerley, Philadelphia
neighborhood, 72
Camp, Charles L., 119
Campbell, Marie, folklorist, 111
Canada, 139
Cante-fable, Negro, 71–72
Cape Ann, Massachusetts, 122
Cape Fear, South Carolina, 122
*Cap'n Simeon's Store* (Wasson),
196
Capp, Al, 92
Captain Kidd, in New
England local history, 149
Carey and Hart, publishers, 82
Carmer, Carl, 6; *The
Hurricane's Children,* 9
Carson, Kit. *See* Kit Carson
Carver, Jonathan, 131
Catherwood, Mary Hartwell, 194
Chadwick, Hector M. and
Nora K., *The Growth of
Literature,* 32
Chaga Indians, 19
Chamberlain, Samuel, 159
Chanfrau, Francis, 101, 105,
106
Chapel Hill, North Carolina,
194
Chapman, John. *See* Johnny
Appleseed
Charlemagne, 130
Chase, Richard, folklorist, 23,
111, 190
Chaucer, Geoffrey, 187
*Chesapeake,* American naval
vessel, 98
Chicago, Illinois, 59
Chicago Folklore Society, 111;
correspondence of, 194
Chico State College, 154
Chief Eight Feathers
(Ne-shaw-so-ge-nebbi), 143
Child, Francis James, folklorist,
21, 110
Chinese-American folklore, 123
Chowning, Ann, 51

Christensen, Erwin O., *Index of
American Design,* 125–26
Christiansen, Reidar, *The
Migratory Legends,* 157
Christmas, Annie. *See* Annie
Christmas
Civil War, 95, 133; legends of,
45, 149
Clark, Thomas D., historian,
116; *The Rampaging
Frontier,* 120
Clay, Cassius, 75
Clay, Henry, 95
Cleaver, Eldridge, 75
Clemens, Samuel L., 6, 81,
117, 180, 190, 193, 196, 204,
205, 207, 208
Cloverton Paper Company, 152
Coal-Oil Johnny, folk
character, 74
Coe Ridge, Kentucky, 61
Cohen, Hennig, *Humor of the
Old Southwest,* 67
Coinage Act, 55
*Coin's Financial School*
(Harvey), 56
Colasacco, Sam, informant, 36
Collecting folk arts, 126
Collecting folklore: in England,
24; from ethnic groups, 36,
122–24; in Finland, 108–9;
in Ireland, 109; legends,
168–71; potential in U. S.,
121–25; regionally in U. S.,
23–24
"Collection and Analysis of
Folk-Lore, The," 16n
*Collections, Historical and
Miscellaneous* (Moore and
Farmer), 175n
Collections of folklore,
discussed, 115
Collectors of folklore, regional,
23–24
Colonial folklore, discussed,
64–66
Colorado, 116, 167, 168

Colorado, University of, 167–68
Columbia University, 146
Comstock Railroad Bridge, 68
"Concept of Regionalism as a
    Tool for Social Research,
    The" (Vance), 41
Concord, Massachusetts, 183
Confederate Army, 132
Confidence-Man, The
    (Melville), 190
Congressional Record,
    denouncements of folklore in,
    51
Connecticut, 31, 122, 147, 167,
    170
Contrast, The (Tyler), 102–3
Conundrums, in newspapers,
    117
Cooper, James Fenimore, 98,
    117, 186, 188
Cooperstown, New York, 126,
    154
Copenhagen, Denmark, 110
Cornell University, 8
Cornish-American folklore,
    dialect jokes, 38
Corombos, George, informant,
    36–37
Corombos, Ted, informant, 37
Corombos family,
    Greek-American family of
    informants, 36–37, 144
Corrido, 136
Cortez, Gregorio. See Gregorio
    Cortez
Course of American Democratic
    Thought, The (Gabriel), 44
"Cousin Sally Dilliard," 181
Couvade, 20
Cowboy, as frontier hero, 68
"Cow Boy's Lament," 68
"Crackerbox philosopher,"
    American character type, 99
Crafts. See Folk arts
Crane, Stephen, 186, 194
Creek Indians, 140
Creffield, Joshua, 170

Crockett, David. See Davy
    Crockett
Crockett Almanacs, 104, 106,
    135. See also Almanacs
Croy, Homer, Jesse James
    Was My Neighbor, 33
Crystal Falls, Michigan, 154, 166
"Current Attitudes towards
    Folklore," 16n
Current-Garcia, Eugene, 116
Curti, Merle, historian, The
    Roots of American Loyalty,
    44
Custer, George Armstrong, 159
"Cut Legs," 25–26
Czech-American folksongs in
    Nebraska, 123

Daily Worker, 46
Dake, Orsamus Charles, 172
Daley, Tom J., informant, 152,
    153
"Daniel Webster and the Sea
    Serpent," 182
Danny and the Boys (Voelker),
    86
Danvis Folks, 178
Darley, Felix O. C., 82
Davenport, John, 147
David Crockett, the Man and
    the Legend (Shackford), 33
Davidson, Donald, folklorist,
    16n
Davidson, Levette J., 5, 116, 187
Davis, Arthur Kyle, folksong
    collector, 111
Davis, Jefferson, 133
Davis, Rose M., 207
Davy Crockett, American
    Comic Legend (Dorson), 4,
    80
Davy Crockett, folk hero, 101,
    136; in the almanacs, 104,
    106; biography of, 32–33;
    folk-epic development of
    legend, 33n; as hero buffoon,

100; as Heroic Age hero, 107; images of, discussed, 91–92; influence of image on literature, 190; as model for tall-tale figures, 82; political career, 103–4; in Zeb Short tale, 84

"Davy Crockett and the Heroic Age," 33n

Day, Holman, 178, 196

Death Car, 155, 170

Declaration of Independence, 95

*Deep Down in the Jungle* (Abrahams), 61, 71–72, 74

Deerslayer, 98

Del Gue, informant, 33

Delmarva peninsula, 122

Denmark, 110

De Pauw, Corneille, *Recherches philosophiques sur les américains*, 65

De Pillis, Mario S., historian, 52–54, 59, 62

Detroit, 123, 155

Deuteronomy Dutiful, Yankee comic hero, 101

Devil, 189

"Devil and Daniel Webster, The," 25–26, 83

"Devil and Tom Walker, The," 25–26, 182, 206

Devil's Rock, 155

DeVoto, Bernard, historian, 79, 190; *Mark Twain's America*, 81; *The Year of Decision: 1846*, 80

Dick, Everett (historian), 34

Dickenson, Emily, 186

*Dictionary of Americanisms* (Bartlett), 99

*Dictionary of American Proverbs and Proverbial Phrases, 1820–1880* (Taylor and Whiting), 117

Dido, 140

Dillingham, William B., *Humor of the Old Southwest*, 67

Disney, Walt, 7, 91

Diviner. *See* Water witch; Oil diviner

*Division Street: America* (Terkel), 59

Dixon Mills, Alabama, 207

Dobie, J. Frank, folklorist, 6, 23, 24, 113; *Legends of Texas*, 163, 164, 170

Doggett, Jim, 180

*Dog on the Sun* (Green), 198

Dorson, Richard M.: on Botkin, 5–7, 13–14; collecting in Gary, Indiana, 74; collecting in Maine, 139, 161; collecting in Michigan Upper Peninsula, 4, 36–37, 43, 85–87, 138, 195; collecting in northern Indiana, 59; criticized by De Pillis, 53; criticized by Soviet ethnologist, 62; early career of, 3–4, 79; fakelore coined by, 3; fakelore defined by, 9; folklore, theory of, summarized, 50; as performing storyteller, 89; as president of American Folklore Society, 13; *America Begins*, 31n; *American Folklore*, 49, 51, 62, 66; *Bloodstoppers and Bearwalkers*, 85, 138, 154, 166; *Buying the Wind*, 169; *Davy Crockett, American Comic Legend*, 4, 80; *Folk Legends of Japan*, 157; *Jonathan Draws the Long Bow*, 4, 120, 160, 161, 164, 187; *Negro Tales from Pine Bluff, Arkansas, and Calvin, Michigan*, 41n; *Negro Folktales in Michigan*, 155

Down-Easter, regional character type, 121
Downing, Jack, 84, 190
Drake, Samuel Adams, 175n; *A Book of New England Legends and Folklore*, 159–60, 161
Driller, as folk hero of the oil industry, 74
Dromgoole, Will Allen, 194
Duell, Sloan, and Pearce, publishing house, 42
Duffy, Judge Hugh C., informant, 164
Duke University, 113
Dundes, Alan, folklorist, *Every Man His Way*, 76, 77
Dybbuk, Jewish demon, 70
Dyer, T. F. Thiselton, folklorist, 26
Dyersburg, Tennessee, 207

East Chicago, Indiana, 59
Eckstorm, Fanny H., folklorist, *Minstrelsy of Maine*, 22
Edinburgh, University of, 4, 80
"Educated Feller," 68
Edwards, Harry Stillwell, 194
Eggleston, Edward, 204
Egypt, 140
Eliade, Mircea, 53, 61
Ellison, Ralph, 75
Emerson, Ralph Waldo, 117, 186
Emrich, Duncan, folklorist, 116
England, 21, 88–89, 95, 108, 136
*English Folksongs of the Southern Appalachians* (Sharp), 27
Enloe, Abraham, 133
Era of Good Feeling, 55
Ericson, Eric, local character, 116
Erikson, Erik, psychologist, 71, 76

Erixon, Sigurd, folklorist, 109n
Escanaba, Michigan, 143, 150–53
Espinosa, Jose E., folklorist, 127
*Essay for the Recording of Illustrious Providences* (Mather), 92
Essex County, Massachusetts, 122
Estancia, New Mexico, 67
Estonia, 140
Ethnographers, of folk legends, 168–69
Ethnological Museum, Haifa, Israel, 127
Ethnomusicology, 21, 53
*Evangeline* (Longfellow), 188
*Every Man His Way* (Dundes), 76, 77
Evil eye, 144

Fairies, Irish supernatural beings, 36
Fairy tales, popularization of, by Grimm brothers, 26
Fakelore: and the American Folklore Society, 11–13; coining of, 3, 7; collections of, 5–6, 10; definition of, 9; discussion of, 6–11
Family saga, defined, 158
Farmer, John, 175n
Farmer's Museum, 126–27
Farrell, Ira, *Haywire: Growing Up in the Upper Peninsula 1905–1925*, 137
Farrell, James T., 187
*Fattura*, Italian spell, 36
Faulkner, William, 186, 188, 204, 206
Featherton, Pete, 182
Febold Feboldson, manufactured folk hero, 10
Federal Writers Project, 6, 112, 116
Felton, Harold, 10

Fenimore House, 126
*Fenman's Story, A* (Barrett),
  88
Ferrisburgh, Vermont, 178
Fife, Alta, folklorist, 22, 69;
  *Saints of Sage and Saddle,*
  89–90; *Songs of the Cowboys,*
  67–69
Fife, Austin, folklorist, 22, 23,
  40, 69; *Saints of Sage and
  Saddle,* 89–90; *Songs of the
  Cowboys,* 67–69
"Fifty Lithuanian Riddles," 123
Figh, Margaret G., 189
Fink, Mike. *See* Mike Fink
Finland, 108–9
Finnish-American dialect jokes,
  38
Finnish Folklore Fellows
  Communications, 109
Finnish Literature Society, 108
Finnish method, 17, 62, 108, 171
Fisher, Miles Mark, historian,
  40
*Fisher's River Scenes and
  Characters* (Boggs), 83
Fishwick, Marshall, *American
  Heroes: Myth and Reality,*
  27n
Fitzgerald Publishing Company,
  81
Fleming, E. McClung, historian,
  63–64
Flint, Michigan, 155
Florida, 123, 155
Folk: definition of, 59–60; in
  the U. S., 174n; use of in
  literature, 187
Folk architecture, 127
Folk arts, in U. S. discussed,
  125–28
Folk beliefs: collecting
  superstitions, 113; dictionary
  of, discussed, 118; Greek,
  144; Hasidic, 70–71; Indian,
  39; Negro, 40; in newspaper,
  117; number three in mass

culture, 76; reference of, 110
*Folk Beliefs of the Southern
  Negro* (Puckett), 61, 205
Folk carpenters, 41
Folk culture: frontier, 120; of
  Maine coast, 42; of Michigan
  Upper Peninsula, 43, 88–89;
  Pennsylvania Dutch, 42; and
  popular culture, 90–92; use of
  in literature, 187
Folk heroes: creation of, 100;
  frontier, 32, 33; historical
  personalities as, 44;
  manufactured, 10–11, 46;
  Negro, 40, 72; oil industry,
  73–74; outlaw, 33; popular
  awareness of, 107
Folk-legend, formation of, 100
*Folk Legends of Japan*
  (Dorson), 157
Folklife museums, Swedish, 109n
Folklore: and American
  nationalism, 107; coining of,
  3, 100, 108; collecting in
  America, 112–13; and
  colonial history, 29–32;
  popular awareness of, 107;
  popularizers of, 5–11; as
  processed product, 107;
  problem of definition
  discussed, 113–14; use of in
  literature, 187–209. *See*
  Anecdotes; Ballads;
  Conundrums; Folk arts;
  Folk beliefs; Folk culture;
  Folk heroes; Folklife;
  Folksongs; Folk speech;
  Folktales; Hoaxes; Jokes;
  Legends
"Folklore and Fake Lore," 7
"Folklore and the American
  West" (De Pillis), 52, 53
"Folklore and the Artist"
  (Stevens), 7
Folklore Fellows
  Communications, 109

*Folk-Lore from Adams County,
Illinois* (Hyatt), 113
*Folklore from the Schoharie
Hills, New York* (Gardner),
87, 115, 168
"Folklore in Eben Holden,"
206
Folklore methodology. *See*
Collecting folklore;
Historical-geographical
method; Indexing folklore;
Printed sources
*Folklore of Maine, The* (Beck)
42
*Folklore of the Oil Industry*
(Boatright), 73–74
*Folklore of Romantic Arkansas*
(Allsopp), 163
Folk-Lore Society, The, 21
"Folk-Lore Society: Whence
and Whither," 19n
Folklore theory, American:
and aborigines and slaves,
38–41; and colonization,
29–32, 64–66; of comparative
folklorists, 17–18; discussed,
110–12; Dorson's, 49–54, 62;
cross-regional comparisons in,
52; during 1940s, 3–4; and
folksong and folkmusic
specialists, 21; and
immigration, 36–41, 69–71;
and industrialization, 72–74;
and literary historians, 24–26;
and mass culture, 45–47,
74–77; and the Negro, 71–72;
and patriotism and
democracy, 44–45; and
popularizers of folklore,
26–27; and regional
collectors, 23; and
regionalism, 41, 67–69; and
special pleaders, 22–23; and
the western movement,
32–35, 66; research techniques
for historians, 117;
techniques compared with

European, 112; thematic
approach of, 115; unique
situation of, 28–29, 50
Folklore theory, general:
anthropological school, 16n,
18–21; British, 147;
comparative approach, 17–18;
Finnish, 16n, 17, 108–9;
Irish, 109; Soviet, 62–64,
109–10
*Folklorist, The,* 111
"Folk malevolence," 59
Folk museums, in the U. S.,
discussed, 125–26
"Folk sayings," 189
Folksongs: Anglo-American, 40;
Archive of, 112; cowboy,
67–69, 111, 124; Czech, 123;
French-Canadian, 40; in
Indiana University Folklore
Archives, 125; in printed
sources, 118; Lithuanian,
123–24; lumberjack, 111, 124;
Mormon, 22; Negro, 74–76,
111; Polish, 69; popular
awareness of, 107; protest,
63, 92; scholarship, 21; of
slaves, 40
Folk speech: collecting, in
U. S., 121–22; frontier, 99;
in newspapers, 117; in printed
sources, 120; regional
boundaries of, 42.
*Folktale, The* (Thompson), 27
Folktales: animal tales, 40;
Armenian, 67; and Brer
Rabbit stories, 190; collecting,
111–12; in Indiana University
Folklore Archives, 125;
Jewish, 127; and legends,
158; in newspapers, 116; in
*Spirit of the Times,* 82; New
England, 120; New Jersey,
114; of the oil industry, 74;
Old Marster and John cycle,
40; protest tales, 63

"Folk Traditions as Historical
    Fact: A Paiute Example," 140
Folkways, use of in literature,
    187
Follo, Charles, informant, 153
Ford, Henry, a bourgeois "folk
    hero," 62; joke cycle about,
    45, 63
Ford, Worthington, *Broadsides,
    Ballads, etc. Printed in
    Massachusetts, 1639–1800*
    118
*Forest Rose, The*, 103
Fort Lincoln, 143
France, 108, 140
Frank C. Brown Archives of
    North Carolina Folklore, 194
Frankie and Johnny, folk heroes,
    168
Franklin, Benjamin, 186; *Poor
    Richard's Almanac*, 104; *The
    Way to Wealth*, 189
Franklin, Colin, 88
Frantz, Ray W., 205
Frazier, E. Franklin, 76
Freeman, Edward A., historian,
    130
Freeman, R. A., 133
French-Canadian folklore, 197
*Frontier Mind, The* (Moore),
    128
Frontier society, as Heroic Age,
    32–33
Frost, Robert, 186, 187, 188
Fry, Gladys, folklorist, 61
Furman University, 133


Gabriel, Ralph Henry,
    historian, *The Course of
    American Democratic
    Thought*, 44
Gaelic revival, and the Irish
    Folklore Commission, 109
Gallacher, Stuart A., folklorist,
    189

Gardner, Emelyn E., folklorist,
    23, 115, 169; *Folklore from
    the Schoharie Hills, New
    York*, 87, 168
Garland, Hamlin, and Indian
    folklore, 194
Gary, Indiana, 59
*General Historie of Connecticut*
    (Peters), 30
George, H. B., historian,
    *Historical Evidence*, 130
*George Washington Harris*
    (Rickels), 66
Georgia, 40, 95, 116, 133
Georgia cracker, regional
    character type, 121
Germany, 108, 110, 137
"Ghost in the Tree, The," 198
Gib Morgan cycle, folktales of
    the oil industry, 74
GI folklore, 20, 46; in Indiana
    University Folklore Archives,
    125
*Glance at New York, A*, 101,
    106
Gold Rush, 106
Gollaher, Austin, 134
Gomme, Allan, folklorist, 19n,
    24
Gordon, Robert, folklorist, 112
Gore, J. Rogers, *The Boyhood
    of Abraham Lincoln*, 133
Gothenburg, Sweden, 109
Gouger's Neck, California, 154
*Grapes of Wrath, The*
    (Steinbeck), 188
*Grass Roots History* (Blegen),
    128, 148–49
"Grateful Dead," rock group,
    162
"Graveyard Wager, The", 154
"Great Carbuncle, The," 183
Greece, 140, 144
Greek-American folklore, 144;
    persistence of, among
    Corombos family, 37;
    potential for collecting,

123–25; supernatural beings
in, 36
Green, Paul, 194, 195, 198, 199;
Dog on the Sun, 198;
Salvation on a String, 198
Green Mountains, 83
Greenway, John, folklorist, 63
Gregorio Cortez, Mexican outlaw
hero, 90, 137
Gregory, Dick, 75
Grimm, Jakob and Wilhelm,
folklorists, 17, 26, 182
Growth of Literature, The
(Chadwicks), 33n
Guide to the Study of the
United States of America, 128
Gullah Negroes, folklore of, 40,
197


Hackett, James H., 105
Haifa, Israel, 127
Haliburton, Thomas Chandler,
84, 191
Hall, James, 182, 186, 193
Hallowell, A. Irving,
anthropologist, 39
Halpert, Herbert, folklorist, 24,
114
Hamilton, Alexander, 55
Hampton Institute, 110
Hand, Wayland, folklorist, 5
Handbook of Irish Folklore
(O'Sullivan), 109
Handwörterbuch des deutschen
Aberglaubens, 110
Hanks, Nancy, 133
Hansen, Harry, New England
Legends and Folklore,
159–60
Hansen, Marcus L., historian,
121
Harben, Will N., 194
Hard, Walter, 179
Hardin County, Kentucky, 134
Harlow, Alvin, A Treasury of
Railroad Folklore, 72

Harris, George Washington,
66–67, 186, 190; Sut
Lovingood, 81
Harris, J. M., 133
Harris, Joel Chandler, 186,
193, 194
Harte, Bret, 186
Harvard Folklore Club, 110
Harvard University, 3, 79–80, 85
Harvard University Press, 87,
115
Harvey, William Hope
"Coin," Coin's Financial
School, 56
Hasidic folklore, 69–71
Hastchian, Old Man, informant,
141
Haugen, Einar, 35
Hawkeye, 98
Hawthorne, Nathaniel, 160,
182, 186, 193, 196
Haywire: Growing Up in the
Upper Peninsula (Farrell),
137
Haywood, Charles, 187;
Bibliography of American
Folklore and Folk Song, 113
Hazard, "Shephard Tom," The
Johnny-Cake Letters, 168–69
Heavenly City of the Eighteenth
Century Philosophers, The
(Becker), 58
Henry, John. See John Henry
Henry, Patrick, as mythical
hero, 97
Herder, Johann Gottfried von,
103
Hero, The (Raglan), 27
Hero in America, The (Wecter),
44, 128
Herskovits, Melville J.,
anthropologist, 18–19, 20, 76
Herzog, George,
ethnomusicologist, 53
Hiawatha, promoted as folk
hero, 86
High Knob, Kentucky, 169

*High Times and Hard Times*
(Inge), 67
Hill, George H. "Yankee,"
Yankee comedian, 103, 105
*Histoire Naturelle* (Buffon), 65
*Historian and Historical
Evidence, The* (Johnson), 130
*Historical Evidence* (George),
130
Historical-geographical method.
*See* Finnish method
*Historical Material* (Salmon),
131
"Historical Tradition and
Oriental Research," 131
*History of Civilization in
England* (Buckle), 130
*History of New York* (Irving),
206
Hoadley, Frank M., 206
Hoaxes: in Indiana University
Folklore Archives, 125; New
England sea serpent, 182; in
newspapers, 117
Hockett, Homer C., historian,
*Introduction to Resarch in
American History,* 129
Hoffman, Daniel G., literary
critic and folklorist, 190, 194,
207, 208
Hofstadter, Richard, historian,
*The Age of Reform,* 135
Holbrook, Stewart, *Murder
Out Yonder, An Informal
Study of Certain Classic
Crimes in Back-Country
America,* 170
Holmes, Oliver Wendell, 188
Homeric question, and Albert
Lord, 58
Hoogasian-Villa, Susie, folktale
collector, 69
Hooper, Johnson Jones, 81, 190
Hoosier, regional character
type, 121, 180
Hosea Biglow, 84
Houston, Sam, 165

"How Annie Christmas
Mourned for Her Gambling
Man," 9
"How Big Lige Got the
Liquor," 177
"How Crystal Falls Stole the
Court-house from Iron
River," 166
"How the Game of Baseball
Was Invented in Greece Two
Thousand Years Ago," 37
"How Sharp Snaffles Got His
Capital and His Wife," 179,
196
Howard, Romey, slave ancestral
hero, 143–44
*Huckleberry Finn* (Clemens),
26, 191, 204, 205
Hudson, Arthur Palmer, 5, 189,
192; *Humor of the Old Deep
South,* 121, 184
Hudson Valley, 98
*Humor of the Old Deep South*
(Hudson), 121–84
*Humor of the Old Southwest*
(Cohen and Dillingham, eds.),
67
Humphreys, Moses, 106
Huntley, Chet, 168
Hurley, Wisconsin, 36
*Hurricane's Children, The*
(Carmer), 6, 9
Hurston, Zora Neale, 6
Hyatt, Harry M., folklorist,
*Folk-Lore from Adams County,
Illinois,* 113
Hyman, Ray, *Water Witching
U.S.A.,* 73
Hyman, Stanley Edgar, literary
critic and folklorist, 8, 22,
23, 27

Iceland, 140
Icelandic saga reciters, 130
*Ideas in America* (Jones), 80
Illinois, 34, 120

Illinois Sucker, regional
  character type, 121
"Ill-Looking Horse, The," 177
*Image, The, or What Happened
  to the American Dream,*
  (Boorstin), 135
Immigrant folklore: comparative
  studies of, 124; ethnic
  inheritance of, 35; immigrant
  groups of Michigan's Upper
  Peninsula, 43; stereotypes
  in, 38
Indexing folklore, 117
*Index to the Burlington Free
  Press in the Billings Library
  of the University of Vermont,*
  116, 175n
Indian folklore: folktales, 140;
  and history, 142–43; and
  lovers'-leap legend, 39; oral
  history of the Mukwitch,
  140–41; pseudo-Indian
  legends, 172; in printed
  sources, 120; stereotypes in,
  39; synthesized with
  European folklore, 39
Indiana, 20, 34, 59, 120
*Indianapolis Star,* 58
Indiana University, 4, 12, 13,
  61, 112, 117
Indiana University Folklore
  Archives, 47n, 125
Indians, in New England
  legends, 149
Inge, M. Thomas, *Sut
  Lovingood's Yarns,* 67, 82
Ingersoll, Charles Jared, 95
International Folktale Congress,
  110
*Introduction to Research in
  American History* (Hockett),
  129
Ireland, 108, 109
Irish-American folklore: dialect
  jokes, 38; fairies in, 36
Irish Folklore Commission, 109

Iron Mountain, Michigan, 26,
  36, 144
Iron River, Michigan, 154, 166
Irving, John Treat, Jr., 172
Irving, Washington, 25, 117,
  172, 181, 186, 190–91, 196,
  204, 205, 206; *History of
  New York,* 206; use of folklore
  by, 98
"Irving's Use of American
  Folklore in 'The Legend of
  Sleepy Hollow,' " 206
Italian-American folklore, 36
Italy, 108
Ithaca, New York, 126
Ives, Burl, 26
Ives, Edward D., folklorist, 171

Jacinto Treviño, Mexican hero,
  137
Jack, Phil R., 52
Jack Downing, 84, 190
Jackson, Andrew, 54, 55, 102
Jackson, Kenneth H., 4, 80
Jacksonian Era, 102, 103–4,
  107
*Jacksonian Persuasion: Politics
  and Belief* (Meyers), 54–55
Jagendorf, Moritz, folklorist,
  12–13, 26
James, Henry, 187
James, Jesse Woodson. *See
  Jesse James*
James, William, *The Varieties
  of Religious Experience,* 92
Jameson, J. Franklin, historian,
  *The American Historian's
  Raw Material,* 129
Janaikis, Greek ancestral hero,
  37, 144
Jansen, William H., folklorist,
  25, 114
Japanese-American folklore,
  supernatural beliefs, 36
Jedediah Homebred, Yankee
  character, 101

Jefferson, Thomas, 55, 65
*Jefferson Image in the American Mind, The* (Peterson), 88
Jesse James, outlaw-hero, 33, 136
*Jesse James Was My Neighbor* (Croy), 33
Jewish folklore: folk art, 127; dialect jokes, 38; Hasidic legends, 69–71. *See also* Hasidic folklore
*Joel Chandler Harris: Folklorist* (Brookes), 190
Joe Magarac, manufactured folk hero, 10, 46
John Brown's Cave, 155
John Henry, folk hero, 168
Johnny Appleseed, folk hero, 11, 136
*Johnny-Cake Letters, The* (Hazard), 168–69
Johnson, Allen, historian, *The Historian and Historical Evidence*, 130
Jokes: *blason populaire*, 63; dialect jokes, 37; Henry Ford cycle, 45, 63; jocular tales, 119; in newspapers, 117; Ozark, 119
*Jonathan Draws the Long Bow* (Dorson), 4, 187, 120, 160, 161, 164
Jonathan Ploughboy, Yankee comic hero, 101, 103
Jonathan the Yankee, hero-buffoon, 100
Jones, Howard Mumford, historian, 79; *Ideas in America*, 80
Jones, John Paul, 97
Jones, Louis C., folklorist, 34, 127–28
Jonesport, Maine, 43, 122, 161
Jordan, Philip D., historian, 116

Josh Strickland, Yankee character, 84
Josselyn, John, 119; *Account of Two-Voyages to New England*, 30
Journalistic sketches, antebellum, 66–67
*Journal of American Folklore*, 5, 8, 12, 49, 52, 140, 170, 204
*Journal of the Folklore Institute*, 14, 54
Judd, Sylvester, 186
Julius Caesar, 130
"Jumping Frog of Calaveras County, The," 180

*Kappa*, Japanese demon, 158
*Kalevala*, 108
Kansas, 53
Katchin, Solomon, 141
Keil, Charles, *Urban Blues*, 61, 74–76
Kennebec, Maine, 139
Kennedy, John Pendleton, 186
Kentuckian, regional character type, 121
Kentucky, 19, 23, 61, 83, 105–6, 116, 120, 139, 169
Kiel, Germany, 110
Kimball, J. Golden, Mormon character, 163
King, B. B., 74
King, Charles H., Jr., 75
"Kiowa-Apache Tales," 141
Kireyevsky, P. V., folklorist, 109
Kirkland, Caroline, 204; *A New Home—Who'll Follow?*, 206
Kirkland, Joseph, 194
Kit Carson, folk hero, 136, 159
Kitchen, Sam, informant, 152
Kittery Point, Maine, 178
Kittredge, George Lyman, 3, 30; *The Old Farmer and His Almanac*, 118

Kluckhohn, Clyde,
    anthropologist, 20
Kornbluh, Joyce, folklorist,
    *Rebel Voices*, 73
Korson, George, folklorist, 22,
    23, 113, 124
Kraft, Joseph, 59
Kramer, Frank R., historian,
    *Voices in the Valley*, 54, 90,
    137–38
Krohn, Julius, folklorist, 17
Krohn, Kaarle, folklorist, 17,
    21
Kroll, Harry Harrison, 204, 207
Kuhn, Madison, historian, 146
Kummer, George, 116
Kurath, Hans, 42; *Linguistic
    Atlas of America*, 121–22

Lafayette, Marquis de, 149
Lake City, Colorado, 167
Landowner, folktype of the
    oil industry, 74
Lang, Andrew, folklorist, 24, 26
Lawrence, Captain James, 98
*Lay My Burden Down*
    (Botkin), 88
Leach, Joseph, 121
Leach, MacEdward, folklorist,
    12, 15
Leach, Maria, folklorist, 114
Leadbelly. *See* Ledbetter,
    Huddy
Leatherstocking, 98, 188
Ledbetter, Huddy, 88
Lee, Dorothy, folklorist, 123
Lee, Hector, folklorist, 165
Lee, John D., 156
"Legend of Sleepy Hollow,
    The" (Irving), 190, 191, 192,
    196
Legends: American comic, 25;
    analysis of, by
    geographical-historical
    method, 171; of Charlemagne,
    130; Civil War, 45; current

usage of term discussed,
    159–60; of Davy Crockett,
    32–33, 91–92; genre defined,
    158; field collections of, 169;
    folk, defined, 160; Indian,
    143, 195; Washington Irving
    and German, 206; of John
    Henry, 168; of Lincoln, 44;
    literary, defined, 160;
    Lovers' Leap, 39, 172; of
    Marblehead, 188; in mass
    media, 167–68; of Mike Fink,
    25; of the Minotaur, 131;
    Mormon, 89–90, 155; New
    England, 120, 149; of New
    Jersey, 114, 194; in
    newspapers, 117; occupational,
    124–25; of Owsley, 162;
    Passaconaway, 175n; popular,
    defined, 160; and printed
    sources, 102; Revolutionary
    War, 45; of Troy, 131; as
    wandering traditions, 146;
    and written history, 129–31;
    Yoho legend, 139; *Legends
    of Texas* (Dobie), 163, 165,
    170; *Legends of the Hasidim*
    (Mintz), 69–71. *See also* Oral
    history and folktales
*Legends that Libel Lincoln*
    (Lewis), 133–34
Leisy, Ernest E., 187–88
Lenapee Indians, 140
Lenox, Massachusetts, 183
Lévi-Strauss, Claude,
    anthropologist, 76
Lewis, Montgomery S.,
    *Legends that Libel Lincoln*,
    133–34
Lewis, R. W. B., historian,
    *The American Adam*, 61
Library of Congress, 112
Library of Humorous American
    Works, 82
*Life of George Washington*
    (Weems), 97

*Life Treasury of American Folklore*, 161
Lincoln, Abraham, 117; legends of, 44; oral history about, 132–34; tale credited to, 83
Lindgren, Ethel John, folklorist, 16n
Lindsay, Harold, informant, 152
Linguistic Atlas of America, 121
*Lion of the West* (Paulding), 91, 104–5
Lipman, Jean, *American Folk Art in Wood, Metal and Stone*, 125
Lippard, George, *Washington and His Generals*, 97
*Literary History of the United States, The*, 128
Lithuanian-American folklore, 123
*Lithuanian Folksongs in America* (Balys), 124
"Lithuanian Folk Songs in the United States," 123
Little, Nina Fletcher, 126
Liver-Eating Johnson, folk hero, 33
Local history and folklore, discussed, 145–46
Lomax, Alan, folklorist, 21, 26, 76, 112
Lomax, John A., folklorist, 21, 88, 111, 112, 113
London, 21, 106
*Lonely Crowd, The* (Riesman), 46n, 142
Longfellow, Henry Wadsworth, 98–99, 160, 186, 188, 204; *Song of Hiawatha*, 193, 207
Long Island Sound, 122
Longstreet, Augustus Balwin, 81
Lönnröt, Elias, folklorist, 108
Lookout, California, 165
Loomis, C. Grant, folklorist, 117
Lord, Albert, folklorist, 58

Lord Raglan. *See* Raglan, Lord Fitzroy Richard Somerset
*Los Pastores*, 42
Louisiana, 19, 42, 117
Louisville, Kentucky, 105–6
Loup-garou, French-Canadian werewolf, 197
Lovel, Sam, 197
Lovelace, Lord, 66
Lovers'-Leap legend, as synthetic folklore, 39
Lowell, James Russell, 84, 117
Lowie, Robert, 140
Lubell, Samuel, 58–59, 132
Lucian, 66
Lufkins, John, informant, 39
Lund, Sweden, 109
Lyly, John, 172
Lyman, Kenneth, 51
"Lynching of the McDonald Boys," 154, 165

McAllester, David, ethnomusicologist, 76
McAllister, J. Gilbert, 141
*Machine in the Garden, The* (Marx), 61
*Machismo*, traditional Mexican quality, 59
Maclachlan, John M., 188
McClary, Ben Harris, *The Sut Lovingood Papers*, 66
McLuhan, Marshall, 76
Mafia, 59, 163
Magarac, Joe. *See* Joe Magarac
*Magnalia Christi Americana* (Cotton Mather), 31, 147–48
*Main Currents in American Thought* (Parrington), 92
Maine, 42, 43, 45, 122, 139, 161, 178, 179, 196
Major André, 193
Malcolm X, 75
Manchester, William, *Death of a President*, 76

*Manifest Destiny* (Weinberg),
44; discussed as American
historical myth, 135–38
*Manifest Destiny and Mission
in American History* (Merk),
136
"Man Who Plucked Gorbey,
The: A Maine Woods
Legend," 171
Marble, Dan, comedian, 103,
104–5, 106
Marblehead, legend of, 188
Märchen, in U. S., 111, 158, 171,
181
Mark Twain: *See* Clemens,
Samuel L.
*Mark Twain's America*
(DeVoto), 81
Marquette County, Michigan,
86
Maryland, 95
Marx, Leo, *The Machine in
the Garden,* 61
Massachusetts, 30, 95, 97, 147
Mass culture: and folklore, 45,
54; heroes, 46
Masterson, James R., folklorist,
30, 121; *Tall Tales of
Arkansaw,* 120
"Materials of Folklore," 19n
Mather, Cotton, 30–31, 160;
*Magnalia Christi Americana,*
31, 147–48
Mather, Increase, 30–31; *Essay
for the Recording of
Illustrious Providences,* 92
Mathews, John Joseph, *The
Osages,* 142
*Mati,* Greek evil eye, 37
Matthews, William, *American
Diaries,* 119
Matthiessen, Francis Otto,
literary scholar, 79; *American
Renaissance,* 80
Mecosta, Michigan, 155
Meighan, Clement W., 140–41
Meine, Franklin J., 192; *Tall*

*Tales of the Southwest,* 24,
67, 81, 184
Melville, Herman, 117, 186,
190, 191, 193
Memorat, defined, 158
Mencken, H. L., 107
Menominee, Michigan, 154,
165
Merk, Frederick, historian, 79;
*Manifest Destiny and
Mission in American History,*
136
Merriam, Alan P.,
ethnomusicologist, 76
Merton, Robert, 76
Mexican-American folklore
and Manifest Destiny, 136–37
Mexico, 136, 137
Meyers, Marvin, historian, 53,
57; *The Jacksonian
Persuasion: Politics and
Belief,* 54–55
Michigan, 36, 42, 49, 120, 122,
143, 144; Upper Peninsula,
4, 43, 85–88, 138–40, 150–54,
165
Michigan State University, 4,
85, 154
Micmac Indians, 140
Midwest: myths and symbols of,
90; pioneer folk-culture of,
34
*Midwest Folklore,* 112
*Migratory Legends, The*
(Christiansen), 157
Mike Fink, folk hero, 23, 25,
100, 101, 195
Miller, Joe, 175
Miller, Perry, historian, 32, 79,
81; *The New England Mind,
The Seventeenth Century,*
80
Mills, Randall V., folklorist, 116
Milton, John, 187
Minnesota, 43
Minotaur, 131

*Minstrelsy of Maine* (Eckstorm and Smyth), 22
Mintz, Jerome R., folklorist, *Legends of the Hasidim,* 69
Mississippi, 133
Mississippi River, 100, 195
Mississippi screamer, 180
Mississippi Valley Historical Association, ix, 88
Missouri, 100, 111, 136
*Mitsveh,* 71
Mobile, Alabama, 195
Modern Language Association, 12, 112
Money Legislation, symbolic treatment of, 55–57
Monroe, Harriet, 194
Monroe Doctrine, 95–96
Montell, Lynwood, folklorist, 61
Mooney, James, *Calendar History of the Kiowa,* 142
Moore, Arthur K., literary scholar, 25, 83, 117, 121; *The Frontier Mind,* 128
*More Tales from the Fens* (Barrett), 88
Morgan, Edmund S., historian, 79
Morison, Samuel Eliot, historian, 79, 131, 146
Mormon folklore: anecdotes, 163; folksongs, 22; legends, 89, 90
Morse, Curt, informant, 139
Morse, Eve, informant, 139
Morton, Thomas, 175n
*Mose in California,* 106
Mose the Bowery b'hoy, hero-buffoon, 100–101, 102, 105–6
Motif analysis, as folklore technique, 62, 63
*Motif-Index of Folk-Literature* (Thompson), 4, 80, 148
Motifs: D1719.1, "A contest in magic," 141; D1766.1,

"Magic fountain produced by prayer," 169; E535.3, "Ghost Ship," 148; K185.1, "Deceptive land purchase: ox-hide measure," 140; X584.2*, "We killed a rabbit," 139
Mountain Meadows Massacre, 155
*Mukwitch,* 140
*Mules and Men* (Hurston), 6
*Murder Out Yonder, An Informal Study of Certain Classic Crimes in Back-Country America* (Holbrook), 170
Murdock, Kenneth B., literary historian, 32, 79
Museums, folklife, 109n, 154
Myth: in American history, 44–45; and the American West, 135–36; as analytic tool in folklore studies, 54; of the cowboy, 68; of early American heroes, 97–98; of George Washington, 96–97; Indian, in *Hiawatha,* 99; institutional, Midwest, 90; of New World, 65; and oral history, 134–38; of "Soul," 75–76
"Mythical and Romantic Elements in Early English History, The," 130
*Myths and Legends beyond Our Borders* (Skinner), 161
*Myths and Legends of Our New Possessions and Protectorate* (Skinner), 161
*Myths and Legends of Our Own Land* (Skinner), 161, 182n

Narragansett Bay, 122
*Narrow Land, The* (Reynard), 6

Nashville, Tennessee, 104
*Nathan Daboll's Almanac,* 118
National Defense Education
    Act, grants to folklore, 51
*Native American Humor,*
    *(1800–1900),* 25
Natty Bumppo, 98
Navajo Indians, 19
Nebraska, 123
Nebraska, University of, 172
*Nebraska Folklore* (Pound),
    171–72
Neely, Charles, *Tales and*
    *Songs of Southern Illinois,*
    169
Negro folklore: antebellum, 61;
    collector of, 23; discussion of,
    40–41, 198; and Brer Rabbit
    stories, 190; folktales, 6, 40,
    41, 143; Gullah Negro
    folklore, 40, 197; and history,
    61, 143–44; John Henry
    legend, 168; organizations
    for, 110; in travel literature,
    119; and racial injustice, 63;
    studies of, 61; urban, 71–72,
    74–76
*Negro Folktales in Michigan*
    (Dorson), 38n ,155
Negro history, and folklore, 61
*Negro Tales from Pine Bluff,*
    *Arkansas, and Calvin,*
    *Michigan* (Dorson), 41n
Nelson, Arvalea, student
    collector, 162
*Nereidos,* Greek supernatural
    being, 37
Nevada, 116
New Bedford, Massachusetts,
    123
New Deal, 57
Newell, William Wells,
    folklorist, 111
*New England Legends and*
    *Folklore* (Hansen), 159–60
*New England Mind, The, the*
    *Seventeenth Century,*

(Miller), 80
"New England Popular Tales
    and Legends," dissertation, 4
New Hampshire, 178, 182
New Hampshire, University of,
    78
New Haven, Connecticut, 31,
    122, 147, 170
*New Home, A—Who'll Follow?,*
    (Kirkland), 206
New Jersey, 100, 114
New Mexico, 20, 67
New Orleans, 9–10, 100
New York, 8, 12, 23, 84, 95,
    126, 154, 178
New York City, 12–13, 101, 104
*New Yorker,* 66
*New York Folklore Quarterly,*
    8, 12, 13, 26, 112
New York Folklore Society,
    12, 13
*New York Herald Tribune,*
    5, 51
New York State Historical
    Association, 126, 154
*New York Times,* 5, 8, 73
Nigger Jim, 205
Nimrod Wildfire, stage comic
    hero, 104, 105
*Nisser,* Norwegian supernatural
    spirit, 36
Noble Savage, 65–66, 172
North Carolina, 113, 116, 122,
    191, 198
Norwegian-American folklore,
    35, 36
*Norwegian Language in*
    *America, The* (Haugen), 35
Noy, Dov, folklorist, 127
Nye, Russel, historian, 93


O'Brien, Mike, 151
Occupational folklore:
    businessman, 45; discussion
    of, 124–25; in Upper
    Peninsula, 43; labor

movement, 72–73; military,
20, 46–47; oil industry, 73;
railroads, 72; sailing and
fishing, 42
Ohio, 116
Ohio Buckeye, regional
character type, 121
Ohio River, 100
Ohio Valley, 11
Oicotypes, in Negro folklore,
71–72
Oil diviner, 73
Ojibwa Indians, 39, 85, 143
*Old Farmer and His Almanac,
The* (Kittredge), 118
*Old Farmer's Almanac, The,*
118
Old Marster, Negro folktale
hero, 40
Old Promoter, oil industry
folk hero, 73
Old Stormalong, manufactured
folk hero, 10
Olmstead, Frederick Law, 119
O'Neill, Eugene, 186, 189
Opler, Marvin, 36
Oral folk history: in England,
88; in the Michigan Upper
Peninsula, 89, 165–66
Oral history and folktales,
138–40; and local legends,
154–56; and minority groups,
142–44; and myth, symbol,
and image, 134–38; project of
Columbia University, 146;
source for popular attitudes,
prejudices, and stereotypes,
132–34; validity for
historians, 131
"Oral Tradition and Written
History: The Case for the
United States," 54
Oregon, 34, 123, 170
"Oregon" Smith, tall-tale hero,
34, 114, 136
Oregon territory, 136

Organization of American
Historians, ix, 88
*Osages, The* (Mathews), 142
O'Sullivan, Sean, *Handbook
of Irish Folklore,* 109
*Other People's Money*
(Brandeis), 56
Otis, James, as mythical hero,
97
Owsley, hippie drug culture
hero, 162
Ozarks, 23, 24, 42, 90, 111, 119
*Ozarks, The* (Randolph), 168
*Ozark Superstitions*
(Randolph), 90

Packer, Alfred E., 167
Paiute Indians, as informants,
140–41
Paragonah, Utah, 140
Paredes, Américo, folklorist, 59,
136; *"With His Pistol in His
Hand,"* 90
Parrington, Vernon Louis,
historian, 55; *Main Currents
in American Thought,* 92
Passaconaway, legend of, 175n
Patch, Sam. *See* Sam Patch
Paterson, New Jersey, 101
"Pat Sheridan's Speech at
Escanaba," 150–53, 166
*Paul Bunyan* (Stevens), 7
Paul Bunyan, manufactured
folk hero, 6, 9, 46, 62, 63, 86,
107, 188
Paulding, James Kirke, 186;
*The Lion of the West,* 91,
104
Pausanias, 66
Pawlowska, Harriet M., folksong
collector, 69
Pawnee Indians, 172
Pawtucket, Rhode Island, 101
Pecos Bill, manufactured folk
hero, 46
"Pecos River Queen," 68

*Pedlar, The* (Wetmore),
    100–101, 104, 106
Peedee River, 122
Pendergast, David M., 140
Pendleton's Civil Service
    Reform Act of 1883, 150
Pennsylvania, 23, 42, 45, 51,
    95, 124
Pennsylvania, University of,
    12, 13, 112
Pennsylvania Dutch,
    folk-culture of, 42, 127
Penrod, James H., 191, 206
Percy, Thomas, 21
Pernetty, Dom, 65
Perry, Oliver Hazard, 97
Perry, Ralph Barton, 78, 79;
    *Puritanism and Democracy*,
    80
Persia, 139
Peterkin, Julia, 186, 197
"Peter Rugg, the Missing Man,"
    181
Peters, Samuel, *General History
    of Connecticut*, 30
Peterson, Merrill D., historian,
    *The Jefferson Image in the
    American Mind*, 88
Peterson and Company,
    publishers, 82
Phantom ships, 31, 147
Philadelphia, 104
Pierpont, James, 147
Pinckney, Charles Cotesworth,
    98
Pine Mountain, Kentucky, 19,
    23, 139
Pine Tree Ballads, 196
Place traditions, 130, 155
*PMLA*, 206
Poe, Edgar Allan, 187
Polívka, Georg, folklorist, 17
Polk, James K., 136
Pollard, Lancaster, historian,
    41
Polly's Peak, 164

Polynesia, oral history in, 131
Pontiac, Michigan, 155
*Poor Richard's Almanac*
    (Franklin), 104
Populist movement, 56, 63
Porter, Kenneth, 45
Portuguese-American folklore,
    123
Potawatomi Indians, 143
Potomac River, 182
Pound, Louise, folklorist,
    *Nebraska Folklore*, 171–72
Powell, Adam Clayton, 75
Printed sources: diffusion of
    folklore by, 174–75, 175n,
    177; folk beliefs in, 118;
    folklore in early newspaper,
    175–80; and folktales,
    173–85; and legend, 102;
    New England, 84; use of, by
    historians, 57, 115; testing
    for folklore in, 185
*Profile of Old New England:
    Yankee Legends, Tales, and
    Folklore* (Taft), 159, 160,
    161
Proverbs, in newspapers, 177
*Providence Journal*, 168
"Publishing Folklore," 88
Publishing folklore, problems
    of, 114–15
Publications of the Texas
    Folklore Society, 165
Puckett, Newbell N., *Folk
    Beliefs of the Southern
    Negro*, 61, 205
*Pueblo*, 136
Pujo Committee, 56
Puritanism, 30–32, 44, 80
*Puritanism and Democracy*
    (Perry), 80

*Quest for Nationality, The*
    (Spencer), 99

Raglan, Lord Fitzroy Richard
    Somerset, folklorist, 140,
    141, 147, 156; *The Hero*,
    27
*Rampaging Frontier, The*
    (Clark), 120
Randolph, Vance, folklorist, 6,
    23, 24, 27, 111, 113, 119,
    120, 163; *Ozark
    Superstitions*, 90; *The
    Ozarks*, 168
*Random Thoughts and
    Musings of a Mountaineer*
    (Alley), 132
Raven Rock, 193
Rawlings, Marjorie Kinnan,
    186
Rayford, Julian Lee, 195–96
Read, Allen Walker, 84
Rebbes (Hasidic miracle
    worker), 70
*Rebel Voices* (Kornbluh), 73
*Recherches philosophiques sur
    les américains* (De Pauw),
    65
Redden, Francesca, 40
Redfield, Robert,
    anthropologist, 20
Regional character types, 121
*Regionalism in America*, 41
Reichart, Walter A., 206
Relic areas, in U.S., 122
Revolutionary War, 45, 97, 103,
    149, 170
Reynard, Elizabeth, 6
Rhode Island, 101, 122
Rhymes, in newspapers, 117
Richter, Conrad, 186
Rickels, Milton, literary
    scholar, *George Washington
    Harris*, 66
Riddles, 117, 123
Ridley, "Uncle" Boney, 132
Riesman, David, *The Lonely
    Crowd*, 46n, 142

Ritson, Joseph, ballad scholar,
    21
Roaring Fork Cafeteria,
    167–68
Roberts, Leonard, folklorist,
    23, 111, 139; *South from
    Hell-fer-Sartin*, 169
Robeson, Paul, 75
Robinson, Rowland, 82, 176,
    178, 198, 207–8; *Uncle
    Lisha's Shop*, 196
Rodes, Sara P., 205, 206
*Romanticism and the Romantic
    School in Germany*
    (Waerner), 183
Roosevelt, Franklin D., 57
Roosevelt, Theodore, 55
*Roots of American Loyalty*
    (Curti), 44
Rosenstock-Hussy, Eugen,
    historian, 131
Rounday Down, 130
Rourke, Constance, *American
    Humor*, 24–25. 27, 186–87,
    190
Routledge and Kegan Paul,
    publishers, 88
Rusk, Ralph Leslie, literary
    scholar, 118
Russell, Irwin, 186
Russia, 62, 108, 109–10

*Sagen*, American, 168–69, 175
Saint Haralampos, Greek
    patron saint, 37, 144
Saint Louis, Missouri, 100
*Saints of Sage and Saddle*
    (Fife and Fife), 90
Salem, Massachusetts, 183
Salmon, Lucy Maynard,
    historian, *Historical Material*,
    131
*Salvation on a String* (Green),
    198

Sam Bass, outlaw hero, 33,
    137, 164
Sam Lovel, 197
Sam Patch, hero-buffoon,
    100–101, 102
Sam Patch; or the Daring
    Yankee, 104–5
Sam Slick, 84, 190
Sandburg Carl, 6, 186, 187
San Francisco, 106, 123, 162
Santos, Spanish-American
    holy images, 127
Sappho, 172
Saturday Rambler, 116
Saturday Review (present
    American periodical), 3
Saturday Review of Literature
    (American periodical before
    1952), 5, 6
Saucier, Corinne L., folklorist,
    23
Saxon, Lyle, 10
Schlesinger, Arthur M., Sr.,
    historian, 79
Schoharie Hills, New York,
    collecting folklore in, 23
Scott, Walter, 21, 98
Seneca Indians, 84
Shackford, James A., David
    Crockett, the Man and the
    Legend, 33
Shadow of History, In the, 165
Shamanism: Indian, 30; in
    urban Negro folklore, 76
Shannon, British naval vessel,
    98
Shapiro, Irwin, 10
Sharp, Cecil, folklorist, 21, 27,
    111
Sheridan, Patrick, local
    character, 150–53, 166
Shine, black folk hero, 72
Shivaree, 20
Shoemaker, Henry W.,
    folklorist, 23
Shooter, oil industry folktype,
    74

Short, Zeb. See Zeb Short
Siberia, 140
Signifying Monkey,
    Camingerley culture hero, 72
Simmons, Merle, folklorist,
    136–37
Simms, William Gilmore, 179,
    196
Simon Suggs, 190
Simpson, Alan, historian, 32
Sioux Indians, 143
Sisu, traditional Finnish
    quality, 59
Sketch Book, The (Irving),
    204, 206
Skinner, Charles M., 175n;
    Myths and Legends of Our
    Own Land, 161, 182n;
    Myths and Legends beyond
    Our Borders, 161; American
    Myths and Legends. 161;
    Myths and Legends of our
    New Possessions and
    Protectorate, 161
Slavery, folklore of. See Negro
    folklore
Sleepy Hollow, 192–93
Smith, E. L., informant,
    143–44
Smith, Henry Nash, historian,
    34, 53, 57, 79; Virgin Land:
    The West as Symbol and
    Myth, 33, 44, 54, 55, 80, 98,
    128, 135
Smith, John, 131
Smith, John T., folklorist, 137
Smith, Joseph, 90
Smith, Merriman, 76
Smith, "Oregon". See
    "Oregon" Smith
Smith, Reed, folksong collector,
    111
Smith, Seba, 84, 191
Smith, Sydney, 99
Smyth, Mary W., folksong
    collector, Minstrelsy of
    Maine, 22

Sogwin, Mike, informant, 143
Solomon Swop, Yankee comic
   hero, 101
*Song of Hiawatha*
   (Longfellow), 99, 193, 207
*Songs of the Cowboys* (Thorp),
   67–69
"Soul," myth of, 75–76
Sources of folklore, printed vs.
   oral, 57–58
South Carolina, 111, 122, 132
Southeastern Folklore Society,
   112
*Southern Folklore Quarterly,*
   5, 92, 112, 188
Southern Methodist University,
   79
*Southern Workman,* 110–11
Southey, Robert, 187
*South from Hell-fer-Sartin*
   (Roberts), 169
*South Italian Folkways in
   Europe and America*
   (Williams), 35, 122
*Soviet Ethnography,* 62
Soviet Union. *See* Russia
Spanish-American folk art, 127
"Speckles," 69
*Spectator,* 172
Specter ships, 31, 147
Spencer, Benjamin T., literary
   scholar, *The Quest for
   Nationality,* 99
Spencer, Dave, informant, 195
Spenser, Edmund, 187
*Spirit of the Times,* 25, 81, 82,
   102, 115, 116, 118, 120, 176,
   177, 178, 190, 191
Stackalee, black folk hero, 72
Stampede Mesa, 164–65
*Standard Dictionary of
   Folklore, Mythology and
   Legend* (Leach), 114, 205
Stanley, Augustus Owsley III.
   *See* Owsley
Star Husband tale, 17
Star Island, 193

Steckmesser, Kent Ladd, *The
   Western Hero in History and
   Legend,* 159
Steinbeck, John, 187, 188
Stevens, Harry, 118
Stevens, James, *Paul Bunyan,* 7
Stockholm, Sweden, 109
Stolen Grandmother tale, 170
Strickland, Josh. *See* Josh
   Strickland
"Struggle between the
   Reactionary and the
   Progressive Forces in
   Contemporary American
   Folkloristics, The,"
   (Zemljanova), 62
*Study of American Folklore,
   The: An Introduction*
   (Brunvand), 50
Suggs, James Douglas, folk
   narrator, 75, 88
Suggs, Simon, 190
Superstitions. *See* Folk beliefs
"Supper for the Dead," 198
Surry County, Virginia, 133
Survivals, theory of, 19
*Sut Lovingood* (Harris), 81,
   190, 191
*Sut Lovingood, Yarns of a
   Nat'ral Born Durn'd Fool*
   (Harris), 66
*Sut Lovingood Papers, The*
   (McClary), 66
*Sut Lovingood's Yarns* (Inge),
   67, 82
Swain County, Virginia, 133
Sweden, 108, 109n
Swedish-American dialect
   jokes, 38
Sydow, C. W. von, folklorist,
   72, 158
"Symbols of the United States:
   From Indian Queen to
   Uncle Sam" (Fleming), 63
Syndicate, popular conception
   of, 59

Taft, Lewis A., *Profile of Old New England: Yankee Legends, Tales, and Folklore,* 159, 160
*Tales and Songs of Southern Illinois* (Neely), 169
*Tales from the Fens* (Barrett), 88
*Tales of Frontier Texas 1830–1860* (Anderson), 67
*Tales of the North American Indians* (Thompson), 114
Tale types: 1030, "The Crop Division," 25; 1036, *Hogs with Curly Tails,* 25; 1833E, *God Died for You,* 139; 2400, *The Ground is Measured with a Horse's Skin,* 140
Taliaferro, Harden E., 83, 186, 191, 204, 206
Talleyrand, French minister, 98
*Tall Tale America* (Blair), 10, 25
Tall tales, in newspapers, 117
*Tall Tales of Arkansas* (Masterson), 120
*Tall Tales of the Southwest* (Meine), 24, 67, 81, 184
Tarpon Springs, Florida, 123
Taylor, Archer, folklorist, 4, 17, 206–7; *Dictionary of American Proverbs and Proverbial Phrases, 1820–1880,* 117
Tebbel, John W., 134
Tengu, Japanese demon, 158
Tennessee, 100, 103, 104, 196, 207
Terkel, Studs, *Division Street: America,* 59
Texan, regional character type, 121
Texas, 23, 24, 104, 136
Texas, University of, 13
"Texas Cowboy," 68
Texas Rangers, 137

"Theory for American Folklore, A," 14, 49, 61
"Theory for American Folklore Reviewed, A," 14
*Theory of the Leisure Class, The* (Veblen), 125
Thomas, Robert B., 30
Thompson, Harold W., folklorist, 178; *Body, Boots, and Britches,* 8, 184
Thompson, Stith, folklorist, 4, 17, 18n, 39, 207; *The Folktale,* 27; *Motif Index of Folk-Literature,* 80, 148; *Tales of the North American Indians,* 114; *Types of the Folktale,* 83
Thompson, William Tappan, 81, 190
Thoms, William John, folklorist, 3
Thoreau, Henry David, 204, 206
Thorp, N. Howard "Jack," *Songs of the Cowboys,* 67–69
Thorpe, T.B., 180, 196, 197
Tidwell, James N., folklorist, *A Treasury of American Folk Humor,* 27
*Time* (current American periodical), 3, 59
Toast, Negro folklore genre, 71–72
Tolles, Frederick B., historian, 79
Tom Sawyer, 205
Tony Beaver, manufactured folk hero, 10
"Toughest Gamecock on Record, The," 178
Travel lie, 65
Travel literature, 119
*Travelers and Travel Liars 1660–1800* (Adams), 64–65
*Treasury of American Folk Humor, A* (Tidwell), 27
*Treasury of American Folklore, A* (Botkin), 5–6, 27, 184

*Treasury of Mississippi Folklore, A* (Botkin), 10
*Treasury of New England Folklore, A* (Botkin), 6
*Treasury of Railroad Folklore, A* (Botkin and Harlow), 72
Treviño, Jacinto. *See* Jacinto Treviño
Trickster: anecdotes of, 102; Old Promoter as, 73; Yankee, 84
*Troubleshooter* (Voelker), 86
Troy, 131
Truman, Harry S., 57
Truzzi, Marcello, 92
*Tsimshian Mythology* (Boas), 18, 27
Tule Lake, California, 36
Turkey, 140
Turner, Frederick Jackson, historian, 32, 135
Tyler, Royall, *The Contrast*, 102–3
*Type and Motif-Index of the Folktales of England and North America* (Baughman), 85
*Types of the Folktale* (Aarne and Thompson), 83

U.C.L.A., 13, 112
Uncle Lisha, 197
*Uncle Lisha's Shop* (Robinson), 196
Uncle Remus, 72, 189
Uncle Sam (American symbol), 64
"Uncle Village, The," 196
Uncompahgre County, Colorado, 167
*Union Jack*, 116
Upanishads, 66
Upper Peninsula, Michigan. *See* Michigan, Upper Peninsula
Uppsala, Sweden, 109

*Urban Blues* (Keil), 61, 74–76
Ur-form, 17, 29. *See also* Finnish method
Utah, 23, 42, 140, 168

Vail, R.W.G., historian, 119
Vance, Rupert B., 41
"Vanishing Hitchhiker, The," 170
*Varieties of Religious Experience, The* (James), 92
Veblen, Thorstei ., *The Theory of the Leisw , Class*, 125
Verbal art, 1ᶜ
*Vergleichendᵉ Märchenforschungen* (Aarne), 18n
Vermont, 83, 178, 179, 196, 197
Viking Press, 166
Virgil, 140
Virginia, 95, 97, 110, 111, 133
*Virgin Land: The West as Symbol and Myth* (Smith), 33, 44, 54, 55, 80, 98, 128, 135
Voelker, John D., 195; *Anatomy of a Murder*, 87; *Danny and the Boys*, 86; *Troubleshooter*, 86
Vogt, Evon, anthropologist, *Water Witching U.S.A.*, 73
*Voices in the Valley* (Kramer), 54, 90, 137
*Vrykólakas*, Greek supernatural being, 36, 37

Waerner, Robert M., *Romanticism and the Romantic School in Germany*, 183n
Wagner, Henry R., 119
*Wall Street Journal*, 51
Walton, Ivan, folklorist, 165, 189
War of 1812, 94, 103, 137

Warville, Brissot de, 65
Washington, D.C., 149
Washington, George, as
    mythical hero, 96, 100, 149
*Washington and His Generals*
    (Lippard), 97
Wasson, George S., 178; *Cap'n
    Simeon's Store,* 196
Waterman, Richard A.,
    anthropologist, 47
Water witch, 73
*Water Witching U.S.A.* (Vogt
    and Hyman), 73
*Way to Wealth, The*
    (Franklin), 189
Weber, Brom, 66
Webster, Noah, *American
    Dictionary of the English
    Language,* 99
Wecter, Dixon, historian, 44;
    *The Hero in America,* 128
Weems, "Parson," *Life of
    George Washington,* 96–97
Weinberg, A.K., historian, 44
Weiss, Harry B., 118
Wells, Phillis, 133
Welsh, Herbert, informant, 143
Wenner-Gren Conference, 76
Wertenbaker, Thomas J.,
    historian, 32
West, Victor, 190
*Western Folklore,* 112, 171
*Western Hero in History and
    Legend, The* (Steckmesser),
    19
Wetmore, Alphonso, *The
    Pedlar,* 100–101, 104–6
Weygandt, Cornelius, 178
Whig party, 104
White-Eye Anderson, informant,
    33
Whiteside Mountain, 132
White Steed of the Prairies,
    164, 182
Whiting, B.J., folklorist, 191;
    *Dictionary of American*

*Proverbs and Proverbial
    Phrases,* 117
Whitman, Walt, 187
Whittier, John Greenleaf, 160,
    186, 193, 194
"Who's Old Cow," 68
Wild Bill Hickok, 159
Wildfire, Nimrod. See Nimrod
    Wildfire
*William T. Porter and "The
    Spirit of the Times"* (Yates),
    82
Williams, Phyllis, *South Italian
    Folkways in Europe and
    America,* 35, 122
Wilson, Edmund, 66
Windham, Connecticut, 167
Windham Frog Fright, 167
Winslow, Ola E., historian, 32
Winthrop, John, 31, 147, 160
Wisconsin, 36, 43, 53, 83
Witchcraft, in early colonial
    writings, 30
*"With His Pistol in His Hand"*
    (Paredes), 90
*With the Bark On* (Anderson),
    67
Wolfe, Thomas, 186, 188
Wood, William, 175n
Wordsworth, William, 103
WPA folklore collecting
    program, 112
Wright, Benjamin, 79
Wright, Conrad, historian, 79
Writers' Congress, Russian, 110
Wyandot Indians, 140

X, Malcolm. See Malcolm X
XYZ affair, 98

Yankee: as folk symbol, 64; as
    regional type, 101, 119; as
    stage figure, 100–3; trickster,
    84

*Yankee Blade,* 102, 116
Yankee Jonathan, stage comic
    hero, 104–5
*Yankee Privateer,* 116
Yates, Norris W., 25–26;
    *William T. Porter and "The
    Spirit of the Times,"* 82
*Year of Decision, The: 1846*
    (DeVoto), 80
Yeats, William Butler, 187

Yoho Cave, 139
"Young Goodman Brown," 183

Zeb Short, Vermont folk hero,
    83
*Zeitschrift für Volkskunde,* 13
Zeke Broadhuss, 198
Zemljanova, L.M., 62–64